DIVIDEND POLICY AND CORPORATE GOVERNANCE

Dividend Policy and Corporate Governance

LUIS CORREIA DA SILVA
MARC GOERGEN
LUC RENNEBOOG

OXFORD
UNIVERSITY PRESS

OXFORD
UNIVERSITY PRESS

Great Clarendon Street, Oxford OX2 6DP

Oxford University Press is a department of the University of Oxford.
It furthers the University's objective of excellence in research, scholarship,
and education by publishing worldwide in

Oxford New York

Auckland Bangkok Buenos Aires Cape Town Chennai
Dar es Salaam Delhi Hong Kong Istanbul Karachi Kolkata
Kuala Lumpur Madrid Melbourne Mexico City Mumbai Nairobi
São Paulo Shanghai Taipei Tokyo Toronto

Oxford is a registered trade mark of Oxford University Press
in the UK and in certain other countries

Published in the United States
by Oxford University Press Inc., New York

British Library Cataloguing in Publication Data

Data available

Library of Congress Cataloging in Publication Data

Data available

ISBN 0–19–925930–5

1 3 5 7 9 10 8 6 4 2

Typeset by Newgen Imaging Systems (P) Ltd, Chennai, India
Printed in Great Britain
on acid-free paper by
Biddles Ltd., King's Lynn, Norfolk

To our families and friends

Preface

The spectacular failures of Enron and Worldcom certainly prove that corporate governance is still a highly relevant and timely topic, even for a capital market, the US market, which is thought to be highly developed and thought to provide one of the highest levels of investor protection and information disclosure. The serious problems of, among others, the Dutch retailer Ahold show that Europe is not immune either to misrepresentation of corporate information. Although the academic literature on corporate governance is developing quite rapidly, little is known about markets other than the UK or USA. We also know very little about the interaction between corporate governance and one of the major financial decisions that companies take, that is dividend policy. This book intends to close these gaps.

Oxford,   Luis Correia da Silva
Manchester and Tilburg   Marc Goergen
September 2003   Luc Renneboog

Acknowledgements

We are grateful to Steve Bond, Bob Chirinko, Marianne Citoyen-Leroy, Julian Franks, Klaus Gugler, Tim Jenkinson, Marina Martynova, Colin Mayer, Joe McCahery, Derek Morris, Steve Nickell, Stuart Ogden, Greg Trojanowski, and Burcin Yurtoglu, who read earlier versions of all or part of the manuscript. All remaining errors are obviously the responsibility of the authors. Our thanks also go to Andrew Schuller, the editor.

Contents

List of Figures

List of Tables

About the Authors

Luis Correia da Silva is a Director of OXERA (Oxford Economic Research Associates) and head of OXERA Finance. He holds degrees in Economics from Keble College, University of Oxford (D. Phil), and from Université Libre de Bruxelles, Belgium (M.Sc. and MBA). His research has focused on financial regulation of banks, security houses, fund management, dividend policy, capital structure, and cost of capital of firms. He has directed OXERA's consultancy work for the Financial Services Authority, London Stock Exchange, Office of Fair Trad (OFT) World Bank, Royal Bank of Scotland, European Asset Management Association (EAMA), the UK Department of Trade and Industry (DTI), Royal Mail, and various utility companies and regulators. His book *Asset Management and Investor Protection: An International Analysis* is also published by Oxford University Press.

Marc Goergen holds an M.Sc. in Economics from the Free University of Brussels (ULB) and an MBA in European Business from Solvay Business School, Brussels. He completed his D. Phil. in Economics at Keble College, University of Oxford, before joining both the School of Accounting and Finance, University of Manchester, and the Manchester School of Management, UMIST as a lecturer. In 1997 he took up a lectureship at the ISMA Centre, University of Reading. He returned to the Manchester School of Management, UMIST, in 1999 and was appointed to a senior lectureship in 2002. Marc is a research associate of the European Corporate Governance Institute (ECGI) and a fellow of the International Institute for Corporate Governance and Accountability. His main research interests are in corporate governance and corporate control, initial public offerings, corporate investment models, and dividend policy. He has had papers published in *European Financial Management*, the *Journal of Corporate Finance*, the *Journal of Business Finance and Accounting*, and the *Journal of Law, Economics and Organization*. He has also written a book on corporate governance entitled 'Corporate Governance and Financial Performance' (published by Edward Elgar) and contributed chapters to numerous other books.

Luc Renneboog graduated from the Catholic University of Leuven with degrees in management engineering (M.Sc.) and in philosophy (BA), from the University of Chicago with an MBA, and from the London Business School with a Ph.D. in financial economics. He is currently Associate Professor at the Department of Finance of Tilburg University, and a research fellow at the Center for Economic Research (Tilburg) and the European Corporate Governance Institute (Brussels). He held appointments at the Catholic University of Leuven (Belgium) and Oxford University, and visiting appointments at London Business School, European University Institute (Florence), Venice University, and CUNEF (Madrid). He has published in the *Journal of Financial Intermediation, Journal of Corporate Finance, Journal of Law and Economics, Journal of Banking and Finance, Journal of Law, Economics and Organization, Cambridge Journal of Economics, European Financial Management*, and others. He has also edited two books, entitled 'Corporate Governance Regimes: Convergance and Diversity' and

'Venture Capital Contracting and the Valuation of High Technology Projects', both published by Oxford University Press. His research interests are corporate finance, corporate governance, dividend policy, insider trading, financial distress, law and economics, and the economics of art.

PART I

CORPORATE CONTROL AND DIVIDEND POLICY

1

Introduction

Although dividend policy is one of the major decisions taken by a firm's board of directors, very little is known about how dividends are set outside the UK or the USA. Even less is known about the link between dividends and corporate governance for companies outside the Anglo-American system of corporate governance.

Nevertheless, cross-country comparisons have been drawn that have raised controversy. For example, it is widely believed that German companies pay out lower and more stable dividends than UK and US firms.[1] In turn, the retained cash flows of German firms are employed to finance the operations and shareholders benefit from a capital gain in the long run. This has led some policy-makers in the UK, such as the former financial secretary to the Treasury, Stephen Dorrell, to argue that 'dividend payouts [in the UK], which have risen substantially since 1979, may have become too high and inflexible'.[2] Although dating back to 1994, Dorrell's statement has lost none of its relevance. In October 2002, Michael McLintock, the chief executive of M&G, which is part of Prudential, one of the most important institutional investors in the UK, wrote a letter to the major UK companies about the importance of maintaining dividends despite shrinking profits. The letter said that 'the investment case for dividends in the majority of circumstances is a strong and well-supported one, has stood the test of time, and is likely to be increasingly appreciated in the economic and stock market conditions which we seem likely to face for the foreseeable future'.[3]

Strikingly, over the last decade, some German firms have started to adopt accounting practices that are close to Anglo-American standards. For example, Daimler–Benz AG, now DaimlerChrysler, one of the largest German publicly quoted corporations, announced in 1994 that it was 'considering changing its dividend policy to come into line with what the group's finance director (Gerhard Liener) described as "Anglo-American" practice . . . In the long term, Daimler–Benz was considering making sure that its dividend was more closely related to the group's earnings'.[4] Although there is a large set of controversial issues involved in this discussion, there is very little empirical evidence to support these statements.

Most of our understanding of the factors that shape dividend policy is based on evidence from the practices of Anglo-American firms. These firms evolve in a financial

---

[1] See, for example, *The Economist*, 29 Jan. 1994.   [2] *Financial Times*, 29 Apr. 1994.
[3] *Financial Times*, 8 Oct. 2002.   [4] *Financial Times*, 8 July 1994.

system (a market-based corporate governance regime) that differs markedly from the blockholder-based regime of other countries such as Austria, France, Germany, Italy, and Japan. The US and the UK capital markets are primarily characterized by a large stock market, publicly traded corporations that rely on transient ownership structures comprised of institutional investors (such as pension funds, mutual funds, and others), who act as agents for widely dispersed shareholders, and reliance on the market for corporate control to accomplish corporate restructuring. In contrast, the Austrian, French, German, Italian, and Japanese corporate governance structures rely on close ties between management, large shareholders, and creditors. The large shareholders hold their stakes for a much longer term and have much higher latitude to exert control. Financial institutions are allowed to hold debt and equity of the same corporation. It has been argued that corporate governance structures of the German and Japanese type have been more successful than the Anglo-American system in resolving the problem of monitoring managers.[5] Owners of large and longer term holdings have the incentive and the ability to engage in information gathering about the companies in which they invest. They are also better placed to assess the ongoing prospects of the company rather than engage in short-term profit-taking actions of buying and selling their shares. As a result, it has been suggested that the Anglo-American system is poor in the allocation of capital to investment whereas Japanese and German firms, in particular, have lower costs of finance.[6]

The above two points are interrelated. Dividends may be lower in Germany because of certain institutional arrangements. Theoretical arguments of dividend policy rely mainly on the idea that dividends serve to mitigate asymmetries of information and agency conflicts between managers and investors. If the German system of corporate governance is itself associated with lower informational and monitoring problems, then dividends may not be necessary devices to reduce these costs. From the above discussion, it emerges that a central driving force of the German corporate governance system is the pattern of ownership and control. Although a large proportion of the corporate sector is associated with large shareholders, there are some firms whose shares are widely dispersed. Furthermore, there is substantial cross-sectional variation in the nature of the large shareholders. This study deals with the way particular forms of control in Germany can act as substitutes for dividends in signalling firms' prospects and aligning the interests of shareholders and managers.

The main objective of this book is to provide more evidence on dividend policy of firms that operate outside the Anglo-American system of corporate governance. Particular emphasis is put on the possible impact of different types of shareholders on the dividend payout as well as its short and medium-term flexibility. The book offers some important insights into dividend patterns in Germany, a country which may serve as a prototype of the blockholder system.

The book consists of two parts. Part I sets the background for the empirical studies contained in Part II of the book. The first chapter of Part I—Chapter 2—reviews the characteristics of the main systems of corporate governance across the world. First, we review

---

[5] See, for example, Porter (1992).

[6] Alternatively, one can argue that, given the higher degree of shareholder protection, the cost of capital of Anglo-American firms should be lower (see, e.g. McCahery et al. 2002).

control and ownership patterns across the world. In particular, we look at the importance of certain types of shareholders across Continental Europe, the UK, and the USA. Second, we highlight the differences between ownership and control and the different devices that cause the deviation from the one-share-one-vote principle. Third, we review the theories and empirical evidence on the various corporate governance mechanisms. In particular, we discuss how different corporate governance devices can act as substitutes or complements to dividend policy.

Chapter 3 reviews the literature on dividends and the impact of control on dividend policy. We start by reviewing theoretical models on the link between dividend policy and control. First, we focus on the models that consider control as an alternative to dividends in their role as a signal of the firm's prospects. Second, we review the theoretical papers that treat control as an alternative monitoring device to dividend policy. A conscious effort is made to contrast the empirical evidence on the UK and the USA with that on the rest of the world. The possible dividend policy impact of banks, which are traditionally thought to dominate the corporate governance systems of France, Germany, Italy, and Japan, is also analysed.

Part II of the book contains the empirical studies. The dividend policy of the quoted industrial and commercial German firms is compared to that of a UK sample. We also compare our results to those found by studies on US firms. The first chapter, Chapter 4, lists our research questions. Chapter 5 sets the scene by discussing existing, cross-country studies on dividend policy and by identifying some of the empirical issues relevant to the study of dividend policy.

The purpose of Chapter 6 is to establish how well the Lintner (1956) partial-adjustment model fits German data and to compare the findings on Germany with previous evidence based on UK and US firms. We use recent developments in econometrics on dynamic panel data estimations to model the dividend behaviour of a large cross-section of firms during a ten-year period from 1984 to 1993. This period is particularly interesting, as it starts with a five-year economic boom followed by a period of recession. Although the model is generally well behaved, there are some inconsistencies. One possible source of problem is the high proportion of unchanged dividends per share, which we term high 'discreteness'. This is in contrast with the dividend behaviour of UK and US firms.

In Chapter 7 we look at *when* German and UK firms change the dividend rather than by *how much* firms change the dividend in response to changes in earnings. In particular, we model the decision to cut and omit the dividend. We also examine how rapidly firms re-establish the dividend payout that was in place prior to omissions and cuts. This approach has three merits. First, it allows us to test the signalling role of dividends in Germany. We investigate the impact of a sudden and transitory deterioration in earnings (such as earnings losses after a period of good performance) on the dividend behaviour of firms. Second, the results can be compared with the US finance literature that has modelled the decision in a somewhat similar way and has found evidence consistent with dividends playing an informational role. Third, a high degree of 'discreteness' in the dividend per share series suggests that this approach is necessary as a cross-check to the panel data estimations.

Chapter 8 draws on the findings of all previous chapters in order to model the relation between dividends and control in Germany. We examine in detail the patterns of control in the ten-year period from 1984 to 1993 for a large cross-section of firms. The chapter reports the controlling shareholders, the extent to which financial institutions are shareholders, and the importance of other corporations as large shareholders. In addition, we document that there is frequent use of 'pyramid' structures of ownership, whereby shares are held in a company which in turn holds shares in another firm. These structures allow shareholders at the top of the pyramid to exert control in public corporations through different layers of ownership. We apply our 'preferred' version of the dividend model from Chapters 6 and 7 to investigate how cross-sectional and inter-temporal variation in control patterns influence the dividend behaviour. In addition, we test the hypothesis that the tax status of the different shareholders has an impact on the dividend policy of the firms in which they invest. The main purpose of this chapter is to provide empirical evidence on whether certain forms of control structures can act as substitute mechanisms to dividends in reducing informational asymmetries and agency conflicts.

In the conclusion, we report a series of stylized facts about dividend policy in Germany, the UK, the USA, and the rest of the world that emerge from our review of the literature. We also draw important conclusions from our empirical analysis on the speed of adjustment of German dividends, their flexibility, the governance role of dividends, and taxes as a determinant of dividend policy.

2

Recent Facts and Developments in Corporate Governance

2.1. INTRODUCTION

A corporate governance regime is usually defined as the amalgam of mechanisms that ensure that the agent (the management of a corporation) runs the firm for the benefit of one or multiple principals (shareholders, creditors, suppliers, clients, employees, and other parties with whom the firm conducts its business). Becht, Bolton, and Röell (2002) regard the corporate governance rules as the outcome of the contracting process between the various principals and the management. Agency problems may arise when the firm is managed contrary to the interests of one or more principals and the management violates the explicit (sometimes implicit) contracts with the principals. The efficiency criterion, which the corporate governance regime is to contribute to, differs across countries. Whereas in many Continental European countries (e.g. Germany) the legal definition of corporate governance explicitly mentions stakeholder value maximization, the Anglo-American view—expressed by, for example, Shleifer and Vishny (1997)—focuses on generating a fair return for investors. Contrary to Shleifer and Vishny, Jensen and Meckling (1976) show that the maximization of shareholder value is equivalent to economic efficiency provided that the following conditions are fulfilled: (*i*) the firm is considered as a nexus of complete contracts with creditors, employees, customers, suppliers, and other relevant parties, (*ii*) the shareholders can claim the residual returns after all other contractual obligations have been met, and (*iii*) there are no agency problems.

The corporate governance devices available to ensure economic efficiency are manifold and comprise the market for corporate control (the hostile takeover market), large shareholder monitoring, changes in blockholdings, creditor (in particular bank) monitoring, internal control mechanisms, such as the board of directors and various non-executive committees, executive compensation contracts and the regulatory framework of the corporate law regime and stock exchanges. Another important corporate governance device is the dividend policy: A high payout policy precommits managers to generate sufficient cash flows and to pay them out to the shareholders. As such, the dividend payout policy can be a substitute governance mechanism to the ones listed above. Conversely, some of the governance devices may be complements to a high dividend payout policy. For example, one may need the presence of large shareholders or a strong board of directors to impose such a dividend policy. Similarly, firms have used high dividend payout policies to ward off hostile takeovers. Consequently, this chapter focuses on the main corporate control mechanisms that are either alternative monitoring devices to dividend policy or important determinants of the payout ratio.[1]

Section 2.2 discusses the differences in ownership and control concentration across countries. Not only does concentration differ across countries, but so does the concentration by type of shareholder. The latter may have important consequences for dividend policy for two reasons: (*i*) Some types of large shareholder are better at monitoring poorly performing companies and may, therefore, be a better alternative governance device to dividend policy and (*ii*) different types of large shareholder may be liable to different tax regimes and thereby influence the payout policy in different ways. Section 2.3 shows that control is not necessarily the same as ownership as there exist several mechanisms which cause deviations from the one-share-one-vote principle. Such deviations may have an important impact on dividend policy. Section 2.4 reviews the theoretical models on the various alternative corporate governance mechanisms and the empirical evidence on their efficiency. Section 2.5 concludes.

2.2. THE PATTERNS OF OWNERSHIP AND CONTROL

2.2.1. *Differences in Control Concentration Across Countries*

The recent literature shows ample empirical evidence that corporate control structures differ substantially across countries. Barca and Becht (2001), who coordinated the work of the European Corporate Governance Institute (ECGI), have published the first exhaustive cross-country study on control patterns. Their focus is on control structures[2] which are distinct from ownership in two respects. First, not all shares have voting rights attached as, for example, non-voting shares do not confer any control rights to their owners. Second, as control is not necessarily exercised at the first tier, the ECGI does not only take direct stakes into account, but also considers indirect control relations. Therefore, they accumulate all voting stakes controlled directly or indirectly by the same ultimate shareholder or investor group.[3] In the remainder of this section, we discuss control rather than ownership.

In most Continental European companies, the majority of the voting equity is held by one shareholder or a shareholder group (Fig. 2.1) and in the vast majority of firms, at least a blocking minority (i.e. 25 per cent) is held by a single shareholder (Fig. 2.2). In contrast, the UK and USA are characterized by dispersed equity and broad discretion on the part of management to run the business.

Table 2.1 confirms that the high degree of control concentration in Continental Europe is striking. In Austrian, Belgian, French, German, and Italian companies, a single shareholder (or a shareholder group) usually owns an absolute majority of the voting shares. This stands in sharp contrast with the UK where the largest shareholder controls on average only 14 per cent. The dilution of ownership and control is even more pronounced in the

---

[1] Another factor which may influence dividend policy and explain differences across countries is taxation, which will be discussed in detail in Chapter 8.

[2] The reason for this is that the EU Large Holdings Directive (88/627/EEC), which governs disclosure of shareholders in the EU member states, requires the disclosure of voting stakes—rather than ownership stakes—exceeding certain thresholds. Hence, information on ownership is not normally available for most EU countries.

[3] For a more detailed account on the use, occurrence, and control consequences of the use of ownership pyramids or cascades see Section 2.3.

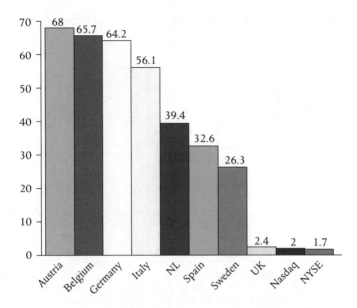

Figure 2.1. *Percentage of listed companies under majority control*
Source: Barca and Becht (2001).

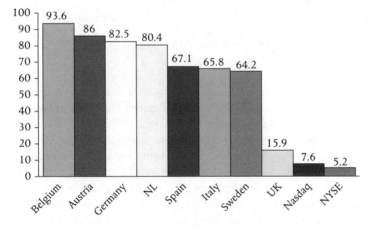

Figure 2.2. *Percentage of companies with a blocking minority of at least 25%*
Source: Barca and Becht (2001).

USA. Whereas a coalition of the three largest shareholders votes for more than 60 per cent in Continental Europe (up to a supermajority, that is, 75 per cent, in France and Austria), a similar coalition can vote for a mere 30 per cent of the shares in Anglo-American countries.

The above stylized facts raise the question as to why the levels of control vary so substantially across countries. Goergen and Renneboog (2003a) provide at least a partial answer to this question. They choose two countries with substantially different corporate governance regimes: Germany (a blockholder-based governance system, that is, a system

Table 2.1. *Ownership distribution of largest shareholders in Europe and the USA*

Country	Sample	Shareholdings			
		Largest	2nd largest	3rd	4th–10th
Austria[a]	600	82.2	9.5	1.9	6.5
France[a]	403	56.0	16.0	6.0	5.0
Italy[a]	214	52.3	7.7	3.5	5.1
Netherlands[b]	137	28.2	9.2	4.3	7.1
Spain[a]	394	38.3	11.5	7.7	10.3
UK[b]	248	14.0	8.3	6.1	9.2
US-NYSE[b]	1,309	8.5	3.7	1.8	0.9
US-NASDAQ[b]	2,831	13.0	5.7	3.0	1.6
		Largest	2nd + 3rd	4th + 5th	6th–10th
Belgium[a]	135	55.8	6.9	0.6	0.2
Germany[a]	402	59.7	8.6	2.6	0.3

Notes: This table gives the average size of the largest control stakes (stakes of voting equity) for European countries and the USA. For all countries, the data are for 1996 apart from Belgium (1994) and UK (1993). The Austrian sample consists of both listed and non-listed companies; the sample companies in all other countries are listed.

[a] Both direct and indirect shareholdings are considered.
[b] Only direct shareholdings.

Sources: Becht and Boehmer (2001); Becht, Chapelle, and Renneboog (2001); Bianchi, Bianco, and Enriques (2001); Bloch and Kremp (2001); Crespi and Garcia-Cestona (2001); De Jong et al. (2001); Goergen and Renneboog (2001); Gugler et al. (2001); Renneboog (2000).

with strong shareholder concentration, complex control structures, few listed companies, and weak shareholder protection) and the UK (a market-based regime with many listed firms, diffuse ownership, and strong shareholder rights). They study how control evolves after the initial public offering (IPO). A first reason for shareholders to hold larger voting stakes in German firms may be the different regulatory and legal environment. A detailed analysis of the German and UK stock exchange regulation, explicit rules on minority shareholder protection, informational transparency and the takeover codes shows that shareholder rights are weaker in Germany. The voting procedure at annual meetings, the composition of the board of directors and fiduciary duties of directors further reinforce the relative weakness of German shareholder rights. As a consequence, control tends to be more valuable to shareholders of German firms to avoid expropriation of their investments and/or to take advantage of private benefits of control. Furthermore, holding large control stakes is less expensive in Germany than in the UK, because ownership pyramids, the possibility of issuing non-voting shares and the nomination of one's representatives to the board of directors ensure that control can be maintained with relatively low levels of cash flow rights.

Although the legal environment predicts stronger levels of control in Germany (see also Section 2.4.3), it does not explain how the differences in control concentration come about.

Given levels of competition in a global economy, it is surprising that corporate governance regulation has not converged more (McCahery et al. 2002).[4] Goergen and Renneboog (2003*a*) explain the lack of convergence (or the slow speed of convergence) by economic factors which determine control retention by large initial shareholders in IPOs, the dissipation of control among many small shareholders, and control transfers. For the latter they distinguish between control transfers to ultimately widely held bidders and concentrated bidders. They select a sample of UK firms and a sample of German firms, which are floated on the stock exchange with high levels of initial control. They then trace possible control changes over time. They find that the initial shareholders in the average German company do not only own much larger stakes than their UK counterparts, but that they also keep majority control over the five years after the IPO. In contrast, the initial shareholders of UK companies lose majority control already two years after going public. Goergen and Renneboog (2003*a*) find strong evidence that corporate characteristics explain differences in the control evolution not only across companies from the same country but also across the two countries. They use Tobit models to estimate the percentage of control held by the initial shareholders, the percentage held by the new large shareholders and the size of the free float six years after the flotation. They find that firm size is an important determinant of control concentration in the UK but not in Germany. Large UK companies evolve towards a more widely held equity structure whereas in large German firms new shareholders hold significantly larger voting stakes. The reason is that wealth constraints become binding for UK shareholders, whereas German ones can avoid this effect by leveraging control via ownership pyramids. If the founder of a German firm is still a major shareholder at the IPO and if there are non-voting shares outstanding, control is likely to remain tight in the hands of the initial shareholders. This is not surprising as founding families often extract (non-pecuniary) private benefits of control and non-voting shares enable them to raise additional equity while maintaining control. Whereas growth does not have an impact on the control concentration of UK firms, strong growth in German firms leads to the transfer of control to new large shareholders.

2.2.2. *The Nature of Control*

As in most European countries, the mandatory disclosure threshold is 5 per cent of the voting equity[5] this subsection only considers holdings of at least 5 per cent. Table 2.2 shows

---

[4] Still, Bebchuk and Roe (2000) claim that the rigidity to changes in control concentration hinges to a large extent on the structures with which the economy started (structure-driven path dependence). The efficient choice of a corporate control structure is influenced by sunk costs. Furthermore, there is an endowment effect as there are advantages to using the dominant form in the economy, which is the one which most players are familiar with. Internal rent-seeking by parties who participate in corporate control may also explain why such parties may attempt to impede change towards a more efficient control structure. For example, the management of widely held companies may prefer to retain a diffuse control structure as this enables them to maintain their private benefits at the expense of the shareholders. Likewise, Bebchuk (1998) argues that concentrated ownership—and hence uncontested corporate control—prevails in Continental Europe because the lax corporate governance regulation allows large shareholders to reap substantial private benefits of control. Hence, as long as Continental European regulation does not change, control will remain concentrated (Bratton and McCahery 1999).

[5] Exceptions are the UK with a threshold of 3% and Italy with 2%.

Table 2.2. *Distribution of largest shareholders in Europe*

Country	Sample	Individuals and families	Banks	Insurance companies	Investment funds	Holdings and industrial companies	State	Directors
Austria[a]	600	38.6	5.6	0.0	0.0	33.9	11.7	0.0
Belgium[a]	135	15.6	0.4	1.0	3.8	37.5	0.3	0.0
France[a]	403	15.5	16.0	3.5	0.0	34.5	1.0	0.0
Germany[a]	402	7.4	1.2	0.2	0.0	21.0	0.7	0.0
Italy[b]	(2/4)	68.6	7.2	0.0	0.0	24.2	0.0[c]	0.0
The Netherlands[d]	137	10.8	7.2	2.4	16.1	10.9	1.3	0.0
Spain[a]	394	21.8	6.6	8.8	0.0	32.6	0.0	0.0
UK[d]	248	2.4	1.1	4.7	11.0	5.9	0.0	11.3

Notes: This table gives the total large shareholdings of voting rights (over 5%) held by different investors classes. For all countries the data cover the year 1996, except for Belgium (1994) and the UK (1993).

[a] Both direct and indirect shareholdings are considered.
[b] Numbers for Italy refer to both listed and non-listed companies.
[c] Of the listed Italian companies about 25% are directly and indirectly controlled by state holdings: this is classified in the table under 'Holdings and industrial companies'.
[d] Only direct shareholdings.

Sources: Becht and Boehmer (2001); Becht, Chapelle, and Renneboog (2001); Bianchi, Bianco, and Enriques (2001); Bloch and Kremp (2001); Crespi and Garcia-Cestona (2001); De Jong et al. (2001); Goergen and Renneboog (2001); Gugler et al. (2001); Renneboog (2000).

that not only is control different across countries, but so are the main categories of share-holders. The main shareholders are classified into (*i*) institutions (banks, insurance companies, investment and pension funds), (*ii*) individuals (excluding directors) or families, (*iii*) directors and their families and trusts, (*iv*) industrial and holding companies, and (*v*) the federal or regional governments. For each of these categories, we sum up the voting blocks (of 5 per cent or more) they control directly (by holding shares directly in a target firm) as well as indirectly (via other companies).

Industrial and Holding Companies
In France, the shareholder category of industrial and holding companies controls on average 35 per cent of the shares (Table 2.2). In Belgium, this number is even higher with 38 per cent.[6] German industrial and commercial companies control an average stake of 21 per cent in other German listed firms. In other words, in 52.4 per cent of the German companies, an industrial shareholder holds a stake of 40 per cent or more (not shown). Similarly, the corporate sector holds high levels of control in Austrian, Italian, and Spanish

---

[6] The distinction between an industrial holding company (or conglomerate) and a financial holding company is often difficult to make across countries. The average cumulative ownership of share stakes in excess of 5%, held by French and Belgian holding companies (financial and industrial ones combined) is 21% and 27%, respectively.

firms. In contrast, the industrial and commercial sector of the UK and the Netherlands owns 6 and 11 per cent, respectively, of the votes in listed companies.

Banks and Financial Institutions

Bank shareholdings in Continental European companies are generally small. Combining direct and indirect stakes, banks control, on average, between 0.4 and 7.2 per cent in Belgium, Italy, the Netherlands, and Spain. In France, bank control is strongest, with an average of 16 per cent of the voting shares (Table 2.2), although direct shareholdings are rare and amount only to about 2.7 per cent. The reason is that some large French banks are the ultimate shareholders of investor groups which comprise intermediate holding companies. In Germany, only 5.8 per cent of the large voting stakes of 5 per cent and more are held (directly as well as indirectly) by banks, resulting in an average of 1.2 per cent of the votes (Table 2.2). However, the influence of banks in Germany is higher than the control resulting from directly and indirectly held share stakes because investors depositing their bearer shares at their bank normally grant the bank the exercise of their votes (the so-called proxy votes). Furthermore, German corporations tend to have a housebank (*Hausbank*) which can exert additional influence on the firm (e.g. through board membership). In Anglo-American countries, bank control is almost negligible.

The avoidance of potential conflicts of interest is the main reason why bank holdings in listed companies are low in most countries (Goergen and Renneboog 2001). Banks owning shares in firms frequently also hold debt in these firms. However, each type of claim may require a different optimal decision process in the wake of financial distress. When there is a danger of bankruptcy and the bank faces a refinancing demand by the firm, creditor claims may encourage the bank to make the firm file for liquidation, whereas the equity claims may lead the bank to revolve its loans. Such conflicts of interest may even be exacerbated by the fact that in countries such as Belgium, France, and Italy, intricate ownership-based networks exist which also comprise banks. For instance, a bank's equity may be controlled by a large industrial holding company that also owns large share stakes in other subsidiaries in which that bank also owns equity or debt (Renneboog 2000).

Investment trusts, pension funds, and insurance companies are the main shareholders in the Netherlands and the UK. The average percentage of voting shares from share blocks of 5 per cent or more amounts to 19 and 16 per cent, respectively (Table 2.2). It should be noted that the true control by financial institutions is much higher, as most of their holdings are below the disclosure threshold of 5 per cent. The lack of large institutional blockholders in most Continental European countries suggests that, in contrast to the Anglo-American countries, little 'shareholder activism' is to be expected from financial institutions.[7] Even in Anglo-American countries, evidence of monitoring by financial institutions is scarce because financial institutions want to avoid active monitoring of firms and gathering non-public information. If financial institutions were to possess such information, they would be prohibited from trading by the insider trading legislation such that the liquidity of their

---

[7] Bratton and McCahery (1999) question whether Anglo-American style institutional shareholder activism would lead to improved corporate results in Continental Europe because, in their opinion, a minimum level of takeover activity is a precondition of relational engagement between institutional shareholders and managers.

investment portfolio would be reduced (Stapledon 1996; Stapledon and Bates 2002). Furthermore, the costs of actively monitoring the many firms included in the institutions' portfolios may also be prohibitive.

Families and Individuals

Table 2.2 shows that individuals and families are one of the main shareholder categories in Continental Europe.[8] In fact, Franks and Mayer (2001) have found that large-scale family control is especially pronounced in the largest German firms. This finding was also documented by Becht and Boehmer (2001): In 37 per cent of their sample, individuals or families control large blocks of, on average, 20 per cent of the voting rights. A particular category of individuals controlling share stakes is that of the directors who are insiders, and therefore possess superior information on the firms' prospects. For most of Continental Europe, hardly any information is known about directors' control for the following reasons: (i) the shareholdings of most directors are below the disclosure thresholds, (ii) although large family blockholders frequently appoint their representatives (which can be family members) to the board, the origin of board representation does not need to be disclosed publicly, and (iii) the use of intermediate investment companies further obscures the picture of directors' control. In contrast to Continental European firms, directors of UK firms[9] are, along with institutional investors, the most important category of owners. The fact that in some UK companies, managers hold large share blocks can make them less unaccountable. For instance, Franks, Mayer, and Renneboog (2001) show that voting rights in the hands of executive directors lead to managerial entrenchment and resistance to disciplinary actions undertaken against this management.

To summarize, (i) the concentration of control is much higher in Continental Europe than in the UK or USA; (ii) the use of pyramids and other complex control structures in Continental Europe enables certain shareholders to retain control over long periods; (iii) the Continental European corporate sector owns large stakes in listed companies; (iv) banks—unless they are part of a financial group—hold, in general, small stakes in all countries; (v) institutional investors and directors are the main shareholders in the UK, but do not hold much voting power in Continental Europe; and (vi) directors' control is relatively high in the UK and can lead to managerial entrenchment.

There are at least three reasons why the patterns of control may have a substantial impact on dividend policy. First, shareholders who control the firm may impose their preferred payout ratio on all the shareholders. The preference for a specific dividend policy may be influenced by the tax status of the controlling shareholder (see Chapter 8). Second, the controlling shareholder may reduce the dividend payout ratio and decrease dividend flexibility given that for him there may be other ways of obtaining a payout of cash flows. Such private benefits of control will be further discussed in the next section. Third, a controlling shareholder may not have to rely on the disciplining effect of a high dividend payout as

---

[8] The higher importance of family control in Austria and Italy can be explained by the fact that the sample consists of both listed and non-listed companies. Still, even after excluding the non-listed Italian firms, a majority of the listed Italian companies is family-controlled.

[9] In contrast to Continental European boards, those of the UK consist of two-thirds of executive directors.

a governance device as it may be more efficient and less costly to monitor the management directly.

2.3. WHY AND WHEN IS CONTROL NOT NECESSARILY IDENTICAL TO OWNERSHIP?

In this section, we highlight the differences between control and ownership and the different devices that cause deviations from the one-share-one-vote rule, which may have an important impact on dividend policy. It is important to realize that the potential agency problems are different in cases where the one-share-one-vote principle is valid compared to situations where that rule is not upheld. When diffuse ownership coincides with weak shareholder voting power, there may be serious agency conflicts between the management and the shareholders as a result of a lack of monitoring. This lack of monitoring may be particularly problematic in countries where shareholder protection is weak. Monitoring the management may be prohibitively expensive for small shareholders as a monitor bears all the costs related to his control efforts but only benefits in proportion to his shareholding (Grossman and Hart 1980, 1988; Demsetz 1983). Therefore, only a large share stake gives sufficient incentives to monitor a company. The advantage of diffuse control is increased share liquidity and the exposure of the company to the disciplining role of the market for corporate control. Conversely, strong ownership and voting power come with low liquidity but the presence of a large shareholder exercising control reduces the likelihood that managers will deviate from the corporate objectives.

The two basic cases where ownership and control coincide are represented by panels A (dispersed ownership and control) and D (concentrated ownership and control) of Fig. 2.3. One would prima facie expect these two cases to represent most Anglo-American companies (dispersed ownership and control) and most Continental European and Japanese firms (concentrated ownership and control), respectively. The question is whether the voting power of large shareholders should be limited or, conversely, whether large voting power should be encouraged to curb managerial discretion.

In practice, panel D does not apply to most companies from Continental Europe because the one-share-one-vote principle is not necessarily upheld. There are several mechanisms causing deviations from that principle: for example, ownership pyramids, shares with multiple voting rights and voting restrictions. Panel C represents the case where the concentration of voting power is lower than that of ownership. This case occurs because of the use of voting caps, designed to prevent large shareholders from exercising control. The use of voting caps improves the protection of small shareholders against expropriation by large shareholders. When a company is in imminent danger of being taken over, voting caps restrictions can also be applied. For example, Franks and Mayer (1998) show that in each of the three hostile takeover battles in Germany since the Second World War voting rights restrictions were used. As a consequence, the voting power of several large share stakes was reduced from, for instance, 30 to 5 per cent. In the cases of Feldmühle Nobel and Continental, the use of voting caps contributed to the failure of the takeover bid.

		Control	
		Weak	Strong
Ownership	Dispersed	Panel A: Dispersed ownership and dispersed voting power	Panel B: Dispersed ownership and concentrated voting power
	Concentrated	Panel C: Concentrated ownership and dispersed voting power	Panel D: Concentrated ownership and concentrated voting power

Panel A: Dispersed Ownership and Weak Voting Power
- *where*: USA, UK.
- *advantages*: a. high potential for portfolio diversification and high liquidity; b. existence of a takeover market
- *disadvantages*: insufficient monitoring: free riding problem
- *agency conflicts*: management vs shareholders

Panel B: Dispersed Ownership and Strong Voting Power
- *where*: countries where a stakeholder can collect proxy votes, where shareholder coalitions are allowed, where non-voting shares are issued and where shareholding pyramids exist: e.g. in Continental Europe.
- *advantages*: a. monitoring of management, b. portfolio diversification and liquidity
- *disadvantages*: a. violation of one-share-one-vote, b. reduced takeover possibility
- *agency conflicts*: controlling blockholders vs small shareholders

Panel C: Concentrated Ownership and Weak Voting Power
- *where*: any company with voting right restrictions; e.g. in some Continental Europe
- *advantages*: protection of minority rights
- *disadvantages*: a. violation of one-share-one-vote, b. low monitoring incentives, c. low portfolio diversification possibilities and low liquidity, d. high cost of capital
- *agency conflicts*: management vs shareholders

Panel D: Concentrated Ownership and Strong Voting Power
- *where*: Continental Europe, Japan, in any company after a takeover, in recently floated companies.
- *advantages*: high monitoring incentives
- *disadvantages*: a. low portfolio diversification possibilities and low liquidity, b. reduced take over possibilities
- *agency conflicts*: controlling blockholders vs small share holders

Figure 2.3. *Ownership and voting power*

Source: Renneboog (1998).

The issuing of multiple voting shares was outlawed in Germany,[10] Italy, Spain, and the UK as of May 1998 (Faccio and Lang 2002; Goergen and Renneboog 2003*a*).

Panel B of Fig. 2.3 shows that it is possible to have dispersed ownership with concentrated voting power. Whereas such a situation combines the incentive for increased monitoring with the advantage of allowing investors to diversify their wealth, there is also

---

[10] Still, for German firms a grandfather clause was put in place in 1998. Prior to 1998, German firms could be authorized to issue shares with multiple voting rights by the Ministry of Economics of the *Land* of their headquarters (Goergen 1998: 71).

an imminent danger that concentrated control will be exercised to extract private benefits from minority shareholders. The corporate law regimes in most Continental European countries include a number of mechanisms that allow controlling shareholders to obtain a return on their investments that covers private benefits of control and exceeds the financial return by the private benefits of control. The most widely used mechanism to obtain control with a limited investment is ownership pyramids or cascades which can enable shareholders to maintain control throughout multiple layers of ownership while at the same time sharing the cash flow rights with other (minority) shareholders at each intermediate ownership tier. Hence, ownership pyramids reduce the liquidity constraints of large shareholders while allowing them to retain substantial voting power. For instance, if a shareholder X owns 51 per cent of the voting equity of firm Y which in turn owns 51 per cent of the voting equity of firm Z, there is an uninterrupted control chain which gives shareholder X absolute majority control at each tier. Still, the cash flow rights of shareholder X in firm Z are merely 26 per cent.[11] This disparity between ownership and control is characteristic of countries that permit the exploitation of private benefits of control.

A second mechanism that yields control with limited cash flow rights (panel B) is proxy votes. For example, German banks are allowed to cast the voting rights of the shares deposited with them by the firms' shareholders. The casting of the votes is conditional upon the bank announcing how it will vote on specific resolutions at the general meeting and upon the lack of receiving alternative instructions by the depositing shareholders. Another example of proxy voting can be found in the USA where the management can make proposals to be voted on at the general meeting and solicit proxy votes for their support.

Starting from a situation of diffuse ownership and dissipated control (panel A), there is a third mechanism to achieve the case of panel B. Voting pacts enable small shareholders to exert a much higher degree of control as a group than the members of the pact could, individually. There is little empirical evidence that long-term shareholder coalitions are formed because such coalitions may bring about substantial costs. For example, the regulatory authorities in the UK consider a long-term shareholder coalition as a single shareholder and the coalition has to comply with all the regulations concerning information disclosure, mandatory tender offer, disclosure of strategic intent, etc. As such, a coalition of shareholders in the UK controlling 30 per cent of the voting rights would be compelled to make a bid on all other shares outstanding. Therefore, most coalitions are formed on an *ad hoc* basis with a specific aim, such as the removal of badly performing management. Crespi and Renneboog (2002) investigate the monitoring role of shareholder coalitions in the UK by simulating the relative voting power of each blockholder in potential voting coalitions using Shapley values. The Shapley values measure the extent to which individual shareholders (or groups of shareholders) are pivotal in potential winning voting coalitions. The authors present evidence that such coalitions play a monitoring role in poorly performing UK firms.

A fourth mechanism to separate ownership and control is the issuance of dual class shares. Grossman and Hart (1988) argue that a significant stake in a company entails benefits of control, which can be partitioned into private benefits and security benefits.

---

[11] For an example of pyramids in the German context, see Chapter 8.

The latter include benefits of ownership and control concentration that are shared and enjoyed by all the shareholders (e.g. the positive effects of monitoring). Although blockholdings are meant to be a mechanism that mitigates agency costs resulting from excessive managerial discretion, they can induce their own types of agency costs as the private benefits usually come at the expense of other shareholders or stakeholders: for example, the squeeze-out of minority shareholders at a price below the value of their shares in a tender offer, and the diversion of resources from security holders to entities controlled by a blockholder (Zwiebel 1995; Pagano and Röell 1998; Johnson et al. 2000). The private benefits of control are usually non-transferable[12] benefits beyond the financial return on investment. For example, if a car producer acquires car seats from a subcontractor, a large shareholding in the subcontractor can yield an important (strategic) advantage. The large shareholder will usually be represented on the subcontractor's board and will, thus, be able to obtain private information on the firm's cost structure or on supply contracts with competitors. The large shareholder could, for example, after obtaining such strategic information, renew negotiations about the price charged by the subcontractor for the car seats. Consequently, such transactions can lead to the creation of another kind of agency conflict, namely the oppression of minority shareholder rights. Another example illustrates the danger of expropriation of minority shareholders: suppose that a shareholder owns 51 per cent of the voting shares in firm A and that he also owns 100 per cent of the equity of another firm, firm B. If firm A is a supplier to firm B, the controlling shareholder may be tempted to reduce the transfer price of goods sold to firm B. Profits are then maximized at the level of firm B over which the shareholder has full control and owns all the cash flow rights. At the same time, profits are not maximized at the level of firm A which harms its minority shareholders. Renneboog (2000: 1991) quotes the following example: 'A blockholder belonging to a holding group will tend to concentrate on the interests of his own group as a whole. He might be tempted to divide the markets over its subsidiaries such that they do not compete too intensively with each other. For instance, the French holding group Suez, could have an interest in dividing the international utility markets over its subsidiaries, the French firm Lyonnaise des Eaux and the Belgian firm Tractebel. This limitation on strategic freedom of the subsidiaries is not in the interest of minority shareholders [who invested directly in these listed subsidiaries] and of investors who are participating in the group via the stock exchange.' Other examples of minority shareholder expropriation are tunnelling in the context of the transition economies (see Johnson et al. 2000).

It is obvious that control over the dividend payout policy may also yield the large shareholder a private benefit of control. For example, she may set a dividend payout ratio which is optimal to her own specific tax situation but not to that of the majority of the smaller shareholders. Also, if a large shareholder has other ways of extracting funds from the company (see, e.g. the examples above), she has an interest in setting a low payout ratio. As such,

---

[12] Zwiebel (1995) argues that private benefits of control can be extracted even if a company has multiple large shareholders. He claims that these benefits may be divisible, and that parties can enjoy them according to their relative control. Above some threshold, the control by large blockholders will not be challenged, as it may be difficult or impossible to build up share blocks of a similar size. Unchallenged control may encourage the extraction of private benefits of control at the expense of dispersed small shareholders.

the monitoring (or precommitment) role of dividend policy is discarded at the expense of the minority shareholders.

Dual or multiple class shares are commonly issued by European firms, but with large differences across EU member states. Under a dual class regime, one class (B-shares) has fewer voting rights than the other class (A-shares). They are used by firms in Germany, Italy, Scandinavia, and Switzerland but rarely so in the UK (Goergen and Renneboog 2001). Faccio and Lang (2002) analyse 5,232 firms from thirteen Western European countries. For instance, in Denmark, Finland, Italy, Sweden, and Switzerland the proportion of firms with outstanding dual class shares ranges from around 35 to 65 per cent. For Austria, Germany, Ireland, Norway, and the UK, the range varies from 13 to 24 per cent (Table 2.3). In France, Portugal, and Spain the proportions are almost negligible. In the USA, dual class shares have become an increasingly important concern to investors since the 1980s, when stock exchanges liberalized the originally restrictive policy on multiple and dual class shares. The range of variation across Europe is considerable with regard to the specification of dual class shares. For example, the voting rights on B-shares in Sweden are typically one tenth of the voting rights on A-shares, while in some countries the B-class shareholders carry no voting rights. Moreover, German firms, as well as firms from certain other countries, can issue preference shares (*Vorzugsaktie*). This is risk-bearing capital without votes, but with special dividend rights. A special case of a multiple voting share is a so-called 'golden share' which gives one or more shareholders (e.g. the government) a veto right in certain clearly defined situations.

Table 2.4 displays the legal restrictions on dual class shares and the average minimum percentage of the book value of equity needed to control 20 per cent of the votes for each country.

Table 2.3. *Dual class shares in Europe*

Country	Number of firms	Number of firms with dual class shares	Percentage of firms with dual class shares (%)
Austria	99	23	23.23
Belgium	130	0	0.00
Denmark	210	70	33.33
Finland	129	47	36.43
France	607	16	2.64
Germany	704	124	17.61
Ireland	69	16	23.19
Italy	208	86	41.35
Norway	155	20	12.90
Portugal	87	0	0.00
Spain	632	1	0.16
Sweden	334	185	55.39
Switzerland	214	109	50.93
UK	1,953	467	23.91
TOTAL	5,531	1,164	21.05

Sources: Faccio and Lang (2002); Bennedsen and Nielsen (2002).

Table 2.4. *Current regulation in Europe*

Voting-rights regulation by country	Details	Number of sample firms	Minimum percentage of equity needed to control 20% of votes	Percentage of firms with dual class shares
One share one vote				
Belgium		130	20.00	0.00
Norway	Exception by government approval	155	19.05	13.16
Proportion on non-voting (and limited voting) stocks capped				
France	< 25% of stock capital	607	19.93	2.64
Germany	< 50% of stock capital	704	18.83	17.61
Italy	< 50% of stock capital	208	18.38	41.35
Portugal	< 50% of stock capital	87	20.00	0.00
Spain	< 50% of stock capital	632	20.00	0.16
Minimum percentage of the votes accruing to shares with limited voting rights compared to voting shares				
Denmark	Minimum ratio: 10%	102	n.a.	51
Finland	Minimum ratio: 10%	129	15.42	37.60
Sweden	Minimum ratio: 10%	245	9.83	66.07
UK[a]	Minimum voting rights[a]	1,953	19.14	23.91
No legal restrictions				
Austria		99	18.96	23.23
Greece		n.a.	n.a.	n.a.
Ireland		69	18.91	28.07
Luxembourg		n.a.	n.a.	n.a.
The Netherlands	Complex	n.a.	n.a.	n.a.
Switzerland		214	15.26	51.17
TOTAL		5,334	18.74	19.91

Notes: Legal restrictions on issuing dual-class shares. 5,232 publicly traded firms.

[a] In UK non-voting shares are outlawed since 1968, but firms are free to issue preference shares with minimum rights. Voting rights are activated (1) if the dividend is in arrears (2) if share capital is reduced or the company is wound up or (3) if the share rights are affected.

Sources: Bennedsen and Nielsen (2002); Faccio and Lang (2002); Rose (2002).

Meanwhile, since the seminal study by Barclay and Holderness (1989), several studies have attempted to quantify the private benefits of control. Most studies measure the size of the private benefits by the premium paid for control blocks in publicly traded companies. Nicodano and Sembenelli (2000) and Trojanowski (2003) argue that this methodology is inappropriate, since it neglects the firm's overall ownership and control structure. Instead, following Zwiebel's (1995) suggestion, they posit that the fraction of control rights being transferred in a block trade should be measured by changes in the strategic importance of shareholders. The relative strength of a shareholder is calculated by measuring the degree to which the shareholder is pivotal in potential voting coalitions, as proxied by changes in Shapley values. Rydqvist (1987) and Zingales (1994) analyse samples of companies with dual class stocks and measure control using power indices. Price comparisons of shares carrying different control rights allow them to make inferences about the value of private benefits of control.

Dyck and Zingales (2002) measure the private benefits of control in thirty-nine countries based on 412 control transactions over the period 1990–2000. They find that the value of control, measured by the difference between the price paid for the block and the share price two days after the announcement of the block transaction relative to the share price, ranges from −4 to +65 per cent with an average of 14 per cent. In some European countries, the size of private benefits appears to be very large (Table 2.5). For example, the mean premium

Table 2.5. *Block premium as a percentage of firm equity*

Country	Mean	Median	Stand. dev.	Min.	Max.	Number of observations	Number of observations positive
Australia	0.02	0.01	0.04	−0.03	0.11	13	9
Austria	0.38	0.38	0.19	0.25	0.52	2	2
Canada	0.01	0.01	0.04	−0.02	0.06	4	2
Denmark	0.08	0.04	0.11	−0.01	0.26	5	3
Finland	0.02	0.01	0.06	−0.07	0.13	14	9
France	0.02	0.01	0.10	−0.10	0.17	5	3
Germany	0.10	0.10	0.13	−0.24	0.32	18	15
Israel	0.27	0.21	0.32	−0.01	0.89	9	8
Italy	0.37	0.16	0.57	−0.09	1.64	8	7
Japan	−0.04	−0.01	0.09	−0.34	0.09	21	5
The Netherlands	0.02	0.03	0.05	−0.07	0.06	5	4
New Zealand	0.03	0.03	0.09	−0.17	0.18	19	14
Norway	0.01	0.01	0.05	−0.05	0.13	14	9
Portugal	0.20	0.20	0.14	0.11	0.30	2	2
Singapore	0.03	0.03	0.03	−0.01	0.06	4	3
Spain	0.04	0.02	0.06	−0.03	0.13	5	4
Sweden	0.06	0.02	0.08	−0.01	0.22	13	12
Switzerland	0.06	0.07	0.04	0.01	0.15	8	8
UK	0.02	0.01	0.05	−0.06	0.17	43	23
USA	0.02	0.02	0.10	−0.20	0.40	47	28
Average/number	0.14	0.11	0.18	−0.04	0.48	412	300
Europe and the USA only							
Average/number	0.13	0.04	0.17	−0.03	0.44	200	140

Note: The block premiums are computed by taking the difference between the price per share paid for the control block and its market price two days after the announcement of the control transaction, and by dividing it by the market price of the block two days after the announcement and multiplying the ratio by the proportion of cash flow rights represented in the controlling block.

Sources: Dyck and Zingales (2002).

in Austria, Italy, and Portugal is 38, 37, and 20 per cent, respectively. In contrast, in most other European countries, the mean premium is below 10 per cent.

Economists studying private benefits of control warn that estimating the value of the control premium is complicated, as the control premium depends on a number of factors, including the degree of competition in the market for corporate control (Dyck and Zingales 2002), the size of the block sold (Barclay and Holderness 1989; Zingales 1994, 1995), the dispersion of shares in the target firm (Barclay and Holderness 1992), the inequality of voting power across shareholders (Nicodano and Sembenelli 2000; Zwiebel 1995), the nationality of the buyer (Nenova 2003), and the financial condition of the firm involved (Berglöf and Burkart 2002). The control premium is lower in the Anglo-American market-based corporate governance system that has widely dispersed owner-ship structures and a high level of legal protection of minority shareholders. The factors measuring differences in legal enforcement in the Dyck and Zingales study are tax com-pliance and product market competition. Almost invariably, the existence of large private benefits of control suggests that large shareholders may be able to obtain a large share of the rents.

2.4. CORPORATE GOVERNANCE MECHANISMS

In this section, we describe the main predictions of the theoretical models focusing on cor-porate governance mechanisms which may act as substitutes (or complements) to dividend policy. We also summarize the main conclusions from empirical research. We focus on inter-nal governance mechanisms, such as large blockholder monitoring and the structure of the board of directors, as well as external mechanisms, such as the market for corporate control, changes in control concentration and creditor monitoring.[13]

2.4.1. *Internal Governance Mechanisms*

Blockholders
The ultimate question is: Do blockholders enhance firm value? Value is expected to be created by the increased monitoring of the management by the large blockholders (see among others: Admati, Pfleiderer, and Zechner 1994; Maug 1998; Kahn and Winton 1998). Furthermore, if directors own blockholdings, this may align their incentives with those of the other shareholders. One of the first papers to investigate the impact of large managerial ownership on firm value is Morck, Shleifer, and Vishny (1988). They measure firm value by Tobin's Q, proxied by the market-to-book ratio of assets, and find a non-linear relation between Q and managerial ownership. Firm value increases as managerial owner-ship increases to 5 per cent, firm value then decreases as managerial ownership increases

---

[13] We have no intention of giving an exhaustive account of all the governance mechanisms. For example, we do not review the governance role of executive compensation contracts. For a detailed survey of the literature see for example Murphy (1999); Becht, Bolton, and Röell (2002); Core, Guay, and Lancker (2001); and Bebchuk, Coates, and Subramian (2002). For an overview of the European mergers and acquisitions market, see Goergen and Renneboog (2003b).

from 5 to 25 per cent and firm value increases again at ownership levels beyond 25 per cent. Hence, at low levels of managerial ownership, an increase in cash flow rights seems to bring about additional incentives for the managers to maximize shareholder value. At levels of ownership between 5 and 25 per cent, additional ownership leads to entrenchment. The entrenchment effect disappears if managerial ownership exceeds 25 per cent. McConnell and Servaes (1990) find different results: Q increases in a non-linear fashion until it reaches its maximum at a level of insider ownership of 40–50 per cent and then gradually declines for higher levels of ownership. In addition, they report a positive linear relation between firm value and the fraction of shares owned by institutional investors. McConnell and Servaes (1995) investigate the relation between a firm's growth opportunities, ownership structure, and leverage. They conclude that the allocation of equity ownership among insiders, institutions, corporate blockholders, and atomistic shareholders is of marginally greater significance in low-growth than in high-growth firms. Even in the context of managerial compensation schemes, the role of blockholders is apparent. For example, Mehran (1995) shows that equity-based compensation is used less extensively in US firms with stronger outside blockholders suggesting that blockholder monitoring is a substitute for equity-based compensation contracts. In contrast, Crespi, Gispert, and Renneboog (2002) find managerial compensation contracts related to share price performance are complementary to outside blockholdings in Spanish firms. In other words, it seems that in Spain one needs a strong blockholder to impose such contracts. In companies without outside blockholders, the managerial compensation contracts are based on accounting performance (which is subject to managerial control, and can thus be manipulated). A similar result is reached by Renneboog and Trojanowski (2003) for the UK in a simultaneous equation system on managerial compensation and turnover.

It should be noted that concentrated ownership may also generate substantial costs. The above studies do not control for these costs (Trojanowski 2003). First, Demsetz and Lehn (1985) and Admati, Pfleiderer, and Zechner (1994) claim that control by a large shareholder may result in reduced risk sharing. Second, as shown above, ownership concentration may reduce the market liquidity of all the shares (Bolton and Thadden 1998). Third, in highly leveraged companies, a large blockholder may require management to take excessive risks especially if the company is performing poorly and the bankruptcy costs are high. In this case, risk increasing investment projects may lead to the expropriation of the debtholders (Jensen and Meckling 1976; Coffee 1991). Fourth, Burkart, Gromb, and Panunzi (1997) and Pagano and Röell (1998) point out that even when tight control by shareholders is efficient *ex post, ex ante* it constitutes an expropriation threat that reduces managerial incentives to exert effort and undertake value maximizing strategies (the so-called 'over-monitoring' effect).

While the studies listed above examine the relationship between ownership or control and corporate performance, a different strand of the literature investigates whether blockholders take corporate governance actions when increased monitoring is necessary (e.g. in the case of poor corporate performance or financial distress). The incentives to correct managerial failure depend not only on the concentration of ownership or control, but also on its nature as specific classes of shareholders may value control differently (Jensen and

Meckling 1976). The thesis that different classes of shareholders have different abilities to extract control rents is empirically supported for the USA by Demsetz and Lehn (1985); Barclay and Holderness (1989, 1991); and Holderness and Sheehan (1988). Franks, Mayer, and Renneboog (2001) investigate whether the presence of blockholders in poorly performing companies is related to increased board restructuring. They find no evidence of increased managerial disciplining in the wake of poor corporate performance when large outside shareholders are present. The only consistent and significantly negative relation is the one between managerial ownership and executive board turnover. The authors interpret this finding as clear evidence of managerial entrenchment as managers with a substantial degree of control are able to ward off successfully any attempts to remove them. Banerjee, Leleux, and Vermaelen (1997) investigate the governance role of French holding companies which constitute the dominant shareholder category in France. They find no evidence that holding companies assume a governance role. On the contrary, the presence of holding companies as major shareholders seems to reduce corporate performance and firm value. Renneboog (2000) examines whether different types of blockholders monitor companies listed on the Brussels stock exchange. As ownership structures are frequently complex and pyramidal, and are constructed for reasons of control leverage, both direct control as well as indirect control relations are taken into account. The 'ultimate' blockholders are classified into the following categories: holding companies, financial institutions, industrial and commercial companies, individual investors, or families and directors. None of these blockholder types are related to executive board turnover apart from industrial and commercial companies which seem to initiate board restructuring when the firm's accounting and share price performance declines. To summarize, the empirical literature provides little evidence of the corporate governance role of large blockholders.

Most of the above studies assume that performance drives corporate governance actions by blockholders. However, Goergen (1998) who reviews the studies that explicitly address the direction of causality between the two shows that this conclusion may be premature. Kole (1996) is one of the studies that call for a reversal of the direction of causality between firm value and ownership or control. She uses the same sample as Morck et al. For each year between 1977 and 1985, Kole regresses the Tobin's Q of each year on the same three board ownership variables as used by Morck et al. measured in 1980. She finds a significant relationship between Q and 1980 ownership for the years 1977–80, but no relationship between Tobin's Q for the years 1981–85 and 1980 managerial ownership. Kole argues that this suggests that a firm's performance determines its ownership structure and not vice versa. Similarly, Köke (2003) argues for a reversal of the causality. Himmelberg, Hubbard, and Palia (1999) give the following example: Suppose that there are two firms, firm A and firm B. Firm A has a higher degree of market power than firm B. If competition has a disciplining effect on managerial decisions, then firm A requires closer monitoring. Therefore, managers of firm A may receive a higher share of equity to align their interests with those of the other shareholders. However, due to its higher market power, firm A also shows higher profit rates than firm B. Empirically, we would then find a positive correlation between managerial ownership and profitability. But the estimated coefficient of managerial ownership will reflect only spurious correlation, not a causal relationship. Consequently, in the light of these caveats, the result of the empirical papers described in this section should be interpreted with caution.

Boards of Directors
The research on the board of directors (and similar internal corporate governance mecha-nisms consisting of (non-) executive directors such as audit committees or remuneration committees) has focused on the following questions:

1. Are boards with specific characteristics better at generating corporate performance and growth?
2. Are boards with specific characteristics more likely to take corporate governance actions? For example, are independent boards better at removing poorly performing managers?
3. What determines the board's composition and characteristics? For example, does good performance lead to the appointment of more insiders to the board, and vice versa, does poor performance lead to the appointment of more independent directors?

Board Composition and Corporate Performance. The most frequently examined relation con-cerning internal governance mechanisms is the relation between board independence from the management, proxied by the number of outside directors, and corporate performance. A high degree of board independence enables non-executive directors to monitor the firm more closely and take appropriate governance actions, which may even entail the removal of some of the top managers. There is little evidence of a positive relation between corpo-rate performance (measured by accounting benchmarks and Tobin's Q) and the proportion of outside directors (see, e.g. MacAvoy et al. 1983; Hermalin and Weisbach 1991; Mehran 1995; Klein 1998; and Bhagat and Black 2000). Still, the lack of a cross-sectional result may be due to the endogeneity of board composition.[14]

Another board characteristic that may have an impact on corporate performance is board size. The idea is that large boards are less effective than small boards because some directors may free-ride on the efforts of others (Lipton and Lorsch 1992). Yermack (1996) finds empirical support for this for a sample of US firms. An interesting study about the added value of the board of directors and its characteristics is the one by Gertner and Kaplan (1996) on reverse leveraged buyouts. Gertner and Kaplan examine the boards of such firms. These are firms which after a period of being privately held are refloated on the stock exchange. They claim that as such firms can start with a clean slate, they are likely to opt for a value-maximizing board. They find that boards tend to be smaller than in otherwise similar firms.

Interlocked directorships may also influence the board's corporate governance actions. There is interlocking of directorships if directors of different companies sit on each other's

---

[14] If poor performance leads to increased board independence, the cross-sectional result on the potential rela-tion between the degree of board independence (independent variable) and corporate performance (dependent variable) may be underestimated. The reason is that more independent directors will be on boards of firms with historically poor performance (Hermalin and Weisbach 1998; Börsch-Supan and Köke 2000). However, attempts to correct for this problem using simultaneous equations (Hermalin and Weisbach 1991; Bhagat and Black 2000) have not yielded a significant relation. An alternative approach is event studies focusing on whether changes in board composition are followed by changes in performance and firm value. The stock price reaction to the announcement of the appointment of outside directors in the USA triggers a significant abnormal return of 0.2% (Rosenstein and Wyatt 1990).

boards. The danger of interlocking is collusion. Hallock (1997, 1999) documents that interlocked CEOs receive a higher remuneration than otherwise similar CEOs. This suggests that interlocked directors may give the CEO a certain degree of control over his own board.[15]

The Board of Directors and its Corporate Governance Actions. The disciplining of top management (and in particular of the CEO) has received considerable empirical attention. The reason is that such disciplining is one of the few observable governance actions by the board of directors whereas most of its other governance actions are not directly observable, due to the fact that the minutes of the board meetings are not publicly available. The negative relation between CEO or executive board turnover and performance has been documented among others by Coughlan and Schmidt (1985); Warner, Watts, and Wruck (1988); Weisbach (1988); Jensen and Murphy (1990); Barro and Barro (1990); Blackwell, Brickley, and Weisbach (1994); Huson, Parrino, and Starks (2000); Brickley and Van Horn (2000) for the USA; Kaplan (1994*a,b*) and Kaplan and Minton (1994) for Japan; Franks and Mayer (2001) and Köke (2003) for Germany; Renneboog (2000) for Belgium; Dherment and Renneboog (2002) for France; and Franks, Mayer, and Renneboog (2001) for the UK. In addition, the studies find that boards dominated by outside directors are more likely to remove the CEO when stock price and accounting performance is poor. In contrast, CEO turnover on insider-dominated boards is not performance-driven. This implies that board turnover in firms with insider-dominated boards occurs for reasons unrelated to corporate performance. This leads to the conclusion that boards controlled by outside directors are better at monitoring the CEO than boards controlled by inside directors. Another measure of independence, the separation of the jobs of CEO and (non-executive) chairman, appears to be an important condition leading to improved corporate governance (Franks, Mayer, and Renneboog 2001).

However, good corporate governance cannot simply be equated to the dismissal of badly performing managers from the board for the following two reasons. First, poor (industry-corrected or business-cycle adjusted) corporate performance may also be the consequence of past poor corporate governance. As such, the dismissal of poorly performing management may come too late. There is evidence that managerial disciplining only takes place when firms are in the lowest quintile of stock price performance and are incurring accounting losses (Franks, Mayer, and Renneboog 2001). Second, the success of the governance action of removing underperforming management should be considered along with the managerial alternative. For instance, Dherment and Renneboog (2002) study how the French stock market reacts to the appointment of CEOs with different backgrounds. They

---

[15] In a related paper, Shivdasani (1993) shows that firms whose outside directors have more non-executive directorships in other companies are less likely to be acquired in a hostile takeover. This may be due to the fact that directors who exert multiple directorships are of higher quality and assume a more active corporate governance role. However, Hermalin and Weisbach (2001) propose an alternative explanation: Directors in higher demand will turn down directorship opportunities at poorly managed firms, which are more prone to being acquired. Furthermore, they argue that 'outside directors who hold many directorships do so because they have established a reputation for supporting management and not "rocking the boat"'.

find that, whereas voluntary resignations do not cause price reactions, the nomination of an external manager following the performance-related forced resignation of a CEO causes a strong significant increase in abnormal returns of more than 2 per cent. The abnormal return at the promotion of an internal candidate to the post of CEO in a poorly performing firm is negative (1 per cent on the day of the announcement), which presumably occurs because the internal candidate is held (partially) responsible for past poor performance. Several papers examine whether the governance action of top management dismissal is followed by improvements in corporate performance. Denis and Denis (1995) document performance increases following forced CEO turnover in the USA, but Renneboog (2000) and Franks, Mayer and Renneboog (2001) do not find evidence of a significant improvement over the two-year period following the CEO's replacement for Belgian and British firms, respectively.

Changes in the Structure of the Board as a Response to Corporate Performance. Hermalin and Weisbach (1998) investigate the factors that lead to changes on corporate boards. They discover three kinds of factors that determine board dynamics. First, poor firm performance increases the likelihood that inside directors are replaced by outside directors. Second, the CEO succession process is intertwined with the board selection process because firms tend to appoint inside directors to the board when the CEO is close to the retirement age. Furthermore, inside directors tend to leave the board just after a CEO replacement, which is consistent with the hypothesis that they are the losing candidates in the line of succession to the position of CEO. Third, inside directors tend to leave the firm and outside directors tend to join the board after a firm leaves a given product market.

Kaplan and Minton (1994) and Morck and Nakamura (1999) analyse whether the fact that a Japanese firm belongs to a *kereitsu* group, an industrial group which usually also includes a bank, influences its board composition. They find that, in the wake of poor performance, banks take a more active role and appoint their representatives to the firm's board. This implies that Japanese creditors are involved in corporate governance especially in times of financial distress when the likelihood that the debt covenants will be violated is high.

Baker and Gompers (2000) study the board-selection process for a large sample of US IPOs. They analyse whether the CEO's bargaining power, proxied by the Shapley value of his voting stake, influences the selection of board members. They conclude that there is a positive relation, especially when the CEO's tenure and bargaining power are high.

2.4.2. *External Governance Mechanisms*

The role of dividends in the context of corporate control can be twofold. First, as pointed out above, the dividend payout may be a bonding mechanism precommitting managers to pursue value maximization. A high dividend payout ensures that managers focus on generating sufficiently high levels of cash flows and that these are not invested into projects with returns below the cost of capital. As such, a tight dividend policy allows shareholders to reduce their monitoring efforts. Second, dividend policy may also constitute an important signal, as 'dividend cuts are interpreted by the market as powerful signals of bad news both about the current situation and about future prospects' (Marsh 1992: 50). Consequently, the failure to meet the anticipated dividend level or payout may activate alternative corporate governance mechanisms which are better suited to deal with poor performance or financial distress. Given that (industry-corrected) underperformance is not only the responsibility of the management but also reflects the failure of the internal monitors (such as the board of directors or the blockholders), other (external) governance mechanisms (such as the market for corporate control) may be activated to commence the board and/or asset restructuring of the firm. It is important to note that a precondition for dividends to be a signal of failing performance and corporate control is dividend stickiness. In Anglo-American companies, there is ample evidence that managers are reluctant to reduce dividends (see Chapter 3), but it is questionable whether the same reluctance applies to Continental European companies, frequently controlled by one single dominant investor group. For example, if dividends in Continental European firms are more volatile, they are also more in line with current earnings rather than the long-term prospects of the firm. Hence, for Continental Europe, it may be the case that dividends are not as strong a signal of poor management and governance. In Chapter 7, we will focus the issue of dividend flexibility for German companies and compare it to that of UK companies.

The Market for Corporate Control

According to Jensen (1986), the fact that managers pursued their own objectives and the failure of internal control systems fuelled the hostile takeover market in the 1980s. The inefficiency was most pronounced in firms and industries generating substantial free cash flow. In principle, free cash flow, which is defined as the cash flow in excess of what is required to finance all positive NPV projects, should be returned to the shareholders via dividends or share repurchases. As this does not always happen automatically, especially in industries with excess capacity and in need of downsizing (Jensen 1993), there is a need for the disciplinary action via the takeover market.

Several studies focus on the disciplinary role of hostile takeovers. The studies investigate whether poorly performing firms are more likely to be the target of a hostile takeover. Following the bid, one expects a higher level of managerial turnover, and financial and asset restructuring. Therefore, the probability of being taken over is expected to decrease with rising profitability. This hypothesis is not overwhelmingly supported in the literature: While poor performance only slightly affects the probability of a takeover, the main determining factor is size (see Morck, Shleifer, and Vishny (1988); Martin and McConnell (1991); Comment and Schwert (1995) for the USA; and Franks and Mayer (1996) for the UK). Franks and Mayer (1996) also cast doubt on the governance role of the market for corporate control given that the pre-bid financial performance of targets of hostile bids is not substantially different from that of targets of accepted bids. Compared to takeovers without board and asset restructuring, takeovers with restructuring display superior abnormal share price performance over periods of five and two years prior to the bid. This is the opposite of what the theory on the market for corporate control predicts. Franks and Mayer (1996) conclude that there is little evidence that takeovers entailing corporate restructuring are the result of poor past performance. In contrast, Franks, Mayer, and Renneboog (2001) show that companies, forced to cut or omit their dividends, are frequently drastically restructured via mergers and acquisitions which lead to the replacement of most of the directors.

All in all, the role of hostile takeovers is controversial. On the one hand, hostile takeovers are considered to be a device to keep managerial autonomy under check and to impose discipline (Grossman and Hart 1980) by enabling the acquirer to reallocate the target's resources more profitably (Burkart 1999). On the other hand, there is little evidence that, in practice, the market for corporate control assumes these tasks.

Still, the role of the market for corporate control may be an indirect one. First, it is possible that the mere threat of a takeover raises efficiency *ex ante* (Scharfstein 1988; Shleifer and Vishny 1986). Second, companies shielded from the takeover market have lower share prices. The setting up of anti-takeover devices generally coincides with a reduction in share value: event studies (Jarrell and Poulsen 1987; Ryngaert 1988; Karpoff and Malatesta 1989.) find significant negative abnormal returns of -2 per cent. This negative impact can be interpreted as evidence that shareholders fear that managers may take advantage of the increased lack of control by not maximizing shareholder value. Alternatively, the fall in the share price may reflect the fact that the probability of the shareholders receiving a takeover premium is now reduced.

In a survey paper on the economics of mergers and acquisitions, Burkart (1999) concludes that although managers shielded from the takeover threat do not behave like empire-builders they tend to become sluggish. For example, Bertrand and Mullainathan (2003) and Borokhovich, Brunarski, and Parrino (1997) show that increased insulation from takeovers leads to higher managerial salaries and lower total factor productivity in US corporations. Garvey and Hanka (1999) provide evidence that anti-takeover legislation leads to fewer new investments and fewer disinvestments. Hence, it seems that the existence of an active market for corporate control is valuable. As pointed out in Section 2.2, the development of the market for corporate control in Continental Europe is hindered given that the vast majority of firms are controlled by a large shareholder.[16] However, for firms with strong control where the market for hostile takeovers cannot play a disciplinary role, a market for partial control (a market for share blocks) may still operate (see next subsection).

Block Trades (the Market For Partial Control Stakes)
Transfers of control by means of block sales are on average accompanied by positive abnormal performance (Sudarsanam 1996; Holderness and Sheehan 1988). Barclay and Holderness (1989) show that the price reaction is positive regardless of the price paid for the share block. The main reason for the positive market reaction is that changes in control may improve corporate governance, especially when the firm is performing poorly and is in need of a substantial reorganization (e.g. board or financial restructuring) (Barclay and Holderness 1991). When performance is poor, shareholders without a distinct interest in monitoring are expected to sell their shares, while those with strong monitoring abilities may increase their stakes in order to reinforce their position as (major) shareholders. Consequently, under such circumstances, block transactions giving the purchaser control

---

[16] For a discussion of the recently proposed takeover legislation by the European Commission, see McCahery and Renneboog (2003).

over the firm may trigger a more favourable market reaction than those transactions that do not confer control to the purchaser. Evidence for this conjecture is provided by Holderness and Sheehan (1988). They also find, that for the USA, the market reaction is more favourable to block transfers that are accompanied by a tender offer on all outstanding shares. In addition, the market reacts more positively to block transactions in those firms that subsequently experience a full acquisition (Barclay and Holderness 1992). Still, even when no subsequent takeover occurs Sudarsanam (1996) documents that the benefits of ownership concentration outweigh the costs.

Some European studies distinguish between different types of acquirers of share blocks. Banerjee, Leleux, and Vermaelen (1997) find that, in general, block deals do not trigger any positive abnormal performance for listed French firms. However, block acquisitions by holding companies result in value destruction. This conclusion is similar to that of Renneboog (2000) for Belgian holding companies. In spite of the fact that institutions and holding companies trade actively in share stakes, ownership increases by these categories are not correlated with changes in board structure. Conversely, acquisitions of substantial share stakes by industrial companies and families are normally accompanied with changes in the management. Such board restructuring takes place when prior performance was poor (as measured by negative market adjusted returns, negative changes or levels of performance, and by unexpected dividend reductions). This suggests that a market for control stakes exists: Poor performance triggers block trades which are followed by corporate restructuring. Franks, Mayer, and Renneboog (2001) examine the impact of block transfers by type of acquirer (among other disciplinary mechanisms) on managerial turnover in the wake of poor performance. They find that block purchases by individuals or families are associated with significant increases in executive board turnover. In a poorly performing company where family control increases substantially (to the highest decile of family ownership), the resulting executive board turnover increases by 8.2 per cent. Increases in the control stakes held by families or corporations are associated with significant subsequent increases in board turnover but also coincide with decreases in institutional ownership. This implies that institutions sell to other outside investors who force board replacements in poorly performing companies. Whereas Franks, Mayer, and Renneboog (2001) emphasize the monitoring role of the market in share blocks, Burkart, Gromb, and Panunzi (2000) argue that an increase in block size via a block transaction, rather than via a tender offer, may be a relatively inefficient transfer of control. The reason is that transferring control through a block trade preserves the low overall concentration of the ownership and the corresponding high extraction of private benefits.

Bethel, Liebeskind, and Opler (1998) show that in the USA the block purchases by financial and strategic investors[17] cause no significant market reaction, while acquisitions of blocks by activist shareholders are accompanied by significant positive abnormal performance. Activist shareholders are defined as those who acquire stakes in poorly performing companies, and subsequently attempt to restructure the firm in order to achieve

---

[17] Bethel, Liebeskind, and Opler (1998) define activist blockholders as 'raiders' intending to influence corporate policy. Strategic blockholders are non-financial investors who are unopposed by management. Financial blockholders include banks, pension funds, and individuals who do not adopt an activist position.

a considerable improvement in its performance. In contrast, strategic investors invest for the long run and do not interfere with management. Keim and Madhavan (1996) distinguish between buyer and seller-initiated block transactions in the USA. They find that the market reaction to transactions initiated by the buyer are usually positive, whereas the market reaction to those initiated by sellers is always negative.

Creditor Monitoring

An important characteristic of some governance regimes relates to the lending relationships. Shleifer and Vishny (1997) argue that large creditors fulfil a role similar to large shareholders because these creditors have large investments in the firm, and therefore a strong incentive to monitor the firm's management. Diamond (1984) formulates a model on the role and incentives of bank monitoring. He shows that delegation of monitoring to banks is efficient as duplication of monitoring by small investors (creditors) can be avoided, provided the bank's lending portfolio is sufficiently diversified.[18] Krasa and Villamil (1992) study delegated monitoring by considering the role of the intermediary who is to satisfy the different portfolio preferences of both borrowers and lenders. They model the incentive structure of the monitor by determining what intermediary portfolio accomplishes optimal asset transformation between borrowers and lenders. Rajan and Diamond (2000) review the assumptions of Diamond (1984) and show that the bank's incentives to monitor are preserved, provided that there is no deposit insurance and that the first-come first-serve feature of bank deposit contracts is maintained. In other words, it is the possibility of a bank-run that preserves the banks' incentive to monitor the firms.

More intense creditor intervention is expected when the probability of defaulting on debt covenants increases or when the company needs to be refinanced. High gearing can be considered as a bonding mechanism for the management (e.g. Aghion and Bolton 1992; Berkovitch, Ronen, and Zender 1997) such that high turnover is positively related to high gearing. Denis and Denis (1995) infer creditor monitoring from the fact that high leverage combined with managerial ownership improves shareholder returns.

Rajan and Zingales (2003) state that relationship-based financing (which can for example, be found in the German bank-based system) performs better when markets and firms are smaller, when legal protection is weaker, when there is little transparency, and when innovation is mostly incremental rather than revolutionary. Large creditors, especially in bank-based economies such as Germany, typically have a variety of control rights, and therefore sufficient power to monitor. Consequently, bank monitoring may act as a substitute to alternative governance devices. For example, a disciplinary change in control is expected to be less profitable, and hence less likely to occur in firms monitored by banks. Köke (2003) analyses corporate governance in the German bank-based economy and confirms that non-market monitoring devices play a larger role because hostile control transactions are rare, and because other constituencies such as large creditors typically have considerable power. The long-term lending relationships give banks considerable power, which is frequently strengthened by bank representation on the supervisory board of the firm. One reason why bank influence is particularly strong is that historically German

---

[18] Hellwig (2000) generalizes Diamond's results, allowing for risk averse banks.

banks have acted as the so-called house banks, providing long-term loans to long-term clients (Lehman 2003).

2.4.3. *The Corporate Governance Regulatory Framework*

The importance of the above governance mechanisms as well as the governance role of dividend policy—including the interactions between different mechanisms—should be studied within a country's specific regulatory context. For example, strong shareholder protection reduces the danger of expropriation of minority shareholders. Consequently, the development of legal corporate governance rules (e.g. mandatory bid rule in the case of takeovers) and self-regulation (e.g. corporate governance codes of best practice) should be priced by the markets. La Porta et al. (1998, 1999, 2000) have developed a new line of research which explains the differences in corporate governance systems by the level of legal protection for minority shareholders and the degree of capital market development. La Porta et al. find that common law systems tend to offer better protection both against expropriation of shareholders by the management and the violation of the rights of minority shareholders by large shareholders than civil law systems. Likewise, creditor protection— measured by creditor rights indices which are based on bankruptcy law and the regulation regarding financial distress—is strongest in common law countries and worst in French civil law countries (see Table 2.6). The Scandinavian and German countries are somewhere in between. The implication of La Porta et al.'s work is that countries should move towards the more efficient common law system based on transparency and arm's length relationships.[19]

Other studies show analogous correlations (Levine 1999; Beck, Demirgüç-Kunt, and Levine 2002). For example, the level of shareholder protection has been shown to relate inversely to the size of the premium over the market price paid for a majority voting block—higher premiums are paid in countries with weak protection (Zingales 1994). A direct connection between strong shareholder protection and the volume of IPOs has also been shown (see Table 2.7). What these studies tend to confirm is the comparative advantage of countries that protect investors' interests. Recent empirical work by La Porta et al. (2000) and Beck, Levine, and Loayza (2000) finds that firms operating in jurisdictions with strong shareholder protection have a higher growth potential, as measured by Tobin's Q.

Furthermore, Lombardo and Pagano (2002) find that better legal institutions influence equity rates of return and the demand for equity finance by companies. They offer two reasons for this relation: good laws and efficient courts (1) curtail the private benefits of managers and (2) facilitate the contractibility of the firm's relations with customers and suppliers and the enforceability of such contractual relations. Better corporate legislation and more efficient courts raise corporate profitability and growth, which in turn increases the

---

[19] Some argue that the framework developed by La Porta et al. (1998, 1999, 2000) is too limited (Berglöf and von Thadden 1999). In particular, by emphasizing the importance of dispersed ownership, the approach of La Porta et al. only appears relevant to the context of developed countries. Others argue that there have been significant changes over the last twenty years in the pattern of developing markets finance. The differences in corporate and legal rules cannot easily account for the differences in financial arrangements in emerging markets (Glen, Lee, and Singh 2000).

Table 2.6. *Shareholder and creditor protection*

	Shareholder protection	One share one vote	Creditor protection
UK	4	0	4
USA	5	0	1
English origin average	3.39	0.22	3.11
France	2	0	0
Belgium	0	0	2
Italy	0	0	2
Spain	2	0	2
Portugal	2	0	1
The Netherlands	2	0	2
French origin average	1.76	0.24	1.58
Germany	1	0	3
Austria	2	0	3
Switzerland	1	0	1
Japan	3	1	2
German origin average	2.00	0.33	2.33
Denmark	3	0	3
Finland	2	0	1
Norway	3	0	2
Sweden	2	0	2
Scandinavian origin average	2.50	0.00	2.00
Overall average	2.44	0.22	2.30

Note: One share one vote is a dummy variable which equals 1 if one share carries one vote (no multiple class voting rights). The shareholder protection index is higher if shareholders can mail their proxy votes, are not required to deposit their shares prior to the general meetings, cumulative voting is allowed, minority shareholders are protected and a minimum percentage of share capital allows a shareholder to call for an extraordinary general meeting. The creditor rights index is higher if absolute priority is upheld in case of financial distress.

Sources: La Porta et al. (1997).

availability of external financing. Lombardo and Pagano show that the imposition of legal limits on transactions with companies related through ownership cascades can preserve the income rights of minority shareholders and lead to a reduction in managerial benefits. Better legislation—via class action suits or voting by mail—leads to a reduction in the legal and auditing costs that shareholders must bear to prevent managerial opportunism. The authors conclude that the size of these effects on the equilibrium rate of return is increasing in the degree of international segmentation of equity markets.

Gompers, Ishii, and Metrick (2003) create a corporate governance index for US firms based on a large set of corporate governance provisions and focus on the relationship

Table 2.7. *External finance and legal origin*

	External capital/GDP	Listed domestic firms/Population	IPOs/ Population	Debt/GDP
UK	1.00	35.68	2.01	1.13
USA	0.58	30.11	3.11	0.81
English origin average	0.60	35.45	2.23	0.68
France	0.23	8.05	0.17	0.96
Belgium	0.17	15.50	0.30	0.38
Italy	0.08	3.91	0.31	0.55
Spain	0.17	9.71	0.07	0.75
Portugal	0.08	19.50	0.50	0.64
Netherlands	0.52	21.13	0.66	1.08
French origin average	0.21	10.00	0.19	0.45
Germany	0.13	5.14	0.08	1.12
Austria	0.06	13.87	0.25	0.79
Switzerland	0.62	33.85		
Japan	0.62	17.78	0.26	1.22
German origin average	0.46	16.79	0.12	0.97
Denmark	0.21	50.40	1.80	0.34
Finland	0.25	13.00	0.60	0.75
Norway	0.22	33.00	4.50	0.64
Sweden	0.51	12.66	1.66	0.55
Scandinavian origin average	0.30	27.26	2.14	0.57
Overall average	0.40	21.59	1.02	0.59

Notes: External capital is defined as the equity capital held by shareholders other than the largest three shareholders. Initial public offerings are companies which are brought to the stock exchange. Debt is here defined as the sum of the issued corporate bonds and the funds provided by banks.

Sources: La Porta et al. (1998, 1999, 2000).

between governance and corporate performance. They provide evidence on 1,500 large US firms that the firms with strong shareholder rights are associated with higher Tobin's Qs, higher profits, higher sales growth, lower capital expenditures, and fewer acquisitions. Consistent with the theory of La Porta et al. (2000), firms that adopt stronger shareholder rights create substantial benefits for shareholders. Similarly, Drobetz, Schillhofer, and Zimmermann (2003) relate the protection of shareholder rights and the long run performance for a cross-section of German firms. They construct a governance index based on five categories of corporate governance rules and provide evidence that better protection of shareholders leads to higher firm valuations (measured by price earnings ratios and market to book ratios).

In general, these studies document a positive effect of better corporate governance protection on financial market development. Some argue that the conclusions that can be drawn from these studies are limited because the direction of causality between the legal system and financial structure may run in the opposite direction, namely, financial structure prompts transformations taking place in the legal regime (Bolton and von Thadden 1998; Bebchuk and Roe 2000).

2.5. CONCLUSION

This chapter has presented an overview of the main corporate governance devices, which have been chosen for their possible relation to dividend policy. First, some corporate governance devices may have a direct impact on dividend policy. For example, ownership, control and their structure (the degree of control concentration, the presence of blockholders of a specific category of owner and hence with specific monitoring abilities, the changes in control through the market of hostile takeover or through block trades), the composition and independence of the board of directors, the concentration of bank debt and board representation of creditors may all have an impact on the payout ratio. In addition, these devices may also have an indirect effect on dividend policy by acting as substitute corporate governance mechanisms to dividend policy. A high dividend payout level may be a bonding mechanism for the management to generate sufficient cash flows in order to sustain the chosen dividend level. Failure to reach the anticipated dividend level may constitute a powerful signal to the market of possible managerial failure calling for intensified monitoring or the disciplining of the management. The presence of some of the above governance mechanisms may make dividend policy as a signalling governance mechanism redundant. Still, for firms operating in countries with weak legal shareholder or creditor protection, without strong blockholders or with passive large shareholders, the dividend policy may play an important corporate control role.

3

A Survey of the Literature on Dividends and Control

3.1. INTRODUCTION

This chapter draws on two important strands in financial economics: dividend policy and the ownership and control of public corporations. Starting with dividend policy, Miller and Modigliani (1961) proved that the market value of the firm is independent of its dividend policy in a world where (*a*) the firm's investment policy is fixed and known by investors, (*b*) individuals can costlessly buy and sell securities, (*c*) there are no personal or corporate income taxes, (*d*) no asymmetries of information exist, and (*e*) there are no agency costs between managers and outside investors. Since the early 1960s, the dividend debate has consisted of analysing the effect of relaxing the various assumptions underlying the Miller and Modigliani (1961) model on the value of the firm. This gave rise to different dividend policy theories.[1] First, signalling theories of dividends relax the assumption of symmetrical information between investors and managers. Second, agency cost explanations of dividends relinquish the assumption that managers' interests are aligned with those of the shareholders. Third, the different tax treatment of dividends and capital gains has given rise to conflicting views on whether dividends affect the market valuation of the firm. A large body of empirical literature testing these theories has shown that in real world capital markets, dividend policy seems to be important to corporations and investors.[2] The inability to reconcile the theoretical framework and the empirical evidence is referred to, in the financial economics literature, as the 'dividend puzzle' (Black 1976).

One important common feature of the signalling and agency cost theories of dividend policy is that they recognize that ownership and control of publicly quoted (Anglo-American) corporations are frequently widely dispersed and that atomistic shareholders receive benefits in proportion to their share stakes. In the context of agency theory, shareholders care primarily about diversifying away firm specific risks, while managers have a propensity to pursue their own interests which may be in conflict with the maximization of shareholder value. This leads to conflicts of interests between managers and shareholders, and dividends may help to resolve these conflicts. Under asymmetric information, dividends can be useful signalling devices of the prospects of the firm in situations where there are many small shareholders in the market.

---

[1] See Edwards (1987) and Lease et al. (2000) for an excellent survey.

[2] See Copeland and Weston (1988) and Lease et al. (2000) for a survey of the empirical literature. Dong, Robinson, and Veld (2002) use an extensive questionnaire on the reasons why individual investors care about dividends. They conclude that one of the main reasons is the signalling role of dividends.

More recently, financial economists have established that there is often considerable heterogeneity in the voting power of claim-holders of a particular firm. Voting power can occur in at least three forms. First, one or a few shareholders may hold large equity stakes that confer some degree of control. It should be noted that not all Anglo-American firms are characterized by dispersed ownership à la Berle–Means (1932). For example, Goergen and Renneboog (2001) report that in most UK firms institutional shareholders hold substantial minority stakes. McConaughy et al. (1998) find that in over 20 per cent of the largest 1,000 US corporations the founding family remains influential. Internationally, dispersed ownership is the exception rather than the norm (La Porta et al. 2000). For instance, Franks and Mayer (2001) and Becht and Boehmer (2001) provide evidence on concentration of ownership in German firms. Prowse (1992) and Berglöf and Perotti (1994) describe large concentration of ownership of Japanese firms. Becht, Chapelle, and Renneboog (2001); Bloch and Kremp (2001); and Crespí-Cladera and García-Cestona (2001) provide evidence on ownership and control concentration in Belgium, France, and Spain, respectively.

As mentioned in Chapter 2, cash flow rights do not necessarily confer control rights, as in many corporate governance regimes the one-share-one-vote principle is not upheld. A second and a third form of unbalanced voting power are dual-class shares and pyramid structures. The presence of dual-class shares,[3] typically one class with voting rights attached (ordinary shares) and another one with only cash flow rights attached (preference shares), allows the holders of ordinary shares to control a firm with a smaller percentage of the equity of the firm. Pyramid structures,[4] in which one firm controls another firm which in turn controls a third firm, may confer control to the (ultimate) shareholder, at the top of the pyramid, although he owns a smaller fraction of cash flow rights. For example, firm A owns 51 per cent of firm B, firm B owns 51 per cent of firm C. A has control of C although it owns merely 26 per cent of the equity of C.

Concentrated voting power gives shareholders the ability to influence the strategic decisions of the firm. For example, Morck, Shleifer, and Vishny (1988); Stulz (1988); and Demsetz and Lehn (1985) analyse the extent to which corporate ownership is related to performance. Franks and Mayer (2001) and Kaplan (1994) look at the issue of whether large shareholders impose higher management and supervisory board turnover in German firms in the presence of bad performance. Holderness and Sheehan (1988) study the issue of whether investment policies differ between majority-owned and diffusely held US firms.[5]

Following the above discussion as well as the one in Chapter 2, we will make a distinction between control and ownership wherever possible. As most of the theoretical models are based on the American context, they normally refer to ownership and ignore the possibility that ownership may not be identical to control and vice versa.[6] Whenever we use the term ownership we implicitly assume that ownership equals control.

---

[3] See DeAngelo and DeAngelo (1985) and Franks and Mayer (2001) for evidence on the USA and Germany, respectively.

[4] See, for example, DeAngelo and DeAngelo (1985); Goergen and Renneboog (2000); Renneboog (2000); and Franks and Mayer (2001).

[5] Refer to Chapter 2 of Goergen (1998) for a critical review of the literature on the link between firm value and ownership.

[6] This is quite puzzling as the USA has many devices (e.g. dual class shares) to disassociate control from equity ownership.

Traditionally, the dividend decision and the governance of corporations have been treated as two separate issues leading to two separate strands in the financial literature. However, a growing literature is emerging which focuses on the interaction between dividends and corporate governance. In fact, there is a strong case to analyse these jointly as (*a*) dividends can be used by managers to signal the performance of their firms to the shareholders, (*b*) dividend policy can assist shareholders in monitoring managers, and last, but not least, (*c*) dividends are 'hard cash' put in the hands of shareholders and are one of two ways (the other one is capital gains) of giving shareholders a return on their investment. However, if ownership is not widely dispersed then the extent to which managers use dividend policy may be different.

We begin by summarizing the extant finance literature on dividends and on ownership separately and then we look at the arguments that suggest a relation between them. The central idea behind our approach is to survey studies which establish to what extent concentration of ownership may reduce informational asymmetries and agency costs which arise when ownership and control are separated. Assuming that dividends are signalling and/or monitoring mechanisms, dividends and concentration of ownership may then be substitute devices used by firms to reduce such costs. Unlike most previous studies, we make a distinction between families and corporations as large shareholders. The rationale for this distinction is the fact that corporations, as shareholders, are in turn agents for their own shareholders. We argue that this leads to a different agency relation. In Sections 3.2 and 3.3, we explore these ideas in the context of signalling theories of dividends and agency costs, respectively.

There is a voluminous theoretical and empirical literature on dividend policy. As the main purpose of this chapter is to describe the arguments that suggest a link between dividends and control, we do not provide a comprehensive list of studies on dividend policy. We will, however, provide a summary of some of the most important contributions to the field. Furthermore, in what follows, we include some of the main institutional features of the different corporate governance systems. For example, one important feature of the block-holder system is the much discussed power of banks which—especially in Germany—may be both shareholders and creditors of firms. In Section 3.4, we briefly summarize the role of banks as major investors in this system, and describe how this can be related to the dividend policy of firms. In Section 3.5, we survey the taxation arguments related to dividends. Section 3.6 provides an overview of the empirical issues addressed in the book. The section also describes the empirical strategy that we follow in order to investigate these issues for Germany and the UK. Section 3.7 summarizes this chapter.

3.2. DIVIDENDS AND CONTROL AS ALTERNATIVE SIGNALLING DEVICES

3.2.1. *The Theory*

Miller and Modigliani (1961) were the first authors to suggest that dividend changes may convey managers' inside information on the prospects of the firm to outsiders. More recently, more formal models of dividends and information signalling have been developed.

A common feature of these models is that in order for a change in dividend policy to signal an increase in firm value, the management must be better informed than the marketplace, and there must be a cost to a 'bad' firm, that is, a firm with bad prospects, mimicking a 'good' firm, that is, a firm with good prospects. The cost–structure properties vary across models. In Bhattacharya (1979) and John and Williams (1985), the major signalling costs that lead dividends to function as credible signals arise because dividends have a tax disadvantage compared to capital gains.

Miller and Rock (1985) design a model in which 'net' dividends (i.e. the dividends minus new equity raised) represent good news. The cost of incorrect signalling with dividends is underinvestment as companies are paying out dividends, a 'cheap' source of funds, and may have to issue new equity, a more expensive source.[7] Edwards (1987) and Ambarish, John, and Williams (1987) generalize some features of the previous models and develop a model in which firms can simultaneously signal with dividends and investments, each subject to a different structure of dissipative costs. Dissipative costs are costs which create a separating equilibrium between firms who can afford to signal via dividends as they have good investment projects and firms for which it is too expensive, given that the investment has too low a return.

Kalay (1980) applies the Ross (1977) signalling model to the dividend decision of firms. He shows that managerial reluctance to cut dividends is a necessary condition for dividends to convey information. Hakansson (1982) refines the understanding of informative signalling and provides the conditions under which dividends can convey useful information in a general equilibrium framework. Ofer and Thakor (1987) develop a model in which firms signal unobserved firm value via share repurchases and dividends. The cost of signalling is the cost associated with raising new capital externally to finance future investments. Bar-Yosef and Huffman (1986) show that the size of the declared dividend is an increasing function of expected cash flows. In addition, they show that the higher the level of expected cash flows, the lower the marginal effects of cash flows on dividends. In a similar vein, Kumar (1988) shows that dividends can only be a coarse signal of firm prospects as firms tend to smooth their dividends.

The above studies suggest that (*a*) an increase in dividends per share can serve as a signal, and (*b*) that the signal is costly. The question we address next is whether insider ownership can also be used as a (substitute) signalling device.

In Leland and Pyle (1977), the owner's willingness to invest in his own project can serve as a signal that helps to resolve informational asymmetries between entrepreneurs and external investors. Given that the entrepreneur has a choice between the market portfolio and his own project, the fraction of the equity in the project which is retained by the entrepreneur is an unambiguous signal of the quality of the project. As a result, the value of his firm increases with the share stake of the firm he holds on. The cost associated with this signalling structure results from the fact that the entrepreneur holds a less diversified portfolio than he would if there were no informational asymmetry.

---

[7] The hierarchy of sources of funds is often called the 'pecking order of financing'. Companies will first use the cheapest source of funds (retained earnings), then bonds and bank debt, and finally new equity (Myers and Majluf 1984).

It is worth describing in more detail the Miller and Rock (1985) model in this context. The authors point out that the criterion for optimal investment by the firm is no longer an equilibrium, once trading in shares by shareholders is incorporated in the model along with inside information. The reasoning is the following: in a world where the market interprets the announced dividends as conveying information about current and future earnings, managers may be tempted to inflate the market value of the firm by paying out more dividends than the market was expecting, even if that is at the expense of the investment policy of the firm. Eventually, the market will learn the truth and the market price will be corrected downwards. However, as the authors show, the gain to the shareholders who sell out at the inflated price may be higher than the loss to those shareholders who did not sell. There is, therefore, an inconsistency problem. Eliminating the possibility of trading does not ensure an equilibrium because if managers cannot personally benefit from signalling until after the performance is observed, they have no incentive to bear the signalling cost. Miller and Rock (1985) go on to show that an informationally consistent signalling equilibrium exists—in a world with asymmetric information and where trading of shares is allowed—which restores the time consistency of investment policy, but leads in general to lower levels of investment. An important feature of the model is that the deviation from the full-information optimal investment is shown to be larger, the greater is the weight that the firm's objective function places on current prices as opposed to the weight placed on long-term returns. The former is the weight given to the interests of the selling shareholders, the outsiders, whereas the latter is the weight placed on those who hold the shares in the long run, namely the insiders. A cross-sectional prediction of this model is that the higher the value of the equity held by the insiders, the lower is the payout ratio and the higher the investment ratio in the signalling equilibrium.

Born (1988) provides an alternative interpretation of the role of insider ownership as a signalling device. Drawing from Miller and Rock (1985), the author argues that insider ownership is relevant to the assessment of dividend signals. If managers signal superior future performance by increasing dividends, they directly receive a financial return on the fraction of the equity they own. The validity of the signal can best be evaluated *ex ante* when a portion of the management's ownership stake cannot be sold out until after the future performance is realized and can be observed.[8] Managers with stakes held for a long period signal only if they view their shares as undervalued. If management has signalled incorrectly, the long-run decline in the restricted shares' market value can exceed the initial gain from the signal. Thus, the cross-sectional prediction that emerges is that market responses to signals should be positively related to the degree of insider ownership that is held for a sufficiently long period.

---

[8] Such restrictions exist in practice. For example, firms that have recently gone public are frequently subject to so called lock-in (or lock-up) agreements. These agreements prevent the initial shareholders from selling additional shares during a fixed period after the IPO. For the case of the UK, Espenlaub, Goergen, and Khurshed (2001) find that, although no such legal requirement exists, the initial shareholders of IPOs often have their shares locked in until the publication of the next financial report. In addition, a significant number of German firms have dual-class shares with the non-voting shares being listed on the stock exchange and the voting shares being in the hands of the large shareholder. As the latter are not listed, this may restrict their trading (at least in the short term).

John and Lang (1991) develop a model which treats dividends and insider trading as alternative signals. Both dividend announcements and insider trading convey private information to the market. Although it is based on the Leland and Pyle (1977) and Miller and Rock (1985) models, the John and Lang model also has some contrasting features. It not only introduces insider trading as an endogenous variable, but it also assumes that the insiders have private information on the firm's future investment opportunities such that dividend announcements and insider trading have to be jointly analysed. Depending on the nature of insider trading at the time of the announcement, a dividend increase may be perceived as a positive, negative, or neutral signal by the markets. In the case of an unexpected dividend increase, the firm's share price will react positively to abnormal insider buying activity, react negatively to unusual selling activity and not react if there is no abnormal trading activity.

To summarize, there is a large body of theoretical literature which points to the role of dividends as signalling devices. Still, this literature also points out that it is important to analyse dividend policy changes along with insider control, possible restrictions on the trading of insider stakes and insider trading activity.

3.2.2. *The Empirical Evidence*

The theoretical literature on the information content of dividends has strong empirical implications. They can be broadly summarized by these three statements: (i) managers tend to increase dividends only when there is a high probability that future cash flows are sufficient to sustain a higher payout rate; (ii) dividends are decreased only when managers believe that future cash flows will be insufficient to sustain the present rate; and (iii) there is a positive correlation between abnormal share price returns and the announcement of dividend changes. There are a considerable number of studies which report at least one of those empirical observations, although almost all of them relate to US firms (see Marsh 1992 for an excellent survey).

The US and UK Evidence

The empirical observation that managers are reluctant to change the firm's dividend policy has its roots in Lintner (1956) and Fama and Babiak (1968) (see Chapter 6 for evidence on how well those models fit German data). This reluctance has been documented for the USA by amongst others, Kalay (1980); DeAngelo and DeAngelo (1990); and DeAngelo, DeAngelo, and Skinner (1992, 1996). Marsh (1992) reports similar reluctance by managers of UK companies to cut dividends. Edwards and Mayer (1986) conduct a survey amongst members of the 'Hundred Group', an association of finance directors of the largest companies with offices in London. One of the stylized facts from their study was that companies indicated that only a persistent decline in earnings was likely to lead to a dividend reduction whereas a temporary decline in earnings was unlikely to elicit a dividend cut.

As far as the evidence on the positive correlation between dividend changes and share price returns is concerned, Pettit (1972) is one of the first documenting such a relation. However, two subsequent studies present conflicting evidence: Watts (1973) and Gonedes (1978) state that there is no real information content of changes in dividends as share prices do not react significantly. In contrast, more recent US studies consistently show evidence that dividends do indeed convey information beyond that already provided by earnings announcements (e.g. Aharony and Swary 1980; Asquith and Mullins 1983, 1986; Healy and Palepu 1988; Kane, Lee, and Marcus 1984; Ofer and Siegel 1987; Christie 1994). As with increases in regular cash dividends, specially designated cash dividends and share repurchases are also accompanied by permanent increases in stock prices (Brickley 1983; Dann 1981; Vermaelen 1981).[9] For the UK, Marsh (1992) finds results that are remarkably consistent both qualitatively and quantitatively with prior US research.

Finally, there is almost no empirical evidence on whether dividends and insider ownership serve as substitute signalling devices. We came across only four studies which investigate this argument, each from a different perspective. A first study is Zeckhauser and Pound (1990). The authors hypothesize that, if the primary function of dividends is to signal, there may be less need for dividends in the presence of a large shareholder. The presence of such a shareholder may serve as a substitute signal regarding future performance, because intensive shareholder monitoring reduces the degree of asymmetric information between managers and the shareholders and reduces managers' propensity to run the firm in the interest of shareholders. Zeckhauser and Pound compute the difference between the dividend payout ratios of firms with a large shareholder (defined as a shareholder with at least 15 per cent of voting equity) and of those without. They find that payout ratios are higher in firms with large shareholders, but the difference is not statistically significant. Still, the authors fail to control for corporate performance such that their conclusions may be premature. Moreover, the study assumes that signalling occurs via the *level* of dividends rather than via the *change* in dividends. Born (1988) provides evidence which supports his hypothesis that the abnormal announcement period returns are positively related to the degree of restricted insider ownership.[10] He interprets this result as being consistent with the idea that the shares that are restricted provide a 'performance bond' against false signals. Downes and Heinkel (1982) examine the relation between firm value and two potential actions by entrepreneurs who intend to signal information about otherwise unobservable firm characteristics to investors. The two signals are equity ownership retained by entrepreneurs and the dividend policy of the firm. They are hypothesized to be positively related to firm value. Using a sample of unseasoned new equity issues, the empirical results are consistent with the entrepreneurial ownership retention hypothesis, but the dividend signalling hypothesis is rejected. This may be interpreted as evidence showing that the two signals are substitutes. John and Lang (1991) test their model based on the alternative signals of insider trading and dividends. They find that dividend increases are greeted positively, negatively, or neutrally by the market depending on whether there is abnormal insider buying activity, insider selling activity, or no trading at all.

---

[9] The fact that specially designated dividends are shown to convey information may be considered as not consistent with the signalling role of dividends. However, Brickley (1983) finds this information effect because labelled dividends (or extra dividends) represent more than just a transitory increase in dividends and earnings.

[10] See Section 3.2.1 for a description of the argument.

Evidence on the Rest of the World

There is little evidence for countries other than the USA and the UK. Using German data, Amihud and Murgia (1997) test the John and Williams (1985) model which predicts that dividends are a credible signal given that they are taxed at a higher rate than capital gains. As there is no such tax disadvantage in Germany, dividend policy is expected to be less informative. Still, they find that the reaction of share prices to dividend news in Germany is similar to the one documented for the USA. Behm and Zimmermann (1993) test the validity of the Lintner model on thirty-two major German firms, during 1962–88, and conclude that it fits both aggregate and individual firm data rather well.[11] Another study by McDonald, Jacquillat, and Nussenbaum (1975) analyses the dividend policy of a sample of seventy-five French firms over the period of 1962–68 and concludes that the Lintner model fits the French data well.

Gugler and Yurtoglu (2003) offer a new explanation of why dividends may be informative: dividends signal the severity of the conflicts between the large controlling owner and the small outsider shareholders. They study 736 dividend change announcements in Germany over the period 1992–98 and find significantly larger negative wealth effects for companies where the ownership and control structure makes the expropriation of minority shareholders more likely than for other firms. Larger holdings of the largest owner reduce whereas larger holdings of the second largest shareholder increase the dividend payout ratio. Finally, they show that deviations from the one-share-one-vote rule due to pyramidal and cross-ownership structures are also associated with larger negative wealth effects and lower payout ratios.

3.3. DIVIDENDS AND CONTROL AS ALTERNATIVE MONITORING DEVICES

3.3.1. *The Theoretical Framework*

The separation of ownership and control gives rise to an agency problem.[12] The *agent* (manager) raises funds from the *principal* (investors). In exchange, the agent is presumed to be working in the interests of the investors by giving the latter a fair return on their investment. However, this relation creates considerable costs. As the managers are not the residual claimants to the firm's cash flows, the managers' interests may diverge from those of the providers of finance. Ideally, the different parties would sign a complete contract specifying in detail what managers ought to do with the funds, and how the returns are divided between them. In practice, however, all future contingencies are not foreseeable and managers and investors have to resort to monitoring devices.

The finance literature suggests several ways to reduce agency costs, two of which are relevant in this study: concentration of ownership, and dividends.[13] We start by discussing how concentration of ownership or control can reduce agency costs. Recent research has

---

[11] König (1991) and Hort (1984) confirm the Lintner model using German data.

[12] See Jensen and Meckling (1976); Fama (1980); Fama and Jensen (1983); and Shleifer and Vishny (1997) for a more detailed account of this problem.

[13] There are other candidates. One is debt (Jensen and Meckling 1976; Jensen 1986). Using more debt financing reduces total equity financing, reducing in turn the scope of the manager–shareholder conflict

pointed out that concentration of ownership also has costs. Therefore, we briefly survey these studies. We then review the literature which explains how dividends can reduce agency costs. We finally discuss the mechanisms by which dividends and concentrated ownership can act as substitute agency-cost control devices.

Concentration of Ownership or Control and Agency Costs

Concentrating cash flow and control rights in the hands of a large investor can align the interests of a firm's management with its shareholders (Jensen and Meckling 1976).[14] However, in a public corporation with many small shareholders, it may not pay for any of them to monitor the performance of the management. Shleifer and Vishny (1986) argue that large shareholders have the incentive to collect information and monitor the management, thereby avoiding the free-rider problem of control and bringing about value-increasing changes in corporate policy.

However, concentration of ownership can also give rise to a particular form of agency costs, the so-called private benefits of control (Grossman and Hart 1988). The concentration of voting rights in the hands of a single investor gives him the opportunity to treat himself preferentially at the expense of other investors and stakeholders (such as employees, suppliers of capital and goods, and customers). In other words, control may give him the possibility of expropriating minority shareholders. Morck, Shleifer, and Vishny (1988), for example, argue that once concentration of ownership is beyond a certain threshold (the point of entrenchment), the concentrated owners gain nearly full control such that they may prefer to generate private benefits of control that are not shared with other stakeholders. The danger of expropriation of the minority shareholders by a large shareholder may be even more pronounced in firms where the large shareholder holds more votes than cash flow rights. As mentioned above, control rights can be inflated by using devices such as non-voting shares, multiple voting shares or pyramids.

Control concentration may create an additional cost. By their very nature, large shareholders tend to hold undiversified investment portfolios. Consequently, this may reduce the risk-taking of the firm and lead to potential distortions in capital budgeting decisions.

Stulz (1988) focuses on the importance of the takeover mechanism as a disciplinary device for managers and formalizes a theoretical argument justifying a curvilinear relation between the value of the firm and the fraction of the shares owned by insiders. The market value of the firm first increases, then decreases as equity ownership is concentrated in the hands of insiders and reaches a minimum when insider ownership reaches 50 per cent. Morck, Shleifer, and Vishny (1988) find a slightly different relationship between firm value

(but increasing the scope of the shareholder–debtholder conflict). Another monitoring device is the composition of the board of directors (Fama 1980). Schellenger (1989) reports that the presence of outside directors on the board and dividends are substitute monitoring devices of agency problems. For an analysis about the effectiveness of different corporate governance devices, see Franks, Mayer, and Renneboog (2001).

[14] In the UK and the USA, it is common to call a large shareholder an individual or corporation with substantial minority ownership stakes, such as 10 or 20 per cent (see, e.g. Morck, Shleifer, and Vishny 1988). In Germany, and in other European countries, a large shareholder owns much larger stakes, typically above 40 per cent.

and managerial ownership. They find a positive effect of management ownership on financial performance if management ownership is between 0 and 5 per cent, a negative effect if it is between 5 and 25 per cent and a positive effect if it exceeds 25 per cent. McConnell and Servaes (1990) also empirically investigate the relation between Tobin's Q and the structure of equity ownership in US firms. They find a relation between Q and the fraction of common shares owned by corporate insiders which is close to the one predicted by Stulz, that is, a quadratic relation. The curve slopes strongly upwards until insider ownership reaches approximately 40–50 per cent and then slopes slightly downwards. Additionally, they find a significant positive relation between Q and the fraction of shares held by institutional investors. However, more recent studies on the link between firm value and ownership, such as Agrawal and Knoeber (1996); Kole (1996); Himmelberg, Hubbard, and Palia (1999); and Coles, Lemmon, and Meschke (2002), doubt the key assumption behind the earlier studies, that is, the assumption that ownership is exogenous (see ch. 2 of Goergen (1998) for a more detailed discussion of this issue). These studies show that these models may suffer from spurious correlation as a result of a reversal of the direction of causality between financial performance and ownership or of a left-out variable bias (Börsch-Supan and Köke 2000).

So far, we have assumed that the agency relations between managers and large shareholders are of the same type, irrespective of the nature of the latter. However, this may not be the case as different types of concentrated owners may have different abilities or expertise to exercise control or to monitor. Shareholders are typically individuals or families, or corporations or financial institutions, or the state. If corporations or financial institutions are the shareholders then there is a further agency relation that has to be acknowledged because the managers of these corporations or institutions are agents themselves. Besides the relation between the managers of a firm and its corporate owners, the corporations and institutions are themselves subject to agency costs between their managers and their shareholders. A particularly interesting type of outside shareholders is a bank. In Germany, for example, the largest banks own equity, are widely held, and may therefore be subject to agency problems. On one hand, they have strong political ties and there may be conflicts of interest between their managers and the firms in which they have invested. On the other hand, they may have more expertise than other shareholders. We will discuss this issue further in Section 3.4.

To summarize, concentration of ownership or control may (*a*) lead to a reduction in agency costs, and (*b*) be costly if there is almost full control by the concentrated owner.

Dividends and Agency Costs

Rozeff (1982); Easterbrook (1984); and Jensen (1986) develop the agency cost explanation of why companies may pay dividends. Rozeff (1982) argues that dividend payments are part of the firm's optimal monitoring/bonding package and serve to reduce agency costs. Easterbrook (1984) lists some of the mechanisms by which dividends and the consequent raising of capital can control agency costs. Agency costs 'are less serious if the firm is constantly in the market for new capital. When it issues new securities, the firm's affairs will be reviewed by an investment banker or some similar intermediary acting as a monitor for the collective interest of shareholders, and by the purchasers of the new instruments' (p. 654).[15] If there is no such verification process by a third party, then dividends may be an ambiguous signal as they do not differentiate growing firms from disinvesting firms. Finally, Jensen (1986) argues that managers with substantial free cash flow can increase dividends and thereby pay out cash that would otherwise be invested in low-return projects, and thus wasted. In other words, higher dividends may reduce the 'agency costs of free cash flow'.

Dividends, Ownership, Control, and Agency Costs

Easterbrook (1984: 657) suggests substitution among agency-cost control devices. One method of dealing with agency costs is for the managers to hold substantial residual claims in the firm. As such managers' claims increase, other things equal, dividends would be less valuable to investors and would decrease. In Rozeff's (1982) model, firms choose a dividend payout ratio that minimizes total costs: agency costs and transaction costs of financing. Agency costs decrease with dividends and transaction costs increase with dividends. Minimization of total costs produces a unique optimum for a given firm.

Schooley and Barney (1994) extend Rozeff's (1982) model, and propose a non-monotonic relation between dividend payout ratios and the percentage of managerial share ownership. The authors point out that this non-monotonic relation is consistent with the monitoring rationale for dividends (or convergence-of-interests hypothesis or even agency costs explanation of dividends) and the managerial entrenchment hypothesis (Morck, Shleifer, and Vishny 1988).[16] When the insiders' shareholdings are low, an increase in the ownership stake tends to reduce agency costs. As agency costs fall, dividend payouts become less desirable as a tool for further reducing agency costs, and thus dividends tend to decrease. At high levels of insider ownership (the managers are entrenched), agency costs tend to increase with an increase in the ownership percentage, and increased monitoring of the firm via higher dividends may again become necessary. Note, however, that the above studies suggest that it is increased managerial ownership which may reduce agency costs. In these models, the owner is essentially the manager, and they do not distinguish cases where the owner is also an agent, that is, the concentrated owner is a corporation acting in the interests of its own shareholders. As was suggested before, this may give rise to a different agency problem.

Jensen, Solberg, and Zorn (1992) claim that insider ownership may itself be determined by many of the same firm-specific features that affect dividend and debt policy. Therefore, insider ownership, debt and dividend policy are simultaneously determined. This reasoning

---

[15] There are some problems with this argument. First, if there are many purchasers of new equity issues, there may be a free-rider problem similar to the one affecting owners of old securities. Second, it is not necessarily true that the investment bank's incentives are the same as the investors' interests.

[16] Morck, Shleifer, and Vishny (1988) investigate the relation between management ownership and market valuation of the firm, as measured by Tobin's Q. They find evidence of a significant non-monotonic relation. Tobin's Q first increases as managerial ownership increases up to 5 per cent, then declines up to managerial ownership of 25 per cent, and finally rises slightly as ownership by the board of directors rises (see fig. 1, p. 301). Still they admit that the 'theory [the convergence-of-interests and entrenchment hypotheses] provides relatively little guidance as to what this relation should be . . .' (p. 294).

follows directly from Demsetz and Lehn (1985), who provide evidence that insider ownership choices are endogenous outcomes of value-maximizing behaviour. The studies by Agrawal and Knoeber (1996); Kole (1996); and Himmelberg, Hubbard, and Palia (1999) corroborate the endogenous nature of insider ownership.

Two other studies point to different aspects of the relation between dividends and concentrated voting power. Eckbo and Verma (1994) argue that shareholder disagreement (arising from, for example, heterogeneous shareholder tax rates, information asymmetries, and agency costs) over dividend policy may be the rule rather than the exception in publicly held companies. The authors develop a 'dividend consensus hypothesis', whereby actual dividend policies represent a compromise solution where the interests of various heterogeneous shareholder groups are represented by the group's voting power. Shleifer and Vishny (1986) present a model of firm valuation in which the payment of dividends serves to reduce agency costs. In their model, dividends serve as a side payment to large shareholders, such as institutional or corporate investors (who, in the USA, have a tax preference for high dividends), to entice them to hold the shares and to monitor managers.

Dividend Payout Policies in a World with Both Agency Conflicts and Asymmetric Information

To conclude this section, we mention the paper by Noe and Rebello (1996) which develops a theoretical approach to understanding financing and payout policies in a world where there is both adverse selection and managerial opportunism. In their model, a firm, initially owned by a large shareholder and managed by an incumbent manager, seeks funding for an investment opportunity. The shareholder and the manager have private information about the firm's prospects and the manager possesses unique rents that give rise to agency conflicts with shareholders. Within this context, the firm has to raise capital to fund its investments (which are supposed to be higher than its internal funds). To obtain outside financing, the firm must issue a mixture of debt and equity. Depending on whether a firm is shareholder-controlled (the large shareholder typically being an institutional investor) or manager-controlled, the authors disclose the least costly financial signals (in the spirit of the 'pecking order' à la Myers 1984), which include a combination of internal funds (restricting dividends), debt, equity financing, and selling underpriced claims. More specifically, it emerges from the model that in shareholder-controlled firms restricting dividends signals favourable information. This happens in spite of the shareholders' preference for a stronger reliance on external capital—and hence more dividends and debt—to reduce managerial opportunism. However, to issue equity will be more costly (the cost of mispricing securities) and therefore, lower dividends are chosen as a signal. In manager-controlled firms, a reversed hierarchy may apply. There, higher dividends convey more favourable information.

3.3.2. *The Empirical Evidence*

The US and UK Evidence

Rozeff (1982) provides evidence which corroborates his prediction that firms establish higher payout ratios when insiders hold a lower fraction of the equity and/or a greater number of shareholders own the outside equity. Several other studies have provided evidence consistent with this observation (e.g. Dempsey and Laber 1992; Crutchley and Hansen 1989). Hansen, Kumar, and Shome (1994) test a similar specification to Rozeff (1982) on data from the regulated electric utility industry. They interpret their evidence as suggesting that dividends promote more intense monitoring of—what they call—the shareholder–regulator conflict. Eckbo and Verma (1994) find evidence indicating that cash dividends decrease as the voting power of owner–managers increases, and are almost zero when owner–managers have absolute voting control of the firm. Jensen, Solberg, and Zorn (1992) and Noronha, Shome, and Morgan (1996) discuss results consistent with the monitoring rationale for dividends in the context of testing the hypothesis of simultaneity between capital structure and dividend decisions.

Born and Rimbey (1993) corroborate the Easterbrook (1984) hypothesis that high dividends are used as a self-disciplining mechanism forcing the firm to raise outside equity and thereby to face the scrutiny of outsiders. Their sample comprises 490 US firms which initiated or reinitiated dividends over the period 1962–89. They find that slightly more than a fifth of their firms (102 firms) raised outside finance over the 12 months preceding the dividend change. They argue that the financing should precede the dividend change so as to avoid an ambiguous dividend signal. Although they find that the dividend announcement of firms raising outside finance generates lower abnormal returns than that of firms that do not raise additional finance, the former firms have a higher abnormal return per unit of the dividend yield than the latter. Filbeck and Mullineaux (1999) carry out a test similar to the one by Born and Rimbey, but focus on bank holding companies. In contrast, they do not find any support for the Easterbrook (1984) hypothesis. They explain their result by stating that monitoring of bank holding firms by the capital market is not crucial given that a bank regulator exists.

Moh'd, Perry, and Rimbey (1995) also test the validity of Easterbook (1984) and Rozeff (1982) but use improved proxies for agency and transaction costs. They measure agency costs by insider control, control by institutional shareholders, and ownership dispersion. They also use a time series—on 341 US firms for the period 1972–89—rather than a simple cross section. They not only find support for Easterbrook and Rozeff, but also find that firms adjust their dividends to reflect changes in their agency and transaction costs.

Chen and Steiner (1999) jointly study dividend policy, managerial ownership, risk taking, and capital structure. Their sample consists of a cross-section of 784 US firms for the year 1994. The results from the estimation of a simultaneous equation system suggest that managerial ownership and risk are jointly determined.[17] The results also indicate that managerial ownership and dividend policy are substitute mechanisms to reduce agency costs. Similarly to Chen and Steiner (1999), Crutchley et al. (1999) examine the joint determination of four devices expected to decrease agency costs: dividend policy, debt leverage, inside ownership, and institutional holdings. They analyse two cross sections of over 800 NYSE

---

[17] They find that, similarly to Demsetz and Lehn (1985), risk determines managerial ownership in a nonlinear way. At low levels of risk, there is a positive relationship whereas at high levels of risk the relationship becomes negative. They also document that higher management ownership leads to increased risk taking. This is in line with the theory that predicts that more managerial ownership increases the agency problem between the shareholders and debtholders.

and Amex listed firms for 1987 and 1993 in order to measure the potentially increasing activism by institutional shareholders. For 1987, they find that the dividend payout and institutional ownership are jointly determined and positively correlated. Inside ownership does not seem to influence the dividend payout. Conversely, for 1993, the dividend is negatively determined by institutional ownership whereas the latter depends positively on the former. The authors attribute the change in the effect of institutional ownership on dividends to the increasing involvement of institutional investors in the firms of which they hold shares.[18]

Short, Zhang, and Keasey (2002) investigate the impact of institutional ownership and managerial shareholdings on the dividends of a sample of 211 UK firms from the Official List. They estimate four dividend models—the full adjustment model, the partial adjustment model, the Wauld model, and the modified earnings trend model—while including a dummy variable which is set to one if there is at least one institutional shareholder owning in excess of 5 per cent of the firm's shares and another dummy variable which equals one if the managers own in excess of 5 per cent of the shares. For each of the four models, they find consistent evidence that high institutional ownership leads to dividend increases whereas high managerial ownership reduces the dividends. The authors argue that institutional investors reduce agency costs not directly by monitoring the management of the firms they invest in, but by forcing these firms to raise outside equity regularly which subjects them to the scrutiny of the capital markets. Furthermore, institutions may pressurize firms into paying higher dividends given their tax status and their own cash flow needs. Similarly, for the USA, Zeckhauser and Pound (1990) find no evidence that large shareholders and dividend payouts are alternative forms of monitoring. In contrast to all the previous studies, Schooley and Barney (1994); Hamid, Prakash, and Smyser (1995); and Crutchley et al. (1999), test a non-linear relation between dividends and insider ownership. Consistent with their theoretical formulations, they discover a convex relation between insider ownership and dividend yields.

Evidence on the Rest of the World

La Porta et al. (2000) study the dividend policy of 4,103 large firms from thirty-three countries. They measure the potential for agency problems by the degree of shareholder protection in the firm's country. They find that firms from countries with high shareholder protection pay on average higher dividends. In addition, the dividend payout ratio of the firms from these countries is negatively related to their investment opportunities (as measured by the sales growth). Conversely, the dividend ratios of firms from countries with low shareholder protection are independent of their growth opportunities. La Porta et al. interpret this as evidence of the agency costs of low shareholder protection.

Faccio, Lang, and Young (2001) argue that the control of continental Western European and East Asian companies is very similar. In both regions, a significant number of firms are controlled by families or by groups of shareholders. Control also tends to be leveraged, as there are frequent violations of one share one vote. Hence, agency problems mainly take the

---

[18] The authors' results also indicate that although in 1987 inside ownership does not determine the dividend, in 1993 there is a quadratic relationship between the two. No reasons are offered though.

form of an expropriation of the minority shareholders by the large controlling shareholder. However, despite the similarities in terms of control, dividend policies are very different: Western European firms tend to pay higher dividends than their East Asian counterparties. Faccio et al. conclude that in Western Europe firms where expropriation of minority share- holders is more likely, such an accusation is warded off by paying high dividends.

Although the two previous studies link dividend policy to agency costs, they are fairly general and they concentrate on the macro level. The following studies focus on the micro level, namely particular types of shareholders (or control structures) and address the question as to whether monitoring by specific types of large shareholders is a substitute mechanism for a high dividend payout policy in order to reduce agency costs.

Gul and Kealey (1999) study Korean companies. They analyse whether there is a link between *Chaebol*, large conglomerates owned by family and bank shareholders, and divi- dends. They do not find such a relationship. Gul (1999a) unveils a positive link between the dividend paid and government ownership for Chinese firms.

Gugler (2003) hypothesizes that different types of shareholders may rely differently on costly dividend signalling and may provide different degrees of monitoring. Government- controlled firms tend to have the highest degree of agency problems and asymmetry of information as they are ultimately owned by the citizens, who tend to have even fewer incentives to monitor the management than the small shareholders of privately owned firms. Hence, the managers of government-controlled firms will prefer a stable dividend policy and high dividends to keep their principals happy and to safeguard their private benefits. Family-controlled firms are subject to lower agency costs and less asymmetry of information. Hence, dividends should be less important as a signal and they should be more flexible. However, it is more difficult to make any predictions about the dividend policy of bank and foreign-controlled firms, as their dividend policy depends on their ultimate con- trolling shareholder, who may differ. Gugler finds evidence for his hypotheses for a sample of quoted and unquoted Austrian firms.[19] If investment opportunities are good, then state- controlled firms have the highest dividend payout and practise dividend smoothing whereas family-controlled firms have lower ratios and do not engage in dividend smooth- ing. The dividend policy of bank-controlled and foreign-controlled firms is somewhere in between. Finally, firms with few investment opportunities pay out high dividends whatever their control structure. Similar to Gugler (2003), Yurtoglu (2000) finds that the dividend payout ratio of listed Turkish firms which are family controlled is lower than that for other firms. However, to the opposite of Gugler, he also shows evidence that state-controlled firms have lower dividend payout ratios.

To summarize, agency cost theories and a fair number of empirical studies suggest that dividends and concentrated ownership act as alternative forms of monitoring. There is evidence that when families are controlling shareholders, agency costs decrease such that one has to rely less on costly dividend signalling. However, there is much less conclusive empirical evidence on whether other types of shareholders act as monitoring substitutes for dividends.

---

[19] Only about a fifth of his sample consists of quoted firms and most of the unquoted firms only have one shareholder.

3.4. THE CORPORATE GOVERNANCE ROLE OF BANKS

3.4.1. *The Institutional Setting and the Conventional Wisdom about the Role of Banks*

Germany, France, Italy, and Japan are traditionally regarded as being bank dominated (Rajan and Zingales 1995: 1445). The universal feature of banks confers two roles on them: the provision of external finance and of corporate control.[20,21] In this chapter we are only concerned with the latter role.[22]

The important role that German banks can play in corporate governance derives basically from three sources. First, banks have direct equity participations in industrial and commercial companies (see Chapters 2 and 8; Becht and Boehmer 2001; Franks and Mayer 2001 for a detailed description of ownership and control in Germany). Edwards and Fischer (1994: 114) provide evidence that the equity owned by German banks is concentrated predominantly in the hands of the largest banks (Deutsche Bank, Dresdner Bank, and Commerzbank). Second, since most German shares are bearer securities, individual shareholders deposit their shares with their bank.[23] As Edwards and Fischer (1994: 196) argue, the banks have control over a considerable proportion of the voting equity of large corporations at the general shareholder meeting, mainly derived from the proxy votes they exercise rather than from their own holdings of shares. A third source is the representation of banks on the supervisory boards of German firms. Franks and Mayer (2001) report that banks have extensive supervisory board representation, especially in widely held firms.[24]

As a result, depending on the extent of their control of voting rights, banks can have a significant influence on the voting outcome at the annual meeting of the shareholders, and in particular on shareholder representation on the supervisory board. Long-term external finance and active control have been regarded as the cornerstones of the merits of the German system of investment finance. According to this view, long-term relations between firms and banks and active corporate control by banks alleviate agency costs and asymmetries of information between investors and managers.[25] Bank representation and control give the banks the power to discipline poor management.[26] In addition, technical expertise,

---

[20] An important contribution to the understanding of this issue is provided by Edwards and Fischer (1994).

[21] A universal banking system is typically characterized by banks which can underwrite, trade, and, in particular hold a firm's equity.

[22] The interested reader is referred to Edwards and Fischer (1994); Mayer (1990); Corbett and Jenkinson (1996); Mayer and Alexander (1990); Rajan and Zingales (1995); Allen and Santomero (2001); and Carlin and Mayer (2002) for evidence on patterns of financing in different countries. Note that it emerges from this literature that German firms do not rely as much on banks for their external finance as is generally believed.

[23] An AG may issue registered shares, bearer shares or both. However, most listed shares are bearer shares, compounding the difficulty of identifying the shareholders (Boehmer 2002).

[24] See also Edwards and Fischer (1994: table 9.2) for further evidence.

[25] Jensen and Meckling (1976) argue that incentive problems raise the cost of external finance. Outside financing dilutes management ownership, thereby exacerbating incentive problems. Myers and Majluf (1984) point out that if managers are better informed than investors about a firm's prospects, the firm's risky securities will typically be underpriced, thereby raising the cost of external financing.

[26] This traditionally contrasts with a market-based financial system, such as the USA and the UK where the hostile takeover mechanism is regarded as performing a key role in disciplining management. See Hart (1995) for

bank representation and long-term relations give the German banks access to superior information.

The central idea that emerges from this view is that, assuming that dividends play a monitoring and signalling role, bank ownership and control may be alternative mechanisms which alleviate information asymmetries and conflicts of interests between firms and shareholders, and therefore reduce the need for high dividends.

In addition, the banks' extensive involvement in widely held firms contributes to the absence of a market for corporate control in Germany (Mayer and Alexander 1990). Hostile takeovers become difficult without the consent of banks at the annual meetings.[27] More specifically, if dividends are an important part of the defence strategy of firms or if the threat of a takeover encourages a higher level of earnings distributions than would otherwise be the case,[28] then the absence of such a threat in Germany (for bank controlled firms) may put downward pressure on the dividend payout of firms. Note, however, that although this argument may explain cross-country variations in payouts, it does not explain the variations observed within Germany.

The institutional setting in Japan suggests a similar set of arguments. Kester (1986); Prowse (1990); Hoshi, Kashyap, and Scharfstein (1990, 1991); and Berglöf and Perotti (1994) argue that the close ties between Japanese management and investors (especially within the *keiretsu* or industrial group, where banks own debt and equity in member firms) substantially reduce information asymmetries and agency conflicts relative to their US counterparts. Accordingly, banks that own both debt and equity have a strong incentive to monitor firm performance closely and reduce the probability that management will engage in behaviour that favours one set of stakeholders over another. Hoshi, Kashyap, and Scharfstein (1991) present evidence suggesting that information and incentive problems in the capital market affect investment. Investment is found to be more sensitive to liquidity in firms where there are weak links to a main bank and which presumably face greater problems raising capital. Dewenter and Warther (1998) suggest that in such a context dividends play less of a signalling and monitoring role and find empirical evidence consistent with this hypothesis. Gul (1999*b*) finds additional support for this. Although there is no statistically significant difference in terms of the dividend payout ratio between *keiretsu* firms and non-*keiretsu* firms, the former have significantly lower dividend yields than the latter.

At first sight Italy seems to have a corporate governance system similar to Germany and Japan. Bianchi, Bianco, and Enriques (2001) document that ownership is concentrated, pyramids occur frequently and hostile takeovers are rare. Banks own about 8 per cent of the market value of listed firms. However, Bianchi, Bianco, and Enriques (2001) and Brunello, Graziano, and Parigi (2003) argue that the Italian system differs substantially in terms of the monitoring role of banks. First, banks were not allowed to exercise their customers'

a brief survey of the mechanisms for controlling management that are available to investors. Nickell (1995) and Shleifer and Vishny (1997) provide a survey of this literature.

[27] Franks and Mayer (1998: 1385) point out that there are only 'three cases of hostile takeovers in Germany in the post Second World War period' and prior to 2000.

[28] See Jenkinson and Mayer (1994) and Dickerson, Gibson, and Tsakalotos (1998) for evidence in the UK that dividends are a defence mechanism against takeovers.

proxy votes from 1974 to 1998. Since 1998, proxy voting has been possible, but it is limited to stakes exceeding 1 per cent and the procedure is complex. Second, banks tend to be government-owned, and therefore their own governance structure may not be efficient. Most firms also tend to have loans from several banks rather than a single bank and collateral is normally required. All this suggests that for the case of Italy there are no strong reasons to believe that banks act as a monitoring substitute to dividends.

Dherment and Renneboog (2002) investigate the control patterns of a sample of 325 listed French companies. They document that industrial and commercial companies are the largest category of owners with an average of 22 per cent of the voting shares whereas the combined direct ownership concentration of institutions—banks, investment and pension funds, and insurance companies—amounts to 20 per cent. Financial and industrial holding companies control 17 per cent of the equity in the average firm. Similar to Germany, Italy, and Belgium, French ownership and control structures are complex with stakes held through multiple tiers of ownership. Dherment and Renneboog find little evidence that institutional investors, banks or the government are monitoring poorly performing firms (those with dividend declines). These results for France are equally valid for Belgium (Renneboog 2000).

3.4.2. *Evidence on the Effect of Bank Involvement on Dividends*

The previous discussion suggested a number of issues to which empirical research can provide an important contribution. Do banks mitigate informational and agency problems, or do they act in their own interest and to the detriment of corporate performance? Apart from the studies discussed below, little empirical analysis is undertaken to answer this important question.

Low et al. (2001) analyse the market reaction to dividend omissions for two samples of large and small US firms which omitted their dividend some time between 1978 and 1996. They find that the announcement of the dividend omission causes a less negative abnormal return for small firms with substantial bank debt than for small firms with no or little bank debt. However, they do not detect such a relationship for their sample of large firms. They also find that non-bank debt has less of a positive effect on the abnormal return at the dividend announcement than bank debt. This suggests that banks reduce informational asymmetry and/or agency costs.

If banks have an impact on the dividend policy of firms in the USA, where banks are not allowed to hold equity stakes in industrial and commercial firms, then one would expect that the influence of banks in a capital market such as Germany would be even more substantial. Cable (1985) estimates the relation between bank involvement and corporate profitability for a sample of forty-eight leading German firms. The author finds a significantly positive relation between bank involvement and profitability, which goes beyond what may be expected from market power enhancement or the provision of financial expertise alone. He interprets this result as consistent with the hypothesis that bank involvement alleviates informational problems and reduces the costs of aligning the interests of shareholders and managers. Gorton and Schmid (2000) test the relation between performance and bank influence in two years: 1975 and 1986. They find that equity ownership by German banks improved performance while proxy votes did not. They argue that this is evidence of the monitoring role of German banks. They interpret the absence of an impact of proxy votes on financial performance as evidence against conflicts of interest arising from the use of proxy votes by banks.

An alternative hypothesis to the hypothesis that banks mitigate informational and agency problems is that banks are no more (or less) likely than corporate management to detect and pursue opportunities for monopoly rents (Cable 1985). Moreover, banks have strong political ties and are themselves widely dispersed corporations subject to agency problems. Edwards and Fischer (1994) summarize extensive evidence suggesting that German banks are not nearly as active in corporate governance as might be expected from their lending and equity voting power. For example, the authors do not find evidence supporting the view that representation on the supervisory boards of firms enables banks to supply more loan finance to these firms. Moreover, they do not find evidence consistent with the view that banks reduce the costs of financial distress and bankruptcy by closely monitoring and controlling the actions of managers of firms in financial difficulty. Another important finding is that banks do not in general exercise a high degree of control in German corporations where there is a non-bank blockholder (see Franks and Mayer 2001 for a similar conclusion).

In contrast with Cable (1985) and Gorton and Schmid (2000), Chirinko and Elston (1996, 2000) do not find a robust positive effect of bank influence on profitability. Franks and Mayer (2001) study the disciplining of poorly performing management and find no evidence of a positive influence of bank ownership on board turnover in poorly performing companies. Furthermore, Mayer and Alexander (1990) discover no difference in the degree of bank lending to large German firms than to large UK firms, which the authors interpret as evidence inconsistent with the asymmetric information hypothesis.

Although an empirically testable and a relevant question, the relation between dividend policy and bank influence in Germany has received even less attention in the finance literature. To our knowledge the only study that has to some extent provided a contribution to this issue is Chirinko and Elston (1996). A probit analysis of the impact of their measure of bank influence on individuals revealed no pattern. They use two different measures of bank influence. The first measure is a dummy variable which is set to one for firms which have a German bank or insurance firm holding at least 25 per cent of their shares and do not have another shareholder owning in excess of 25 per cent of their equity. The second measure is similar, but uses the higher threshold of 50 per cent.

3.5. THE TAXATION ARGUMENT

Perhaps the most controversial issue in the dividend literature is whether taxes affect dividends.[29] The USA explicitly double-taxes corporate income, once at the level of the firm and a second time when it is received by shareholders. Until 2003 in this 'classical' tax system

---

[29] Litzenberger and Ramaswamy (1982) survey the theoretical taxation arguments and empirical evidence. See Copeland and Weston (1988) for a see also Chapter 5 Lease et al. (2000) survey of the debate.

dividends were taxed at a higher rate than capital gains at the personal level.[30] This raises the question as to why dividends are paid at all. In contrast, in the UK, the dividend income earned by pension funds from their investments was tax exempt until the fiscal reform of July 1997. Until then, tax-exempt shareholders had a strict preference for dividend payments (Bond, Chennells, and Devereux 1995).[31] Similarly, in Germany, corporate shareholders have a clear preference for dividends, but this is not the case for domestic individuals in the highest marginal income tax brackets. So, it might be argued that there is a tax rationale for dividend payments. In Chapter 8 we describe in more detail the tax status of different classes of shareholders in Germany.[32]

Previous studies on the taxation argument of dividend policy have shed some light on at least one of the following questions: (1) 'Do firms with high dividend yields have higher or lower share prices?', (2) 'Does the dividend policy affect specific types of shareholders? (in other words, does a tax-induced dividend clientele exist?)', and (3) 'Do certain types of shareholders (with their specific tax position) influence corporate dividend policy?'

A different way of describing the first question is to ask whether investors require higher rates of return on ordinary shares with high dividend yields (i.e. dividend per share over share price). Under the assumption that dividends and capital gains are taxed differently, Brennan (1970) derives a model of share valuation in which shares with high payouts have higher required before-tax returns than shares with low payouts. However, the empirical tests of Brennan's model yield ambiguous results: the impact of the dividend tax on share price returns depends on the definition of dividend yield employed.[33] Although Black and Scholes (1974), and Miller and Scholes (1978, 1982) argue that the value of the firm is independent of its dividend yield, the empirical work by Litzenberger and Ramaswamy (1979, 1982) and Poterba and Summers (1984) shows that capital gains are valued more highly than cash dividends. Two recent studies on the USA and the UK, however, show mixed evidence. Hubbard and Michaely (1997) analyse the effect of the US tax reform of 1986 on Citizen Utilities. Citizen Utilities have two classes of shares. Class A pays a cash dividend and class B pays a stock dividend. They find that the decrease in the tax rate applied to cash dividends compared to capital gains did not have an impact on the valuation of the two classes of shares. Conversely, Bell and Jenkinson (2002) find strong support that the UK tax reform of 1997 has an effect on the valuation of high-yield firms.

Miller and Modigliani (1961) suggest the existence of a dividend clientele. The empirical evidence on the existence of a clientele effect is also mixed. Elton and Gruber (1970) and Litzenberger and Ramaswamy (1982) provide evidence for US firms which is consistent with the idea that investors in high tax brackets prefer low dividend shares, presumably because they pay lower taxes when receiving their return in the form of capital gains.

---

[30] See Brealey and Myers (2003) and McDonald (2001) for an overview of the tax treatment of dividends in the USA. In 2003, the Bush administration stopped the top dividend tax rate to 15%, below the top rate for capital gains of 20%.

[31] Bell and Jenkinson (2002) find that, prior to 1997, pension funds were the marginal investors for firms with high dividend yields. They predict that the UK tax reform of 1997 will cause changes in the investment allocation of pension funds as well as the valuation of high-yield firms relative to low-yield firms.

[32] See also McDonald (2001) for a comparison of the German and US tax systems.

[33] Copeland and Weston (1988: 588–96) provide a more detailed account of the issue.

However, Lewellen et al. (1978) find a very weak clientele effect in US firms and Lasfer (1996) finds no evidence of a tax-induced clientele effect in UK firms.

Although we acknowledge the relevance of the two previous questions, we do not address them further in this book. Instead, we focus on the third question, that is, whether a firm's dividend policy is affected by the tax status of its shareholders. The intuition is the following. If the argument is true and there is a shareholder with high voting power, or a vast amount of small shareholders with the same tax status, then we would expect to observe firms adopting dividend policies according to the tax status of their shareholder(s) (Eckbo and Verma 1994). Lasfer (1996) and Poterba and Summers (1984) report findings suggesting that UK firms consider their shareholders' tax position when setting their dividend policies. Bond, Chennells, and Windmeijer (1996b) provide evidence consistent with the proposition that the higher the voting power of institutional investors in the UK, the higher is the dividend payout of the firms these institutions invest in. Finally, Eckbo and Verma (1994) provide evidence on Canadian firms suggesting that the controlling shareholder's tax position has an economically important effect on the dividend payout of firms.

Germany provides us with a very rich field of experiment because, as we have discussed previously, there is high concentration of ownership in the hands of a few shareholders. Moreover, there is some degree of heterogeneity in the tax preference for dividends across different classes of shareholders. To test the tax clientele effect for German firms, we need to (*a*) establish the tax status of the different shareholders in Germany, (*b*) investigate the voting power of the different classes of shareholders, and (*c*) compute a tax discrimination variable associated with each class of investors. We investigate these issues in detail in Chapter 8.

3.6. SUMMARY

This chapter surveyed the mechanisms by which dividends and control structures can be related and examines the insights that can be drawn from an analysis of the different dividend theories. Dividends can convey information about the prospects of the firm. Still, when control is high, dividends may become less important signalling devices. Hence, dividend signalling is important in widely held corporations whereas control concentration can act as a substitute in closely held corporations. This argument calls for two qualifications. First, it is not clear how one should define control in a context where the principle of one-share-one-vote is not upheld (due to pyramiding, proxy votes, etc.). Therefore, in the empirical analysis in Chapter 8, we use different definitions of control. Second, strong control may lead specific classes of owners (e.g. insiders, other corporations, families or individuals) to capture private benefits of control, possibly at the expense of other (small) shareholders. In such cases, strong control causes different agency problems, namely those between major and small shareholders. Committing to a high dividend payout may reduce the potential externalities of control concentration. In this context, dividend policy and control concentration are not substitutes, but are complements. Therefore, there may be a need to consider the costs of dividend signalling and control concentration simultaneously.

Agency costs explanations of dividends and control provide a more straightforward set of hypotheses regarding the relation between dividend policy and control. Theory suggests that both dividends and control can reduce conflicts between managers and shareholders, but are costly. In turn, high concentration of ownership or control can give rise to agency problems related to the private benefits of control, and high dividend payouts can generate high transaction costs. We also argued that when the concentrated owner is himself an agent (i.e. a corporation), concentration of ownership or control may give rise to an agency relation with higher costs than when the main shareholder is a family or an individual. One particularly interesting class of shareholders in Germany is banks. German banks, presumably long-term providers of equity and debt, may alleviate agency conflicts and asymmetries of information. In such a framework, the need for dividends to perform that role may be reduced. Although an empirically pertinent and testable hypothesis, it has received little attention in the finance literature.

Finally, we briefly reviewed the taxation argument for dividends. We put forward the argument that if the tax status of different shareholders is an important consideration in the dividend setting of firms, firms where large shareholders have sufficiently high voting power will follow dividend policies in line with the tax status of their controlling shareholders. Consequently, we expect that taxation on dividends will induce tax clienteles.

PART II

DIVIDEND FLEXIBILITY ACROSS CORPORATE GOVERNANCE SYSTEMS

4

Research Questions

This chapter serves the following purposes: to draw a set of empirically testable hypotheses which we will formally test in the next chapters and to describe the empirical strategy followed in the second part of this book. The survey of the theoretical and empirical literature from the previous chapters suggests that different mechanisms exist by which dividends and control may be related. We focus our discussion on the following forms of corporate control: control by families or individuals, by banks, by other corporations (each of which is corrected for the control effects of pyramiding) and the lack of control due to share dispersion across many shareholders.

4.1. SIGNALLING, DIVIDEND POLICY, AND CONTROL CONCENTRATION

As we have documented in Chapter 3, there is a vast body of literature which claims that unexpected changes in dividends convey additional information about the prospects of a firm, over and above the one provided by earnings. Furthermore, firms are reluctant to cut or omit dividends as this signals bad prospects. As signalling by changing the dividend may be costly, specific control structures may reduce the need for dividend signalling. For example, in Leland and Pyle (1977) it is suggested that a higher equity stake held by the manager–entrepreneur reduces the informational asymmetries between outside investors and the manager. In firms with strong concentration of ownership or control, dividend policy may be less informative to the market, and hence have less of a signalling role.

Information theories suggest that closely held firms are less reluctant to cut or omit the dividend (Hypothesis 1)

The signalling hypothesis is tested by using two estimation methods. In Chapter 6, we test Lintner's (1956) 'partial adjustment model' on German data. This model provides evidence on the degree of managerial reluctance to change the dividend. As a complement to this analysis, we follow a discrete choice modelling approach which allows us to estimate the probability that German firms increase, decrease, or omit the dividend. We also estimate the likelihood that German firms cut or omit the dividend in the presence of established good past performance, current losses, and concentration of ownership. The results are reported in Chapters 7 and 8.

4.2. AGENCY COSTS, DIVIDEND POLICY, AND CONTROL CONCENTRATION

Widely dispersed shareholdings can give rise to severe agency costs. On the one hand, the existence of a large shareholder may align the interests of shareholders and managers, and reduce those costs. On the other hand, a higher dividend payout ratio can also reduce agency costs, by increasing the likelihood that the firm has to raise outside financing and, in turn, be subject to outside monitoring. Following Rozeff (1982) and Easterbrook (1984), concentrated holdings can mitigate the need for costly dividends to reduce agency costs.

According to the monitoring rationale for dividends and concentrated control, there is a negative linear relation between the level of dividends and the level of concentration of control. As such, dividends and control concentration are substitute monitoring mechanisms (Hypothesis 2)

However, Morck, Shleifer, and Vishny (1988) suggest that once control goes beyond a certain threshold (the point of entrenchment), the controlling shareholder may treat himself preferentially at the expense of outside minority shareholders. Following Schooley and Barney (1994), beyond this threshold the increased monitoring placed on the firm by higher dividends may become necessary.

According to the convergence-of-interests and managerial entrenchment argument, the relation between dividends and concentration of control is downward sloping over some initial range of control and then upward sloping (Hypothesis 3)

The agency costs hypotheses are examined by using an estimation method that permits us to establish by how much the level of dividends changes following a change in the ownership structure. To do so, we model the dividend behaviour of German firms using a 'partial adjustment model' à la Lintner (1956), and subsequently, incorporate different shareholder control variables into this model. The results are reported in Chapter 6.

Whereas the above hypothesis refers to managerial control, control by other classes of large shareholders may also give rise to different agency relations and costs. Three classes are worth distinguishing: families or individuals, banks, and other corporations. A controlling stake in the hands of a family or individual, rather than a corporation, may give rise to agency costs of free cash flow (Jensen 1986; Eckbo and Verma 1994). If the largest shareholder holds control over the firm's operations, it is possible that he decides to spend current cash on low-return projects or pay himself a high salary, instead of investing this cash flow in the projects yielding the highest net present value. Furthermore, as will be discussed in Chapter 8, German citizens in the highest marginal income tax bracket have a slight tax preference for long-term capital gains versus dividends.

In the presence of a tax disadvantage of dividends versus capital gains, corporate control held by a family or individual may be associated with lower dividend payouts (Hypothesis 4)

An alternative hypothesis has to do with the costs associated with a lower portfolio diversification as the individual's share stake in the firm increases. A possible implication of this cost is that families need to pay themselves 'hard' cash so that, for example, they can pay the large personal borrowings to finance the larger stakes.

Risk-averse individuals may have a preference for a high dividend payout in order to compensate for a less diversified portfolio (Hypothesis 5)

The two previous hypotheses are tested in Sections 8.3 and 8.6 of Chapter 8, respectively. Both tests consist of a panel data analysis and address the question of how much dividends change when the control held by families increases.

Control by banks is particularly interesting in the light of the alleged corporate governance role played by German banks in industry. The traditional view presented in this chapter is that long-term relations between firms and banks (in their role as both creditors and owners of equity) alleviate agency costs and asymmetries of information between outside investors and managers (see, e.g. Cable 1985).

Bank control is associated with lower dividend payouts and less reluctance to cut omit the dividend in firms in which they invest (Hypothesis 6)

This hypothesis is examined in Chapter 8.

One source of corporate control available to German banks is proxy voting (i.e. German banks can act as delegated exercisers of equity control rights. See Chapter 8 for further details). However, Gorton and Schmid (2000) argue that proxy voting can create a conflict of interests between banks and small shareholders on behalf of whom banks exercise the votes. 'Because banks themselves seem impervious to external control, the concentration of power in banks is seen as allowing them essentially to run firms in their own interest. For example, banks can refuse to allow cash to be paid out of firms in order to maintain 'hidden reserves'. Or a bank may force a value-reducing merger between a distressed and a non-distressed firm, both of which it controls.'(p. 30)[1] Proxy votes are usually more important in firms that are widely held. If banks act in the interests of widely dispersed shareholders, proxy voting may be a substitute for dividends in reducing agency and informational costs.

Proxy votes and dividends are substitute monitoring and signalling devices in widely held firms. Thus, proxy votes are negatively related to the level of dividends and the reluctance to cut or omit dividends (Hypothesis 7)

We examine this issue further in Chapter 8.

A final class of large shareholders is industrial or commercial corporations which are in turn agents to their own shareholders. Therefore, they may themselves be subject to agency conflicts and be less effective monitors than other classes of shareholders. Furthermore, in Chapter 8 we show that corporations have a strong tax preference for dividends.

(a) Assuming that dividends and large shareholdings are substitute monitoring devices, firms owned by other corporations may have higher payouts than firms owned by other classes of shareholders; (b) assuming that the tax status of shareholders is a determinant of dividend policy, firms controlled by domestic corporations have higher payouts than firms controlled by domestic individuals (Hypotheses 8(a) and (b))

Hypothesis 8(a) is tested in Section 8.3.3 (the monitoring hypothesis) and hypothesis 8(b) is tested in Section 8.6 (the taxation argument) of Chapter 8.

As Franks and Mayer (2001) argue, one of the main features of the German capital market is the extensive use of complex shareholding structures (pyramids)—shares held in one

---

[1] Wenger and Kaserer (1998) subscribe to the idea that banks increase rather than reduce agency costs.

company which in turn holds shares in another company. Majority or large minority stakes at each level of the pyramid may enable the ultimate shareholder to retain control. This leads us to a final hypothesis which says that

Complex shareholdings do not dilute control at intermediate levels of the pyramid, such that concentrated owners at the ultimate level are the controlling shareholders of corporations. In other words, control as mentioned in the previous hypotheses should be measured and interpreted as ultimate control (Hypothesis 9)

Alternatively, long chains of intermediate control (tall pyramids) dilute control exerted by the shareholder at the ultimate level. The higher the ownership tier from which the ultimate control is exerted, the less effective may be the monitoring performed by an ultimate shareholder in comparison to the monitoring by a large shareholder at the first tier. This competing hypothesis is examined in Chapter 8, where we compare the results of the estimations when we use first-tier shareholder structures with the results obtained when we use control at the ultimate level. The results on the latter are reported in Sections 8.3–8.5, and the findings on the former are described in Section 8.6.

5

Empirical Issues on Dividend
Payout Ratios

5.1. INTRODUCTION

This chapter is an introduction to the empirical chapters of this book. Its purpose is threefold: first, to discuss some of the stylized facts on dividend policy around the world; second, to provide a methodological framework for analysis by describing issues related to corporate and personal taxes and to company law that are relevant to the study of the dividend policy of German firms; third, to challenge some conventional views on how low dividends are in Germany compared to the UK and the USA. For that, we look at the dividend policy of all the German industrial and commercial publicly quoted companies, a large sample of UK firms, and published evidence on US firms. The evidence we provide in this chapter is an attempt to address the following questions: (*i*) what proportion of firms' cash flows and net profits are paid out as dividends; (*ii*) how has the dividend payout ratio evolved during a 10-year period, from 1984 to 1993; (*iii*) how stable are dividends in Germany; (*iv*) how do these results compare with evidence from the UK and the USA; and (*v*) do dividend payout ratios differ significantly across different patterns of ownership and control?

The structure of the chapter is as follows. In Section 5.2, we review patterns on dividend policy around the world and discuss some of the methodological problems arising from the analysis of dividend policy across countries. In Section 5.3, we briefly describe the German tax treatment of dividends and capital gains.[1] This section also discusses some important issues relating to German dividend policy. For example, some provisions of the German company law have important implications for this study. Section 5.4 describes the data used in Chapters 6–8. We start by looking at how the dividend policy of German firms changes in line with profits. We determine the proportion of firms' reported earnings and internal sources of funds that is paid out as dividends. A particular reference is made to the importance of zero dividend payout policies. The results of these analyses are mainly compared with a selected sample of UK firms but also, to a lesser extent, with UK and US published evidence. The section also shows how dividend payout ratios vary across different size distributions, industries, and patterns of ownership. Section 5.5 summarizes the main findings of the chapter.

---

[1] The German tax treatment of dividends and capital gains is discussed in greater detail in Section 8.6 of Chapter 8.

5.2. STYLIZED FACTS ON DIVIDEND POLICY ACROSS THE WORLD

Lease et al. (2000) review the empirical studies on the dividend yield in particular countries. They find that shareholders of firms from Germany, France, Italy, Switzerland, and Japan earn lower dividend yields than those of firms from the UK and USA. To our knowledge, La Porta et al. (2000) is the only cross-country study on dividend policy.[2] They study the dividend policy for a cross section of 4,103 listed firms from thirty-three countries. They categorize these countries in two groups depending on the origin of their legal system, civil law versus common law. They argue that civil law countries provide on average a lower degree of shareholder protection than common law countries. Furthermore, they find that firms from civil law countries pay out lower dividends as compared to those from common law countries. They interpret this as evidence of the agency cost of low shareholder protection.

However, a close analysis of their data (see Table 5.1) shows that this pattern is not as clear-cut as the authors may believe. They use three different measures of dividend payout: the ratio of dividends over cash flows, the ratio of dividends over earnings, and that of dividends over sales. Although, the medians of these three measures are significantly lower for the civil law countries, there are some countries that stick out and do not seem to conform to this simple pattern. For example, Germany and Japan, both civil law countries, have dividend payouts—as measured by dividends over earnings—that are higher than the median payouts of the common law countries. Taiwan, another civil law country, has a dividend payout which—depending on the measure used—is between 2.5 and 6 times the level of the median dividend payout of the common law countries. Conversely, Canada, a common law country, has a dividend payout which is lower than the median dividend payout of the civil law countries.[3]

The review of the La Porta et al. (2000) study raises some important issues. First, the way the dividend payout is measured is important as the use of different measures tends to lead to different conclusions. This issue will be further discussed in Section 5.3. Second, low shareholder protection may come hand in hand with low accounting standards. Again, this calls for a thorough comparison of the different measures of dividend payouts. Third, cross-sectional studies of dividend policy miss out one important element, namely, year-to-year changes in dividends. It may very well be the case that the anecdotal evidence (see Introduction), stating that dividend policy of German firms is more flexible, is true. These three issues are among those which we will further develop in the following section of this chapter.

5.3. INSTITUTIONAL FRAMEWORK

The purpose of this section is to provide a brief overview of some important issues relevant to this study on German dividend policy. The issues relate to: (*i*) 'control agreements' which

---

[2] Other studies that analyse the dividend behaviour in more than one country, but not across as large a number of countries as La Porta et al. (2000) do, are: Leithner and Zimmermann (1993) (France, Germany, Switzerland, and the UK), and Dewenter and Warther (1998) (Japan and the USA).

[3] In the empirical chapters of this book we find that there is no simple, linear relationship between dividend payouts and ownership or control in Germany. This constitutes a clear refinement to La Porta et al. (2000).

Table 5.1. *Dividend payout ratios around the world*

Country	N	Low production	Div/CF (%)	Div/Earn (%)	Div/Sales (%)	GS (Annual)	Div. tax adv.
Panel I: Medians							
Argentina	3	0	12.65	27.36	4.32	14.32	1.00
Austria	9	1	5.85	24.83	0.77	13.31	0.78
Belgium	33	1	11.77	39.38	1.09	3.78	0.74
Denmark	75	1	6.55	17.27	0.71	4.32	0.67
Finland	39	1	8.08	21.27	0.77	−2.14	1.07
France	246	1	9.46	35.55	0.63	4.54	0.64
Germany	146	1	12.70	42.86	0.83	5.88	0.86
Indonesia	1	1	8.72	25.11	0.77	32.62	0.76
Italy	58	1	9.74	21.83	0.92	−1.38	0.77
Japan	149	0	13.03	52.88	0.72	6.19	0.70
South Korea	2	1	7.33	18.49	0.66	5.29	0.79
Mexico	14	1	19.47	46.44	3.59	8.02	1.00
The Netherlands	96	1	11.29	30.02	0.74	4.13	0.40
Norway	50	0	10.74	23.91	0.98	4.43	1.08
Philippines	4	1	6.72	10.47	2.45	−7.29	1.05
Portugal	17	1	0.64	38.01	0.64	8.20	0.98
Spain	33	0	15.77	30.45	1.04	1.32	0.72
Sweden	81	1	5.59	18.33	0.78	−0.63	1.03
Switzerland	70	1	10.38	25.30	0.98	3.73	0.56
Taiwan	3	1	48.97	68.89	11.54	1.62	0.60
Turkey	6	1	8.61	22.64	2.08	0.16	0.90
Civil Law Median	*33*	*1*	*9.74*	*25.11*	*0.83*	*4.32*	*0.78*
Australia	103	0	22.83	42.82	2.22	2.21	0.90
Canada	236	0	8.00	19.78	0.78	−0.62	0.89
Hong Kong	40	0	35.43	45.93	7.51	7.94	1.00
India	1	0	25.69	49.34	1.55	−0.09	0.59
Ireland	16	0	17.39	27.28	0.96	9.96	0.77
Malaysia	41	0	15.29	37.93	3.12	16.31	0.68
New Zealand	17	0	19.16	35.60	2.26	3.11	1.00
Singapore	27	0	22.28	41.04	2.14	11.02	0.96
South Africa	90	0	16.16	35.62	1.90	3.47	0.85
Thailand	10	1	32.83	52.56	3.35	17.73	0.90
United Kingdom	799	0	16.67	36.91	1.89	2.44	0.83
United States	1,588	0	11.38	22.11	0.95	3.15	0.58
Common Law Median	*40*	*0*	*18.28*	*37.42*	*2.02*	*3.31*	*0.87*
Sample Median	*39*	*1*	*11.77*	*30.02*	*0.98*	*4.13*	*0.83*
Panel II: Test of medians (z-statistic)							
Civil vs Common Law			3.97***	−3.29***	−1.722*	−2.36**	−0.34	−0.09

Notes: Panel I classifies countries by legal origin and presents medians by country. Definitions for each of the variables can be found in Table 5.2. Panel II reports tests of medians for civil versus common legal origin.

* Indicates significance at the 10% level.

** Indicates significance at the 5% level.

*** Indicates significance at the 1% level.

Source: La Porta et al. (2000).

may exist in firms with a large shareholder; (*ii*) preference shares which earn a guaranteed dividend; (*iii*) share repurchases; and (*iv*) German accounting rules.

Some quoted German companies have 'control agreements' with their parent company.[4] There are two types of control agreements that can exist between a controlling company and a subordinate stock corporation (*Aktiengesellschaft-AG*): a Profit and Loss Agreement (which we call PLA) (*Gewinnabführungsvertrag*) and a Subordination of Management Agreement (SMA) (*Beherrschungsvertrag*).[5] SMAs require losses to be absorbed by the controlling company but the transfer of profit is optional. In the case of a PLA, there is always a transfer of the profit or loss to the controlling company.[6] The relevant question is, thus, whether the controlled companies should be included in this study.

We opt for their exclusion from the analysis for two reasons. First, the main purpose of these two control contracts is to take advantage of possible tax losses carried forward at the level of the subordinate company.[7] The controlling company can then absorb these losses and offset them against the annual profits so as to reduce its taxable profit. This is advantageous because, in Germany, like the UK but unlike the USA, the taxable profit is established solely on the basis of the accounts of the individual companies in the group. Thus, the amount transferred to the parent company is not a dividend *per se*, but is the result of an opportunity to reduce the tax liability of the parent company. Second, financial reporting is very complex and hard to interpret in these cases. Often, there is no profit disclosed and what is shown is the amount (which may be positive or negative) that is transferred to the parent company (*Gewinnabführung*) as well as the dividend per share paid to the 'free' shareholders (the minority shareholders of the controlled company). One way of circumventing this sample exclusion bias is to use consolidated accounts. If the parent firm is publicly quoted, the transfers from the subordinate firm to its parent company will be accounted for in the parent firm's financial reporting, and therefore these subordinate firms will be recorded (indirectly) in our sample. This is one reason why consolidated accounts have been used in this study. The other reason has to do with provisions concerning the profit distribution, to which we now turn.

---

[4] In a sample of all 477 German industrial and commercial quoted companies in 1993, we came across sixty-one companies which fall into this category. See Section 5.4.

[5] Both agreements require the approval of at least 75% of the voting capital represented at general meetings of both the controlling and subordinate companies. Note that the existence of a controlling shareholder does not necessarily imply the existence of either PLA or SMA type of agreements.

[6] The minority shareholders of the subordinate company are offered protection against expropriation by the group. They must either be offered a guaranteed dividend, or given the opportunity to sell their shares, either for cash or, if the controlling company is a German company, shares in the controlling company. In legal terms, there is no guarantee that a positive dividend will be paid to 'free' shareholders, that is, the minority shareholders of the subordinate company. However, in practice, it is usually the case that positive dividends are paid even if there are losses at the subordinate company level. In some cases, the 'free' shareholders of the subordinate company are offered a fixed percentage of the dividend per share that the shareholders of the controlling company receive (e.g. shareholders of Audi AG receive 100% of the dividend per share received by the VW AG's shareholders).

[7] The German corporate tax system stipulates that Net Operating Losses for corporation tax purposes must first be carried back and offset up to the amount of DM10 million against taxable income of the preceding two years to the extent that such income has not been distributed. Remaining losses can be carried forward without time limit.

The regulation of the profit distribution is referred to in paragraph 150 of the German Stock Corporation Act (AktG §150). According to this provision, the corporation is obliged to build up from its profits a legal reserve (*gesetzliche Rücklage*) in the balance sheet.[8] The annual profit, after transfer to the legal profit reserve is then the basis for distribution according to the provisions of AktG §58, which basically state that the management board (*Vorstand*) and the supervisory board (*Aufsichtsrat*), without consulting the shareholders,[9] can retain part, but no more than half, of the annual profits. In other words, this provision requires companies to pay out at least 50 per cent of their current profits as dividends. However, this is not the case for all companies as other requirements such as legal reserves and special provisions (such that the management board may be authorized to transfer up to 100 per cent of the year's profit to profit reserves) in the articles of association of companies mitigate the impact of AktG §58.

An implication of these provisions is that profits shown in group accounts are generally larger than those shown in the unconsolidated, parent AG. Legally, when deciding on the dividend policy of the firm, the (parent's) management only has to take into consideration the profit of the parent (unconsolidated) company. However, in practice, group accounts play a fundamental role in the dividend payout decision. If the holding company's results were substantially lower than the group's accounts, shareholders could demand either an explanation or a higher dividend. Thus, for the purposes of this study, we opted for the group's profit as the profit measure.[10]

Preference shares (*Vorzugsaktie*) are frequently issued by German corporations.[11] In almost all cases, they carry no voting rights,[12] but are entitled to a minimum cumulative preferred dividend. In general, if this dividend is not paid during two consecutive years then the preference shares become voting shares. Preference shares, relative to ordinary shares (*Stammaktie*), are not only given priority in terms of the dividend they receive, but also receive an excess dividend of usually between DM1 and DM2 per share.[13] These stock corporation provisions basically ensure that firms which are fully controlled by one or a few shareholders and which have issued quoted preference shares, do not adopt dividend policies that favour the large shareholders at the expense of the minority non-voting shareholders.

---

[8] To this legal reserve are transferred 5% of the year's profits (reduced by any losses brought forward) until the sum of the legal reserve and the capital reserve reaches 10% of the share capital (or any higher percentage specified in the company's statutes).

[9] As long as there is no control agreement between the controlling and subordinate companies.

[10] Harris, Lang, and Möller (1994) show that consolidation increases the value relevance of accounting measures for German companies.

[11] For example, of all 477 industrial and commercial quoted firms in 1993, ninety-eight had preference shares issued.

[12] Except in a few cases where the term *preference share* refers to shares with multiple voting rights rather than to a preferential dividend.

[13] In other words, where there are dual-class shares of this type, distributed profits are first accorded to preference shares and in case there is current profit left, ordinary shares start to receive a dividend. Once the amount paid to ordinary shares reaches the amount accorded to preference shares and if there is further profit left, the marginal increase in dividends paid is the same for both types of shares although the preference shares generally receive a small premium in excess of the ordinary shares.

In Germany, public corporations are generally not allowed to buy their shares back (AktG §§ 71–71e). There are a few exceptions. For example, a company can acquire its own shares up to a total of 10 per cent of its share capital if this repurchase is necessary to avoid serious damage to the company (i.e. loss of property or assets), or with the intention of offering them to the employees of the company.

Finally, one further issue. German accounting rules are often considered to be particularly deficient in the information disclosed to investors.[14] Relative to the Anglo-American approach to financial reporting, the German system has traditionally encouraged a certain degree of conservatism (see Harris, Lang, and Möller (1994) for an overview of the system). In particular, three factors contribute to a conservative bias in the profit figure disclosed. First, there is some degree of prudence in asset valuation. The imparity principle (*Imparitätsprinzip*) requires unrealized losses to be recognized but not unrealized gains. Second, as a consequence of the link established by the AktG §58 (see above) between dividends and earnings, managers have incentives not to report earnings that attain a desired dividend policy because higher reported earnings may create shareholder pressure for higher dividends.[15] Third, the existence of pension provisions may also account for a certain downward bias in the published profit figure. We will shortly come back to this point.

In the light of conservative reporting of accounting information, we provide an alternative measure of corporate profitability throughout the following chapters. We define cash flows as zero distribution profits, gross of depreciation, and changes in long-term provisions. As this definition merits an explanation, we briefly discuss: (*i*) zero distribution profits and dividend related taxation; (*ii*) depreciation; and (*iii*) pension and other provisions.

1. *The German tax system affects measured profits and dividend payout ratios.*[16] If dividends are taxed differently from retained earnings, then corporate tax liabilities are sensitive to dividend distributions. The convention that has been used in this case is to measure profits by zero dividend distribution profits and these are defined as

$$\frac{D(1-t_c)}{(1-t_d)} + R \tag{5.1}$$

where t_d accounts for the tax rate on dividends distributed, t_c for the tax rate on retained profits, $D(1-t_c)$ are net dividends (i.e. dividends net of tax), $D/(1-t_d)$ are gross dividends and R are earnings retentions. In order to understand how dividends in Germany affect tax liabilities, assume that a firm makes a loss. If it omits its dividend, then there will be no tax liability. However, if it decides to pay out a dividend despite its loss, then there will be a tax liability (equal to t_d times the dividend distribution).

---

[14] See, for example, Waller, D. 'Germans Draw Line at two Sets of Accounts', *Financial Times*, 19 Mar. 1992; The Lex Column, 'German Accounting', *Financial Times*, 6 Feb. 1995.

[15] Although one should bear in mind all these difficulties when interpreting German accounts, there is no empirical evidence that reported earnings in Germany have less value relevance than those in other countries. For example, Harris, Lang, and Möller (1994) argue that German reported earnings have informational content similar to those of the USA.

[16] See Mayer and Alexander (1990) for a more detailed discussion of the issue.

A detailed discussion of dividend taxation on the corporate and shareholder level is given in Chapter 8.

2. Depreciation is included as it is merely a bookkeeping transaction that does not involve cash inflows or outflows.

3. Long-term provisions are defined as the sum of provisions for pensions (*Pensionsrückstellungen*),[17] and other provisions (*Sonstige Rückstellungen*). The inclusion of pension provisions in the calculation of the cash flow deserves a comment because, for example, in the UK this item is not significant. In one respect, the pension provisions should be regarded as a liability (from the company towards the employees) and therefore it should not be part of retentions. However, in our view, there is a strong case for considering it as a form of cash flow. Edwards and Fischer (1994, table 3.4, p. 66) report that, between 1970 and 1989, this amount accounted for approximately 6 per cent of the non-financial enterprise sector internally generated funds. The authors also argue that firms frequently have a high degree of discretion over the way in which pension provisions are invested. This is another reason why the bottom line profit figure may be so conservative in Germany. Therefore, we opt for the inclusion of this item in the cash flow figure. The item 'other provisions' is net of tax provisions, such as deferred taxation.

5.4. SAMPLE AND DATA

As of the end of 1993, there were 655 companies listed on the German stock market. This compares with a number of 2,412 in the UK; 1,777 in Japan (Tokyo); 6,973 in the USA (Nasdaq and New York combined); and 677 in France (Paris) (Quality of Markets Review 1994). This shows that the German stock market is small compared to the Anglo-American and Japanese markets.

Our sample consists of all 477 German industrial and commercial quoted companies reported in *Saling Aktienführer* published by *Hoppenstedt* at the end of September 1993. These firms are quoted either on the official market (*Amtlicher Handel*) or the unofficial regulated market (*Geregelter Markt*) in one or more of Germany's eight stock exchanges. We exclude financial firms (insurers, banks, financial holdings, etc.) as these firms follow investment and dividend policies that are arguably different from industrial and commercial companies. From the same source, we collect data on published after-tax net income, depreciation, changes in pension provisions and in other provisions, cash dividends per ordinary share and per preference share, number of ordinary and preference shares, share prices at the end of each quarter of 1993, as well as a detailed description of all holdings of voting equity.

---

[17] These take the form of a direct commitment by the firm to its employees: An enterprise makes provision for its employees by investing its contributions to employee pensions within the enterprise itself. The pension payments are financed by making provisions in the firm's balance sheet. When the provisions are made by the firm they reduce its profits, and hence its tax liability, whereas when the pensions are paid out to the employees they are adjusted with no effect on profits. See Edwards and Fischer (1994: 53–8) for a more detailed overview of the German system of pension provisions.

In our sample, there are sixty-one companies which have control agreements with their parent companies;[18] thirty-nine companies with only preference shares quoted; and ninety-eight companies with dual-class shares with at least one class of shares quoted. Control agreements and dual-class shares are simultaneously present in only three companies. Because of the reasons mentioned in Section 5.3, the sixty-one companies with control agreements are excluded from the analysis. This reduces our sample to 416 companies. To control for industry differences, we use the trade and industry classification provided in Commerzbank's *Wer gehört zu wem* of 1991.[19] We were able to partition 397 of the 416 companies into fourteen different industries (see Table 5A.1 in the appendix to this chapter) with the remaining twenty-three firms making up a category labelled 'other industries'.[20]

We use three different definitions of dividend payout ratios. The first definition is the ratio of total gross dividends to total published profits. We take gross instead of net dividends because the former reflect the total amount the firm pays out to both shareholders and the tax authorities. As the sample is drawn from all quoted companies in 1993, some firms were not quoted in previous years. For these firms, the average payout ratio refers only to the years in which they are quoted. A problem with the calculation of payout ratios arises from the fact that companies sometimes pay dividends even though they incur losses or are only just breaking even. Therefore, we calculate the aggregate dividend payout ratio as the sum of the total dividends across all firms divided by the sum of all profits across all firms.[21] Two other payout ratios are calculated on a cash flow basis. One is defined as zero distribution profits gross of depreciation and changes in pension provisions. The second one is essentially the same as the previous one but also considers changes in 'other provisions'.

In order to draw a comparison with dividend payout ratios of UK firms, we draw a sample of 250 UK industrial and commercial quoted firms from *Extel Financial Handbook* (June 1993). The whole population of 1,090 domestic UK industrial and commercial quoted firms reported in *Extel* is partitioned in five different size quintiles, ranging from a market capitalization of £0.436 m to a maximum of £26,532.8 m. Next, we draw a sample of fifty

---

[18]   Generally, in these sixty-one cases, the controlling shareholder has more than 90% of the subordinate company. The question as to why these subordinated companies, or others not under these agreements but similarly closely held, are quoted is a very interesting one. Some possible explanations have to do with the fact that because they are mainly small and regional companies, a flotation brings many advantages: a managerial labour market, because a flotation increases the publicity about the company and may therefore attract better managers; more effective monitoring, because of the requirements in terms of supervisory board representation; and, more equity can be raised.

[19]   The choice of this year has to do with the fact that this book is only published every three years.

[20]   The other nineteen firms were not listed in *Wer gehört zu wem*.

[21]   In other words, it is defined as

$$\frac{\sum_{i}^{N} D_{it}}{\sum_{i}^{N} P_{it}}, \qquad i = 1,\dots N \text{ firms},$$

where *D* are cash dividends paid to shareholders of ordinary and preference shares (including bonuses), *P* are published profits.

industrial or commercial firms from each size quintile. From *Datastream*, we obtain data on retentions, ordinary and preferred dividends, changes in long-term provisions (net of deferred tax), irrecoverable Advance Corporation Tax (ACT)[22] and depreciation.[23]

Analogous to the method used in the calculation of the profit figure of German firms, an after-tax profit on a zero dividend distribution basis is calculated in order to avoid the endogeneity of after-tax profits, which depend upon dividend-induced tax liabilities. In the case of the UK, this affects calculated profits only for those firms which reported irrecoverable ACT during the study period. We follow Edwards et al. (1986) for the calculation of zero distribution profits. Essentially, these are obtained by adding back irrecoverable ACT to net published profits.[24]

5.5. DIVIDEND PAYOUT RATIOS

5.5.1. *The Dividend Decision*

In Germany, dividends are normally declared once a year.[25] Formally, the management board (the finance director in particular) and the supervisory board together propose a dividend per share to the annual meeting of shareholders, which normally approves the proposal. In case the supervisory board does not reach an agreement with the management board, it is up to the shareholders' meeting to decide on the amount of the dividend per share.

---

[22] Until 1997, the UK operated an imputation system of corporation tax, under which part of a company's corporation tax liability is regarded as a prepayment of personal income tax on dividends to shareholders. A company is required to pay dividends net of personal income tax charged at the rate of imputation (which has always been set equal to the basic rate of income tax, i.e. 25% since 1988): this gives rise to a tax charge known in the UK as Advance Corporation Tax (ACT). Shareholders are then liable to personal income tax on the notional gross dividend, credit being given for the tax deducted at source. The company's overall liability to corporation tax thus comprises two elements: ACT and the remainder known in the UK as mainstream corporation tax. The company can offset ACT against its mainstream liability subject to the restriction that the amount of ACT set off cannot be greater than the amount which would, together with the dividend distribution to which it relates, equal the company's taxable profits. If taxable profits are not large enough for ACT to be fully offset then some part of the company's ACT is unrecovered. Usually unrecovered ACT is carried back or forward or even deducted from the balance of deferred tax. It is irrecoverable if its recoverability is not 'reasonably certain and foreseeable', that is the carry-forward should normally not extend beyond the next accounting period. Companies have to disclose the amount of irrecoverable ACT but not the amount of unrecovered ACT. Thus, as a proxy for unrecovered ACT, irrecoverable ACT data were collected. See Edwards et al. (1986) for an excellent description of the UK imputation system of taxation. See Bell and Jenkinson (2002) for a study on the impact of the tax reform of 1997 on UK dividend policy.

[23] The *Datastream* codes (noted DS in what follows) are the following. Retentions (i.e. published after-tax profits, after deducting dividends)—DS196. Ordinary dividends-DS187. Ordinary dividends per share—DS190. Depreciation—DS136. Irrecoverable ACT—DS164. Other long-term provisions (i.e. long-term provisions such as pensions, self-insurance, and provisions for risks and charges)—DS313.

[24] La Porta et al. (2000) fail to adjust their 1994 date for this.

[25] This is to be contrasted with the USA, where they are usually declared on a quarterly basis, and with the UK where they are usually declared twice a year. Lease et al. (2000: table 9.1) provide a more extensive overview of the payment frequency of dividends.

Table 5.2. *Distribution of changes in dividends* (ΔD_t) *conditional on* ΔCF_t *and* ΔCF_{t-1} *in Germany and the USA*

ΔCF_t	ΔCF_{t-1}	ΔD_t (%)					
		−		0		+	
		Germany (%)	USA	Germany (%)	USA	Germany (%)	USA
+		13.9 (16)	20.3	49.5 (47)	13.9	30.9 (36)	65.8
−		36.5 (47)	39.5	54.7 (41)	17.9	8.9 (11)	42.6
+	+	13.5 (15)	13.8	55.1 (49)	11.4	31.5 (36)	74.8
−	−	37.7 (58)	48.8	59.4 (38)	19.4	2.9 (4)	31.8

Note: US figures are reported in Fama and Babiak (1968) and, unlike in the German case, report net profits instead of cash flows. Sample sizes: US—392 major industrial firms; Germany—397 firms all German industrial and commercial firms for which data were available on cash flows, defined as zero distribution profits gross of depreciation and changes in pension provisions. Tables 5A.2 and 5A.3 (Appendix) provide all results for Germany both on a cash flow and zero distribution profit basis. The figures in parentheses concern the distribution of ΔD_t excluding firms where $\Delta D_t = 0$ coincides with zero dividends.

5.5.2. *Some Facts on the Dividend Behaviour of German Firms*

'Dividend smoothing' is the practice by which companies adjust only partially their dividends to changes in current earnings. To provide a somewhat crude measure of the importance of dividend smoothing by German companies, we follow Fama and Babiak's (1968) approach.[26] This consists of computing the distribution of increases and decreases in the dividend per share in period $t (\Delta D_t)$ conditional on a change in the profit per share or cash flow per share [27] in periods t and $t-1$ (ΔE_t and ΔE_{t-1}, and ΔCF_t and ΔCF_{t-1}, respectively).

Table 5.2 and Tables 5A.2 and 5A.3 in the appendix, show that the majority of German companies do not change the dividend per share, irrespective of whether an increase or a decrease in the earnings per share (Table 5A.2) or in the cash flow per share (Table 5A.3) occurs. More importantly, even if there are two years in which there is a successive increase or decrease in earnings or cash flows, dividends remain constant in most cases. This stands in contrast with evidence on US firms provided by Fama and Babiak (1968) (see Table 5.2). The authors report that only between 11 and 19 per cent of the firms do not change the dividend in time t. Probably even more striking is the fact that in the case of two consecutive increases in profitability an overwhelming 75 per cent of US firms increase their dividends per share whereas our results show that the comparable figure for Germany is only 32 per cent. Another striking difference has to do with the proportion of companies increasing their dividends even though earnings decreased in two consecutive years: 32 per cent for the USA and only 3 per cent for Germany.

---

[26] This issue will be extensively discussed in Chapter 6. There, we estimate the Lintner (1956) and Fama and Babiak (1968) dividend models, which provide a classical test of the dividend smoothing proposition.

[27] Defined as zero distribution profits gross of depreciation and changes in pension provisions.

An analysis of the UK sample of 250 firms for the years 1990–92 (see Section 5.4 for the construction of the sample), reveals that 53 per cent of all firm-year observations correspond to dividend per share increases. The proportion of decreases and maintained dividends are 18.2 and 28.8 per cent, respectively.

In summary, German firms seem more reluctant than UK or US firms to increase their dividends in response to superior performance, but they are comparably flexible in cutting the dividend in the wake of a consistent decrease in profitability. Moreover, the German data suggest that there is a high degree of 'discreteness' in the dividends-per-share time series as opposed to the 'smoothness' (i.e. frequent annual small adjustments in the dividend per share) that we observe in the USA and the UK. The question we address next is to what extent this stable dividend behaviour is associated with the fact that some firms have zero dividend payout policies.

5.5.3. *Zero Dividends*

Table 5.3 reports that in 1991–92, approximately one quarter of all German firms do not pay out dividends whereas only 10–12 per cent of UK firms pay no dividends over that period. Devereux and Schiantarelli (1990) report that in a sample of 720 UK firms over the period 1969–86, the frequency of zero dividend payments is approximately 6 per cent. Using the sample of 600 UK manufacturing firms reported in Bond, Chennells, and Windmeijer (1996*b*), we calculate that the proportion of zero dividend payouts during 1984–90 amounts to 6.7 per cent of all firm–year observations. These numbers suggest that the German sample has a higher frequency of zero dividends. Table 5.3 shows that this not due to worse performance by German firms as the proportion of German firms reporting earnings losses is similar to that of UK firms. The table also shows that the proportion of German firms which do not pay dividends in case of earnings losses is higher than in the UK. This issue is discussed in greater detail in Chapter 7.

One reason why a high proportion of unchanged dividends in Germany is reported in Table 5.2 is because many German firms adopt a zero dividend payout policy. How does the dividend behaviour of German firms change if we exclude the zero dividend firms? The numbers in parentheses in Table 5.2 show, that although the proportion of firms that do not change the dividend per share at time *t* is now smaller, the number of firms leaving their

Table 5.3. *Proportion of firms with zero dividend payouts in a sample of all German industrial and commercial quoted firms and 250 UK industrial and commercial quoted firms*

	1990 (%)	1991 (%)	1992 (%)
Zero dividends	14.7 (6.5)	22.0 (9.9)	26.4 (11.6)
Negative earnings	9.8 (9.2)	15.8 (13.3)	23.7 (19.4)
Proportion of firms with zero dividends *and* negative earnings	63 (50)	66 (49)	79 (60)

Note: The figures in parentheses are the UK figures.

Table 5.4. *Average dividend payout ratios of 250 German industrial and commercial quoted firms, 1990–92*

	Definition of payout ratio		
	Gross dividends / Published profits (%)	Gross dividends / (ZDP + Dep + ΔPensProv) (%)	Gross Dividends / (ZDP + Dep + ΔPensProv + ΔOtherProv) (%)
Average	82.7	28.4	25.0
1990–92	(69, 416)	(31, 409)	(39, 250)
1990	80.7	29.5	27.0
1991	84.4	28.6	26.3
1992	83.0	26.4	21.5

Note: The table records three measures of gross dividend payout ratios. ZDP are zero distribution profits, Dep is depreciation, ΔPensProv are changes in pension provisions, and Δ OtherProv are changes in other provisions. The three ratios are calculated as $\Sigma D_{it}/\Sigma P_{it}$, where P is one of the three measures of profits. The figures in parentheses are the standard deviation of the ratio and the size of the sample.

dividend policy unchanged is still high compared to the USA. The fact that German firms may be more reluctant to increase the dividend per share than to decrease is reinforced by these results.

5.5.4. *The Aggregate Dividend Payout Ratio*

Table 5.4 records the size of the dividend payout ratio according to our three different definitions. Dividends as a proportion of published profits are substantially higher than dividends as a proportion of cash flows, 82.7 vs 28.4 or 25 per cent (depending on the definition of cash flow), respectively. The third and fourth columns reveal that the inclusion of other provisions brings the payout ratio on a gross dividend basis down only by a small percentage.

Behm and Zimmermann (1993) report that for thirty-two major listed German firms during the years 1962–88, the dividend payout ratio defined as *net* cash dividends over reported earnings is as high as 60 per cent. Similarly, Harris, Lang, and Möller (1994) find, for a sample of 230 quoted companies, that the average payout ratio, defined in the same way as in Behm and Zimmermann's (1993) study, is 55 per cent. We obtain a payout ratio of 52.9 per cent between 1990 and 1992. On a gross basis, the size of the payout ratio is as high as 94 per cent in Behm and Zimmermann (1993), 85.9 per cent in Harris, Lang and Möller (1994) and 82.7 per cent for our sample.

We now document how the payout ratio has evolved over the ten-year period from 1984 to 1993 for Germany and the UK. Panel I of Table 5.5 shows the dividend payout ratios defined as gross dividends divided by zero distribution profits gross of depreciation and changes in provisions.[28] In column 5 we report the *t*-statistics for the difference between the

---

[28] It should be noted that the results reported in panel I may reflect the business cycle. Therefore, panel II provides a cross-check to panel I as it records the evolution of the payout ratio over a ten-year period for Germany,

Table 5.5. *Dividend payout ratios in Germany and the UK*

Sample	Year	Country		t-statistics
		Germany %	UK %	
Panel I				
250 industrial and	1992	21.5 (22.4)	32.5 (31.8)	−3.068
commercial firms	1991	26.3 (25.9)	32.4 (33.6)	−2.416
	1990	27.0 (27.1)	28.2 (31.2)	−1.411
Panel II				
Germany: 221 industrial	1993	20.7	n.a.	n.a.
and commercial quoted firms	1992	23.7	n.a.	n.a.
	1991	20.8	n.a.	n.a.
UK: 600 manufacturing firms	1990	23.7 (24.1)	28.1 (30.1)	−2.405
	1989	23.1 (24.0)	34.5 (34.0)	−4.088
	1988	23.5 (21.5)	33.5 (32.1)	−4.708
	1987	24.3 (23.5)	33.2 (34.8)	−4.788
	1986	22.2 (22.5)	33.7 (32.9)	−4.755
	1985	19.8 (20.6)	32.5 (33.1)	−5.548
	1984	17.2 (17.9)	33.9 (31.8)	−6.298

Note: Panel I records a comparison of payout ratios defined as gross dividends divided by zero distribution profits gross of depreciation and changes in provisions, for two samples of 250 industrial and commercial quoted German and UK firms, respectively. The German figures correspond to the figures reported in Table 5.4. Panel II records a ten-year period from 1984 to 1993 for a sample of 221 German industrial and commercial quoted firms out of the 250 firms that are recorded in panel I. The definition of the payout ratio is the same as in panel II. The UK sample is the one reported in Bond et al. (1996a). It consists of a sample of 600 UK manufacturing firms during the period 1984 to 1990. In panel II, the definition of the payout ratio is nevertheless different from the German one. It is defined as gross dividends divided by zero distribution profits gross of depreciation. In parentheses, we report the dividend payout ratio obtained when we calculate the average ratio of firms. For that, we used the following exclusion criteria: (*a*) firm-year observations with ratios of above 500% were excluded; (*b*) firm-year observations where the profit figure is negative or zero and the dividends paid are strictly positive were excluded. This calculation is necessary to the calculation of the t-statistics of the difference between the averages reported in column 5.

German and the UK dividend payout ratios. To control for outliers, we exclude firm-year observations (*a*) with dividend payout ratios above 500 per cent, and (*b*) where the profit figure is negative or zero and the dividends paid are strictly positive (in which case the ratio would be negative).

and a seven-year period for the UK. For Germany, we drew a sample of 221 firms out of the 250 firms reported in panel I, for which data were available for at least five consecutive years between 1984 and 1993. For the UK, we used a sample of 600 manufacturing companies (as described in Bond et al. 1996b), for the period 1984–90. The definition of the payout ratio is the same for Germany as in panel I, but differs for the UK. In panel II, the payout ratio of UK firms is based on a cash flow gross of depreciation only, rather than gross of changes in provisions too as it is computed in panel I. This is because data on changes in provisions are not available from the data set of the Institute for Fiscal Studies (IFS).

Panel I of Table 5.5 shows that the UK firms paid out a higher proportion of cash flows as dividends. Although in 1990 the difference between the payout ratios of the two countries is not statistically significant ($t = -1.4$), the difference increased significantly to 11 per cent in 1992. Panel II shows a similar pattern: The payout ratio is consistently higher in the UK over the years 1984–90. Finally, the table suggests that during the second half of the 1980s, the German payout increased from 17 to approximately 24 per cent. The t-statistics reveal that the difference between the UK and German ratios was statistically more significant at the beginning of the period than at the end.[29]

A final remark concerns a comparison between published results on US firms and our results for Germany. Harris, Lang, and Möller (1994); Michel (1979); and Michel and Shaked (1986) report for the USA that dividend payout ratios, defined as gross dividends to reported earnings, are in the range of 39–41 per cent, that is, much lower ratios than the German figures in Table 5.5 suggest.

To summarize, dividend payout ratios are lower in Germany than in the UK on a cash flow basis. However, the difference is around 10 per cent and is not as large as it is commonly thought.[30] Furthermore, on a published profits basis, dividend payout ratios are considerably higher in Germany then in the UK or the USA. However, this may reflect the higher degree of conservativeness of earnings reporting in Germany and the company law provisions that impose a minimum payout ratio on a published profit basis.

5.5.5. *Size*

Presumably, a large, well-established firm with a record of profitability and stability of earnings has easier access to capital markets than a small, riskier firm. The latter is expected to retain more of its annual earnings to finance its operations and to show a smaller payout ratio than a large firm. Panel I of Table 5.6 shows some evidence that the smallest German firms have lower than average payout ratios. Although the t-statistic between the payout ratio of the firms in the smallest quintile and the average across firms is not significant, the smallest firms have a higher frequency of zero dividends than firms in the two largest size quintiles. The largest firms also show lower payout ratios than the average. The UK figures (panel II) show that the smallest firms have significantly lower payout ratios than the average of all firms and the frequency of zero dividends is much higher than in any other size quintile. Devereux and Schiantarelli (1990) report that the frequency of zero dividend payments in the sample of the smallest UK firms is also higher (10.8 per cent) than in the sample of the largest firms (2.5 per cent). The table also suggests that the UK payout ratios are a monotonic increasing function of size.

Perhaps more strikingly, the table reveals that it is only in the two largest size quintiles that the dividend payout ratios in the UK are substantially higher than the payout ratios of

---

[29] Although not reported in the table, we also computed the payout ratios on a published profits basis for the two samples reported in panel I. The UK ratio varied from a minimum of 48.2 (in 1989) to a maximum of 65.7% (in 1984). The average for the period 1984–90 was 58%. The German figures varied from 71.2 (in 1985) to 91% (in 1991), and the average for the period 1984–93 was 86%.

[30] See, for example, *The Economist*, 29 Jan. 1994, p. 17.

Table 5.6. *Dividend payout ratios in Germany and the UK partitioned by size, 1990–92*

	Number of companies	Range of Market Capitalization (Germany: million DM; UK: million UK Sterling)	Average Dividend Payout Ratio (*t*-statistic, proportion of firms with Div = 0 in at least two consecutive years) (%)
Panel I: Germany			
Size Quintile 1	50	2.4–42.5	20 (−1.3, 35)
Size Quintile 2	50	41.3–97.4	26 (0.2, 24)
Size Quintile 3	50	100.5–249.5	31 (1.4, 16)
Size Quintile 4	50	256.0–722.9	29 (0.6, 9)
Size Quintile 5	50	729.2–37,262.2	21 (−1.3, 11)
Panel II: UK			
Size Quintile 1	50	0.4–10.4	21 (−3.0, 22)
Size Quintile 2	50	10.6–27.1	28 (−0.9, 8)
Size Quintile 3	50	27.4–62.7	29 (−0.7, 11)
Size Quintile 4	50	63.0–212.5	34 (1.2, 4)
Size Quintile 5	50	214.0–26,532.8	39 (2.1, 3)

Note: The samples are the same as reported in panel I of Table 5.5. Dividend payout ratios are defined as zero distribution profits gross of depreciation and changes in long-term provisions, average of 1990–92. The *t*-statistics reported in column 4 record the test statistic of the difference between the average of each size quintile and the whole sample. The market capitalization is calculated as the average of the year 1993.

German firms. Although not reported in the table, the *t*-statistic of the difference between the averages of UK and German ratios in the largest size quintile is −3.146, whereas in all other size quintiles, the *t*-ratio was lower than 1 in absolute value. A final observation is that the frequency of zero dividends in German firms is higher than in the UK sample across all size quintiles.

5.5.6. *Industry*

It is easier for a firm in a non-cyclical industry to predict its future cash flows and, therefore, it can afford a higher dividend payout ratio. Conversely, in industries where earnings are very volatile, a high payout ratio can be very costly to maintain in years of bad business cycles. One could thus expect to find higher than average payout ratios in the energy sector, say, and lower than average payout ratios in the construction, automobile, and chemical sectors.

As we can see from Table 5A.1 in the appendix, the most represented industries are mechanical engineering and electrical engineering and electronics with 20 and 26 per cent of the companies, respectively. There is some evidence that firms in cyclical industries such as the construction and automobile (industry X and VI, respectively) have lower than average ratios, but no evidence that the energy sector (industry II), typically a non-cyclical sector, shows higher than average ratios. The substantially higher than average payout ratio for firms in the industrial holdings sector is consistent with the fact that there is a smaller need to plough cash flows back into the business relative to other industrial companies.

5.5.7. *Dividends and Ownership*

In this section we briefly describe the calculated payout ratios across ownership and control structures, for almost all industrial and commercial quoted German firms, between 1990 and 1992. A more thorough analysis of the relation between dividends and control is undertaken in Chapter 8, where we estimate this relation for a ten-year period to benefit from the inter-temporal variation in control patterns.

Of the original sample of 416 German industrial and commercial quoted companies, the degree of concentration of ownership of voting shares was available for 408 firms and the type of large shareholder could be identified in 404 firms. We categorize shareholders as a German family, another German industrial or commercial company, a German bank, a German insurer, the German state/other public authorities, a German industrial/financial holding, a foreign company, and widely held companies, that is, firms without a concentrated owner holding at least 25 or 50 per cent of the voting shares.[31]

Table 5.7 shows that the vast majority of quoted companies in Germany are closely held. This is in contrast with the UK (Franks, Mayer, and Renneboog 2001). The most important groups of large shareholders are families and other corporations. However, this does not take into consideration the fifty-nine companies subject to control agreements with other companies, domestic, or foreign. Hence, the importance of these two categories of large shareholders is underestimated in the table.

The next question we address is the extent to which payout ratios vary across the control patterns (for a more detailed analysis see Chapter 8). Widely held firms seem to have lower payout ratios than closely held firms (Table 5.8). Firms controlled by banks have dividend payout ratios (on a cash flow basis) significantly lower than the sample average. Firms controlled by other corporations have the highest payout ratios. Firms controlled by foreign companies, families, the state, and holding companies are somewhat in the middle, all with virtually identical payout ratios.

5.6. SUMMARY

This chapter has reviewed the institutional framework of the dividend decision by describing the main German company law provisions regulating the (profit) relation between

---

[31] In Germany, control of more than 25% of the voting rights allows a shareholder to block many major decisions such as changes to the company's articles of association. A shareholding that carries more than 50% of all voting rights allows control of elections of shareholders' representatives to the supervisory board. Finally, control of 75% of the share capital confers the ability to take most major decisions affecting the company (e.g. the dismissal of members of the supervisory board, changes to the articles of association). Until 1995, disclosure rules in Germany required shareholdings above 25% and 50% of the voting capital to be disclosed. From 1995 onwards, firms had to disclose stakes in excess of 5% of the votes.

Table 5.7. *Patterns of ownership of voting rights of a large cross-section of industrial and commercial quoted firms in Germany, 1993*

Shareholdings larger than:	25 (%)	50 (%)
I. Companies without a large shareholder	9.7 (39)	29 (117)
II. Companies with a large shareholder, the largest shareholder being . . .		
Family	37.45 (151)	30 (121)
Another German company	26.5 (107)	21.8 (88)
German bank	4.2 (17)	1.7 (7)
German public authorities	4.7 (19)	3.2 (13)
Foreign company/Institution	6.7 (27)	6.7 (27)
German holding	7.7 (31)	5.7 (23)
German insurer	2.2 (9)	1.0 (4)
German foundation (*Stiftung*)	0.7 (3)	0.7 (3)
Employees	0.2 (1)	0.2 (1)
TOTAL	100 (404)	100 (404)

Note: The table records the proportion of firms that are closely held/widely held, i.e., firms that do/do not have a large shareholder owning at least 25% or 50% of the voting rights of a firm. The table also records the origin of the largest shareholder of closely held firms. Of the total of 416 firms (excluding firms with control agreements) we were not able to find information on ownership structures on fourteen firms, leaving us with a final sample of 404 firms. Number of firms are reported in parentheses.

parent companies and subsidiaries, some aspects of the German accounting rules (e.g. those on pension fund provisions) and the tax system, as well as the role of preference shares. There are three legal provisions which influence the payout ratio. First, some corporations have control agreements with their parent companies, whereby they transfer the profit and/or loss to their parent companies. We argued for the exclusion from our sample of these types of parent-subsidiary structures on the grounds that these transfers are not dividends *per se*, but an opportunity for the parent company to benefit from tax losses at the subsidiary level. Second, German corporations are usually required to pay out at least 50 per cent of their published profits as dividends, although there are some special provisions that may mitigate the impact of this provision. Finally, German firms are usually not allowed to buy back their own shares.

German accounting rules by influencing profit reporting also influence dividend policy. German accounting rules are often considered to be deficient in the information disclosed to investors relative to the Anglo-American approach to financial reporting. Under the German system managers have incentives not to report earnings that attain a desired dividend policy because higher reported earnings may create shareholder pressure for higher dividends. Pension provisions may also account for a certain downward bias in the published profit figure.

The chapter presents the following findings. First, German firms pay out a lower proportion of their cash flows than UK firms. Second, on a published profits basis, the pattern is reversed, with German firms exhibiting significantly higher payout ratios. La Porta et al.

Table 5.8. *Average dividend payout ratios of all German industrial and commercial quoted companies partitioned by category of largest shareholder, 1990–92*

Panel I: Widely held firms		
Widely Held, i.e., no	25	22
concentrated owner with		(−1.5,38, 18)
at least	50	26
		(−0.1, 116, 20)

Panel II: Closely held firms	Largest shareholder owning (of the voting shares) (%)	
Largest shareholder	**(25%, 50%)**	**(25%, 100%)**
Family	27	29
	(−0.2, 30, 27)	(0.2, 150, 19)
Another German company	34	32
	(0.6, 19, 16)	(1.0, 106, 22)
German bank	11	20
	(−7.1, 10, 40)	(−1.1, 17, 35)
German state/Other public authorities	36	28
	(0.4, 6, 34)	(0.0, 19, 11)
Foreign company	n.a.	28
		(0.0, 25, 36)
German holding	22	29
	(−1.3, 8, 0)	(0.0, 29, 14)
German insurer	27	24
	(−0.4, 5, 0)	(−0.9, 9, 11)

Note: The table records the dividend payout ratios, defined as gross dividends divided by zero distribution profits gross of depreciation and changes in pension provisions, of different groups of firms classified according to their ownership structure. Panel I records the payout ratio of widely held firms, when the ownership threshold is 25% and 50%. Panel II records the payout ratios according to the concentrated owner. For example, the group of firms where the largest shareholder is a family holding a voting stake between 25% and 50%, pays out 27% of cash flows as dividends. t-statistics, size of sample and proportion of firms with zero dividends in at least two consecutive years are the figures reported in parentheses. The t-statistics report the test statistic of the difference between the average of each category of ownership and the whole sample of 397 firms.

(2000) uncover a similar pattern, but do not present any reasons for these patterns. The company law provisions described above partly account for these two conflicting results. Third, an analysis of the payout ratios on a cash flow basis across different size quintiles establishes that the main difference in dividend payout ratios between German and UK firms is situated in the quintile of the largest firms. The conventional wisdom that German firms have significantly lower dividend payout ratios is not supported by our results. Fourth, not only are the payout levels different for German and UK firms, but so is the dividend behaviour of these companies. For example, 50 per cent of German firms do not change the dividend per share every year which is contrary to the evidence from UK and US firms. German firms are more reluctant than their Anglo-American counterparts to increase their dividends in response to superior performance. However, they tend to be more willing to cut the dividend in the wake of a consistent decrease in profitability. Moreover, the German data suggest that there is a high degree of 'discreteness' in the dividends-per-share time series as opposed to the 'smoothness' (i.e. frequent annual small adjustments in the dividend per share) observed in the USA and the UK. Fifth, dividend payout policy is related to the degree of control concentration. Bank-controlled firms pay out fewer dividends (as a percentage of cash flow) than firms controlled by other corporations.

APPENDIX A

Table 5A.1. *Average dividend payout ratios (gross dividends / cash flows) of German industrial and commercial quoted companies categorized by industry*

Industry	Average 1990–92 (%)
I. Mining and petroleum productions	34 (30, 14)
II. Energy	31 (23, 28)
III. Iron, steel, and metals	22 (20, 19)
IV. Mechanical engineering	20 (19, 51)
V. Electrical engineering and electronics	26 (27, 37)
VI. Shipbuilding, production of rail and road vehicles, and aircraft	12 (16, 12)
VII. Chemicals	27 (22, 25)
VIII. Textiles, clothing, woodworking, and leather production	30 (28, 45)
IX. Food and beverages	19 (16, 32)
X. Construction	24 (19, 14)
XI. Wholesale and retail	33 (25, 30)
XII. Transport	14 (16, 15)
XIII. Industrial holdings	43 (56, 36)
XIV. Housing and real estate	61 (52, 13)
XV. Other	31 (38, 23)

Note: Industry classification according to the Trade or Industry Code provided in Commerzbank '*Wer gehört zu wem*' 1991. Standard deviation and size of sample in parentheses.

Table 5A.2. *Distribution of changes in dividends (ΔD_t) conditional on ΔE_t and ΔE_{t-1} for all German industrial and commercial quoted companies in 1990–92*

| | | $\Delta D_t = D_{1992} - D_{1991}$ | | | | | |
| | | − | | 0 | | + | |
ΔE_t	ΔE_{t-1}	Nr of cies	% of row	Nr of cies	% of row	Nr of cies	% of row
+		4	2.4	96	58.2	65	39.4
−		97	40.8	126	52.9	15	6.3
+	+	1	1.5	39	57.4	28	41.2
+	−	2	2.3	51	58.6	34	39.1
−	+	46	39.0	59	50.0	13	11.0
−	−	48	42.9	62	55.4	2	1.8

Table 5A.3. *Distribution of changes in dividends (ΔD_t) conditional on ΔCF_t and ΔCF_{t-1} for all German industrial and commercial quoted companies in 1990–92*

| | | $\Delta D_t = D_{1992} - D_{1991}$ | | | | | |
| | | − | | 0 | | + | |
ΔCF_t	ΔCF_{t-1}	Nr of cies	% of row	Nr of cies	% of row	Nr of cies	% of row
+		27	13.9	107	49.5	60	30.9
−		74	36.5	111	54.7	18	8.9
+	+	12	13.5	49	55.1	28	31.5
+	−	11	12.9	49	57.6	25	29.4
−	+	39	33.4	63	53.8	15	12.3
−	−	26	37.7	41	59.4	2	2.9

6

Dividend Policy, Earnings, and Cash Flow: A Dynamic Panel Data Analysis

6.1. INTRODUCTION

Lintner's (1956) empirical observation that firms gradually adjust dividends in response to changes in earnings, has acquired the status of a stylized fact of corporate dividend policy.[1] His seminal work suggested that managers tend to change dividends primarily in response to unanticipated and non-transitory changes in their firm's earnings, and that firms have reasonably well-defined policies in terms of the speed with which they adjust dividends towards a long-run target payout ratio. Subsequent studies, such as Fama and Babiak (1968), confirmed Lintner's original findings.

As most of the empirical evidence on dividend models uses US and UK data, less is known about dividend policy and the explanatory power of models for continental European countries. In this chapter, we estimate the empirical relation between dividends and earnings in Germany by applying Lintner's 'partial adjustment model' and using a Generalized Method of Moments (GMM)-in-differences approach with instrumental variables. One of the previous studies that addresses this issue is Behm and Zimmermann (1993), but their results are based on a limited sample of thirty-two of the largest German firms. They estimate the validity of the Lintner model for the period 1962–88 and conclude that it reasonably fits both aggregate and individual firm data.

We examine whether the changes in dividend policy are based upon a long-term target payout ratio. In addition, we investigate whether this target payout ratio is founded on published earnings or on cash flow. We also study how the dividend adjustment process takes place. This study improves on earlier research by using a more appropriate estimation methodology, a larger and more representative sample, a longer time window and different proxies for profitability. Specifically, we improve the methodology along these lines. First, we use panel data on 221 industrial and commercial quoted firms for the ten-year period from 1984 to 1993. This sample corresponds to more than 50 per cent of the German industrial and commercial quoted companies. The reason why we opt for this period is that it encompasses a five-year period of economic boom followed by an economic recession. Unlike earlier studies (e.g. Behm and Zimmermann 1993), we exclude financial companies as these firms may have different considerations in establishing their investment and dividend policies. Second, earlier studies on German dividend policy did not control for unobserved firm-specific effects which

[1] See Marsh and Merton (1986) and Brealey and Myers (2003).

might be correlated with other explanatory variables causing Ordinary Least Squares (OLS) and Within-Groups (WG) estimators to be biased and inconsistent. We use the GMM technique developed by Arellano and Bond (1991); Blundell and Bond (1998); and Arellano and Bover (1995). Finally, we do not only use published bottom line earnings as an explanatory variable but also cash flows which have the advantage that they are less subject to conservatism in German accounting methods (e.g. the legal requirement to add earnings to reserves).

This chapter is structured as follows. In Section 6.2 we describe the dividend models estimated in previous studies. We then describe our data set and provide descriptive statistics in Section 6.3. In Section 6.4, we start by discussing the econometric issues relevant to these dividend models. We subsequently report the econometric results and present some tests to ascertain the robustness of these results. Section 6.5 concludes.

6.2. DIVIDEND MODELS

Marsh and Merton (1987: 3) argue that the controversy regarding normative theories of dividends [namely, based on the relaxation of the assumptions underlying the Miller–Modigliani (1961) theorem of dividend irrelevance] has led empirical researchers to rely heavily on positive approaches to specify their models. Lintner (1956) was the first to propose a positive dividend-earnings model and his work laid the foundations of the vast subsequent dividend literature. He conducted interviews with twenty-eight carefully selected US companies to investigate the rationale behind the determination of their dividend policy. His fieldwork revealed considerable differences in dividend policies across companies but he also unveiled some common patterns. Marsh and Merton (1987) summarize these patterns as follows:

(1) managers believe that firms should have some long-term target payout ratio;
(2) in the dividend decision, managers focus on the change in current payouts and not on the dividend level;
(3) a change in dividends is usually triggered by a major unexpected and persistent change in earnings;
(4) most managers try to avoid changing the dividends if there is a high probability that this dividend change may be reversed within one year or so.

Based upon these facts, Lintner (1956) formalizes corporate dividend behaviour as a *partial adjustment model*. For any year t, the target level of dividends, D_{it}^* for firm i, is related to current earnings, E_{it}, by a desired payout ratio r_i:

$$D_{it}^* = r_i E_{it}. \tag{6.1}$$

In any given year the firm will only *partially* adjust to the target dividend level. We have:

$$D_{it} - D_{i,t-1} = a_i + c_i (D_{it}^* - D_{i,t-1}) + u_{it}, \tag{6.2}$$

where

- a_i is a constant;
- c_i is the speed-of-adjustment coefficient, with $0 < c_i \leq 1$;

- $D_{it} - D_{i,t-1} = \Delta D_{it}$ is the actual change in the dividend and;
- $(D_{it}^* - D_{i,t-1})$ is the desired change in the dividend.

If $a_i = 0$ and $c_i = 1$, the actual changes in dividends coincide with the desired changes. Conversely, if $c_i = 0$, no changes in dividends towards the desired level are undertaken since the actual change at time t is the same as the one observed in the previous time period. The hypothesis that firms gradually adjust dividends in response to changes in earnings and thus apply dividend smoothing implies that the speed-of-adjustment coefficient c_i is within the range $0 < c_i < 1$. Furthermore, a positive a_i represents the management's resistance to reduce dividends.

The adjustment process eqn (6.2) can be written as

$$D_{it} = a_i + c_i D_{it}^* + (1 - c_i)D_{i,t-1} + u_{it}. \tag{6.3}$$

Now substitution of eqn (6.1) into eqn (6.3) gives

$$D_{it} = a_i + c_i r_i E_{it} + (1 - c_i)D_{i,t-1} + u_{it}. \tag{6.4}$$

One obtains the following empirically testable equation:

$$D_{it} = a_i + b_i E_{it} + (1 - c_i)D_{i,t-1} + u_{it}, \tag{6.5}$$

with $r_i = b_i/c_i$ being the payout ratio and c_i the speed of adjustment coefficient.

Alternatively, the empirically testable eqn (6.5) can be obtained by using an *adaptive expectations model*. In this model, current dividends are assumed to be a function of long-run expected earnings:

$$D_{it} = r_i E_{it}^* + u_{it}. \tag{6.6}$$

As the expectations variable E_{it}^* is not directly observable, we assume that earnings expectations are formed according to the following process:

$$E_{it}^* - E_{i,t-1}^* = d_i(E_{it} - E_{i,t-1}^*), \tag{6.7}$$

where d_i is the coefficient of earnings expectations. This equation signifies that the expectations about earnings are revised each period by a fraction d_i of the discrepancy between the earnings observed in the current period and those that had been anticipated in the previous period. By substitution, eqn (6.5) is obtained (but without the constant term).

A *combination of the adaptive expectations and partial adjustment models* yields a different model. Here, we assume that dividends follow the adjustment mechanism posited in eqn (6.3). Furthermore, target dividends are proportional to long-run expected earnings

$$D_{it}^* = r_i E_{it}^*, \tag{6.8}$$

with long-run expected earnings given by

$$E_{it}^* - E_{i,t-1}^* = e_i(E_{it} - E_{i,t-1}^*). \tag{6.9}$$

We finally obtain an empirically testable equation with a constant, E_{it}, $D_{i,t-1}$ and $D_{i,t-2}$.

Fama and Babiak (1968) extend the partial adjustment model by incorporating a lagged earnings variable. They assume that the process generating the annual earnings of firm i can be represented as

$$E_{it} = (1 + \lambda_i)E_{i,t-1} + v_{it}, \tag{6.10}$$

where v_{it} is a serially independent error term. Target dividends are defined as in the partial adjustment model (6.1). A further assumption is that there is full adjustment of dividends to the expected earnings $\lambda_i E_{i,t-1}$, and partial adjustment to the remainder:

$$D_{it} - D_{i,t-1} = a_i + c_i[r_i(E_{it} - \lambda_i E_{i,t-1}) - D_{i,t-1}] + r_i\lambda_i E_{i,t-1} + u_{it}, \tag{6.11}$$

which rearranged, gives

$$D_{it} = a_i + (1 - c_i)D_{i,t-1} + c_i r_i E_{it} + r_i\lambda_i(1 - c_i)E_{i,t-1} + u_{it}, \tag{6.12}$$

yielding the following empirically testable equation

$$D_{it} = a_i + (1 - c_i)D_{i,t-1} + b_i E_{it} + d_i E_{i,t-1} + u_{it}, \tag{6.13}$$

where $b_i = c_i r_i$ and $d_i = r_i \lambda_i (1 - c_i)$.

There has been extensive (early) empirical research confirming Lintner's findings (amongst others: Fama and Babiak 1968; Pettit 1972; Watts 1973).

There are two microeconometric approaches to model dividend behaviour. The first one uses long time series of data for individual firms and allows the slope coefficients to be firm-specific. The second one uses large cross sections and short time periods, and imposes common slope coefficients. The latter allows the target dividend payout ratio to vary across firms in a restricted way, which is fine as the dividend behaviour is likely to be firm-specific. For example, clientele effects (as originally suggested by Miller and Modigliani 1961) and signalling issues can be influential in an individual firm's dividend decision. Given that the length of our time series is limited to ten years of data, we will opt for a panel data approach.

An alternative approach is the macroeconometric model developed by Marsh and Merton (1987). They assume that permanent economic earnings, as proxied by stock market prices (and not accounting earnings), are the fundamental determinant of dividends and apply this insight to firms listed on US stock exchanges.

6.3. SAMPLE AND DATA DESCRIPTION

6.3.1. *Sample*

We select all of the 221 industrial and commercial firms that are quoted in at least one of the eight German Stock Exchanges (GSE), and for which there are at least five years of accounting data available over the ten-year period from 1984 to 1993. The reason why we choose this period is that a five-year period of economic growth is followed by a period of economic slow down. In our sample, thirteen firms leave the stock market and go private, six go bankrupt, five are taken over and two put in place a 'control agreement' during the period of analysis. Thirty-six firms obtain a listing in a year after 1984, but all sample firms are quoted in 1989. Overall, the sample consists of an unbalanced panel data of 2,098 firm-year observations (see Table 6.1).

Table 6.1. *Overall sample composition*

Panel I

Sample period	1984–93
Number of firms	221
Number of firm-year observations	2,098

Panel II

Number of records per firm	Number of firms
10	174
9	13
8	15
7	8
6	9
5	2

Accounting data are collected from *Saling Aktienführer*. This is an annual publication by *Hoppenstedt & Co.* which provides information on balance sheet and profit and loss account items, historical data on equity raised on the stock exchanges, shareholdings, share prices, date of first quotation, etc. From this source, the following data are gathered for the ten-year period 1984–93: published after-tax earnings, depreciation, changes in pension provisions and other provisions, dividends per share for both preference and ordinary shares, and the number of ordinary and preference shares at the end of the accounting year to which the dividend per share refers. The dividend per share figures are adjusted for share splits.

6.3.2. *Definitions and Data Issues*

We use gross dividends, defined as cash dividends gross of corporation tax levied on dividend distributions. Preference shares are often issued on the GSE: in 20 per cent of our sample (forty-four cases out of a total of 221), preferred stock was listed in at least one year during the period 1984–93. To account for dividends on preferred stock, we calculate a weighted average of the dividend paid on ordinary and preference shares. The weights consist of the ratios of the share capital issued as preference shares and ordinary shares, respectively, divided by the total market value of the total equity capital outstanding.

The weighted average dividend per share is hence calculated as follows. Let N_T be the total number of shares outstanding, N_o the number of ordinary shares, and N_p the number of preference shares. Thus, $N_T = N_o + N_p$. Moreover, let DPS_o be the dividend per share paid on ordinary shares, and DPS_p the dividend per share paid on preference shares, then the weighted average dividend per share (WDPS) equals

$$WDPS = \frac{DPS_o \times N_o + DPS_p \times N_p}{N_T}. \tag{6.14}$$

Using this formula, the weighted total dividend per share exceeds the dividend per ordinary share by approximately 4.5 per cent. Thus, this finding confirms what was described in Chapter 5: Dividends paid on preference shares have a premium of between 2 and 5 per cent over and above the dividend paid on ordinary shares.

The UK studies generally consider only dividends on ordinary shares (see, for example, Edwards et al. 1986; Bond, Chennells, and Windmeijer 1996). Even for Germany, the issue of dividends on preferred equity may be less empirically relevant in the context of panel data estimations because the movements in dividends per share are equal for the two classes of shares in virtually all our sample firms. In other words, when dividends per ordinary share increase, for example, the dividend per preference share increases by a similar percentage. Only in three German firms (out of the forty-four with preference shares), the change in dividends per ordinary share was different from the change per preference share. Furthermore, the change is only different in situations of dividend omissions or dividend initiations, which is consistent with the fact that there is generally a dividend premium paid on preference shares even in the wake of poor performance. To conclude, our data suggest that the degree of flexibility in choosing the level of dividends on preference shares is similar to the one on ordinary shares.

A striking fact is the high incidence of 'specially designated dividends' paid by German corporations. We find that such payments occurred in 191 of the 2,098 firm-year observations, that is, 9 per cent of the whole sample. These special dividends predominantly reflect shifts in the dividend policy rather than transitory increases in dividends and earnings. Brickley (1983), who studies the dividend payouts and earnings of a sample of US firms in the year following the announcement of special dividends, also subscribes to this view. In ten firm-years, we observe large one-off payments (*Sonderausschüttung*) associated with either 'special anniversaries', or with sales of subsidiaries (in one case), or with distributions of reserves previously accumulated at a different rate of taxation.[2] The fundamental problem with these large payments is one of timing, that is, to which accounting years should these payments be allocated? As we do not have enough information allowing us to allocate these payments to specific accounting years, we exclude these payments (as do Behm and Zimmermann 1993).

Two earnings figures are employed: (*a*) after-tax earnings as published in the annual reports, and (*b*) cash flows defined as zero distribution earnings gross of depreciation and changes in provisions.[3] Both measures of earnings were divided by the number of shares outstanding at the end of each accounting year to obtain a per-share figure.

We use consolidated data for the following reasons. First, the use of consolidated data ensures that the fact that we exclude firms under 'control agreements' (as discussed in Chapter 5, Section 5.3) does not create a sample exclusion bias. These firms are indirectly included in our data via the accounts of the quoted parent company if the latter is in our

---

[2] Between 1990 and 1993, firms could claim a tax refund of 6 per cent on past years' tax bills from the tax authorities by distributing reserves accumulated during previous years. This refund results from the fact that the corporation tax on retentions was reduced from 56 per cent until 1990 to 50 per cent until 1993. From 1994, the tax refund was no longer granted.

[3] Behm and Zimmermann (1993) use 'net profits', a figure that is suggested by the German Financial Analysts Association (*Deutsche Vereinigung für Finanzanalyse und Anlageberatung, DVFA*). However, data on net earnings are not available for all firms in our sample and negative 'net profits' are not reported.

sample. Second, the dividend policy of the parent company is, in practice, determined after consideration of the annual consolidated accounts. However, a problem arises from working with consolidated accounts. We have fourteen sample firms that are owned by other corporations which, in turn, are also in our sample. Such a double-counting issue may create a bias in our estimations. A typical example is Renk AG, who was owned by MAN AG over our sample period. The size of these fourteen firms is usually very small compared to their parent companies. The average market capitalization of Renk AG is 8 per cent of the market capitalization of the average sample firm, and only 3 per cent of the market capitalization of MAN AG (which is three times as large as the average listed firm). We will investigate whether the double-counting problem biases our results, by performing a re-estimation excluding these fourteen firms.

We use the Commerzbank Industry Classification and classify all 221 firms into nine industry categories. As a proxy measure for size, we calculate the market capitalization for all firms on an annual basis by averaging the market capitalization at the end of each quarter.[4]

6.3.3. *Some Descriptive Statistics*

Some descriptive statistics of the dividends, earnings and cash flow series for the whole period are summarized in Table 6.2. A first striking result is that published earnings account for only 25 per cent of the cash flow. Hence, the mean dividend payout ratio on a published earnings basis is significantly higher than the equivalent ratio on a cash flow basis: 86 and 21.4 per cent, respectively. This also suggests that the published earnings figure is rather conservative. Behm and Zimmermann (1993) find similar figures for a sample of thirty-two major quoted German firms. They report mean net dividends of DM7.31, that is, DM11.4 on a gross basis, slightly lower than our figure of DM12.3. Their mean published earnings per share figure is also found to be slightly lower than ours, DM12.5 versus DM14.3, respectively. Table 6.2 also reveals that the dividend per share figure has a coefficient of variation (i.e. defined as the standard deviation of the series over the mean) of 0.75, which is lower than the coefficient of variation of published earnings (1.07) and cash flows (0.95). The variance ratio of dividends over published earnings equals 0.36 ($= 9.2^2/15.3^2$) and the one of dividends over cash flows equals approximately 0.03. This provides a rough estimate of the degree of 'dividend smoothing'. Cash flows have a slightly lower coefficient of variation than published earnings but the variance ratio of published earnings over cash flows equals 0.079 providing some evidence of what we can call 'published earnings smoothing'. As these figures per share may be influenced by firm size, we also show the correlation coefficient between firm size, on the one hand, and dividends, published earnings, and cash flows per share, on the other. We observe that cash flows per share are positively correlated with firm size (coefficient of 21.1 per cent). The correlation coefficients between size, and dividends per share and published earnings are smaller, but are also positively related (8.3 and 14.7 per cent, respectively).

---

[4] As for seventy-six firm-year observations, the ordinary shares are not quoted whereas the preference shares are, we multiply the total number of ordinary and preference shares by the price of the listed preference share.

Table 6.2. *Descriptive statistics on dividends, published earnings, and cash flows*

	Dividends per share	Published earnings per share	Cash flow per share
Mean	12.3	14.3	57.6
Standard deviation	9.2	15.3	54.6
Coefficient of variation	0.75	1.07	0.95
Median	12.5	12.2	46.4
Maximum	76.6	684.2	695.7
Minimum	0	−222.9	−198.5
Correlation coefficient with firm size (%)	8.3	14.7	21.1

Note: Sample period: 1984–93. Sample: 221 German industrial and commercial quoted firms. Dividends are gross dividends per share. The cash flows are defined as zero distribution earnings gross of depreciation and changes in provisions. The par value of all shares is standardized to DM50 (approximately €25). The coefficient of variation is defined as the standard deviation of the series over its mean.

Table 6.3. *Number of increases, decreases, and maintained dividends*

	Nr of firm-year observations	% Of total
Dividends *Maintained*	955	50.9
Thereof, cases of zero dividends in at least two consecutive years	203	10.8
Dividends *Increased*	615	32.8
Thereof, dividend *Initiations*	65	3.5
Dividend *Cuts*	307	16.4
Thereof, dividend *Omissions*	107	5.7
Total	1,877	100

Note: Sample period: 1984–93. Sample: 221 German industrial and commercial quoted firms.

An important stylized fact on German dividends is the high incidence of unchanged dividends every year. As Table 6.3 reports, almost 51 per cent of the firm-year observations in our sample correspond to cases of maintained dividends. The frequency distribution of dividend changes during 1984–93 looks normal with the average firm changing its dividends per share every 2 years.

Table 6.3 shows that approximately 11 per cent of the firm-years correspond to cases where there are zero dividend payouts in at least two consecutive years. The table also reveals that in 21 per cent of observations (i.e. 203/955), the zero dividend payout is maintained. The proportion of dividend cuts (including omissions) is approximately 16 per cent of the total sample. Approximately 30 per cent of the dividend cuts are dividend omissions,

Table 6.4. *Distribution measures of percentage changes*

	Increases (%)	Cuts (%)
Mean		
Percentage of dividend increases[a]/cuts[b]	31	−30.5
Median		
Percentage of dividend increases[a]/cuts[b]	15.4	−25
Standard Deviation		
of Percentage of dividend increases[a]/cuts[b]	63.4	20.4
Number of dividend increases[a]/cuts[b]	550	200
Nr of Dividend *Initiations*	65	
Nr of Dividend *Omissions*		107
Distribution (%)		
of size of dividend increase[a]/cut[b]		
[0; 10] dividend increase/cut	166 (30.2)	29 (14.5)
[10; 25]	247 (44.9)	76 (38)
[25; 50]	74 (13.5)	69 (34.5)
[50; 75]	29 (5.3)	18 (9.0)
[75; 90]	7 (1.3)	8 (4.0)
[90; 100]	27 (4.9)	

Notes: Sample period: 1984–93. Sample: 221 German industrial and commercial quoted firms.

[a] Excluding dividend initiations.
[b] Excluding dividend omissions.

suggesting that in German firms dividend policy is not very rigid. Only five firms do not pay any dividends throughout the whole sample period, whereas 116 firms always pay a strictly positive dividend (not reported in the table).

In Table 6.4 we show the characteristics of the distribution of changes in the dividends per share. We observe that the mean increase and cut (excluding dividend initiations and omissions, respectively) are almost identical in absolute value (31 per cent). Half of the dividend cuts amount to 25 per cent or more, whereas the median of increases is lower, at 15 per cent. To summarize, we observe: (i) a high frequency of changes in dividends per share; (ii) a frequent occurrence of dividend omissions and zero dividend payout policies; (iii) some evidence of dividend smoothing; and (iv) the median of dividend cuts is higher than the median of dividend increases.

6.4. ESTIMATION AND RESULTS

Our basic, empirically testable, model is based on the discussion in Section 6.2:

$$D_{it} = \alpha D_{i,t-1} + \beta \Pi_{it} + \text{YEAR}_t + \eta_i + V_{it}, \tag{6.15}$$

where

- D_{it}, $D_{i,t-1}$ are the dividends per share at time t and $t-1$, respectively, for firm i;
- Π_{it} is earnings or cash flow per share at time t for firm i;
- $YEAR_t$ are time dummies that control for the impact of time on the dividend behaviour of all sample firms;
- η_i is a firm-specific effect to allow for unobserved influences on the dividend behaviour of each firm and is assumed to remain constant over time. There are several possible sources of these unobserved influences. For instance, this firm-effect can be viewed as a firm's component of the 'normal' signalling constraint which quoted firms may have to satisfy;
- V_{it} is a disturbance term.

6.4.1. *Estimation*

In this subsection we briefly describe the estimation techniques used in this chapter. A more detailed account of these techniques is given in the appendix to this chapter, where we illustrate them in the context of a simple autoregressive specification model. In dynamic panel data models such as eqn (6.15), where there is a large cross-section of firms and a small number of time series observations, an estimation problem arises because the earnings variable, Π_{it}, is likely to be correlated across firms with the firm-specific effect, η_i. In addition, the lagged dependent variable is most likely to be correlated with these firm-specific effects. Thus, if we estimate eqn (6.15) using OLS, the estimators are inconsistent and biased because $\mathrm{cov}(D_{i,t-1}, \eta_i) \neq 0$ and $\mathrm{cov}(\Pi_{it}, \eta_i) \neq 0$ (Hsiao 1986). A WG estimator, that is, OLS on the equation with each observation expressed as the deviation from the time mean, will eliminate the firm-specific effect. However, the estimators will still be inconsistent and biased since $\mathrm{cov}(D_{i,t-1}, V_i) \neq 0$, where V_i is the deviation from the time mean of the disturbance term V_{it} (Nickell 1981).

To obtain consistent estimators, the model is first-differenced to eliminate the fixed-effect, η_i:

$$D_{it} - D_{i,t-1} = \alpha(D_{i,t-1} - D_{i,t-2}) + \beta(\Pi_{it} - \Pi_{i,t-1}) + (YEAR_t - YEAR_{t-1})$$
$$+ (\eta_i - \eta_i) + (V_{it} - V_{i,t-1}). \tag{6.16}$$

We then use an instrumental variable approach (Anderson and Hsiao 1981) to estimate eqn (6.16) as suggested by Arellano and Bond (1991).

Provided there is no serial correlation in the disturbance V_{it}, we can use all lagged values of the dependent variable, that is, $D_{i,t-2}$, $D_{i,t-3}$, ..., $D_{i,1}$ as valid instruments in the first-differenced equation. Similarly, allowing for a possible correlation between Π_{it} and V_{it}, only lagged values dated $t-2$ and earlier will be used as instruments (Arellano and Bond 1991). In other words, we allow for the endogeneity of the regressors as it is likely that shocks affecting dividend choices may also affect measured earnings and cash flows. Arellano and Bond (1991) develop a GMM technique in-first-differences to obtain such an estimator.

A further refinement is developed by Arellano and Bover (1995) and Blundell and Bond (1998). Their Monte Carlo analysis shows that in dynamic panel data models where the autoregressive parameter (i.e. α in eqn 6.15) is moderately large and the number of time series observations is moderately small, the GMM-first-differences-IV estimator is poorly behaved.[5] In this case, lagged levels of the series provide weak instruments for the first-differenced equation. The authors propose a linear GMM estimator in a system of first-differenced and levels equations that offers significant efficiency gains in situations where the GMM-first-differences performs poorly. The resulting linear estimator uses lagged differences of the series as instruments for the equations in levels, in addition to lagged levels of the series as instruments for equations in first differences. Specifically, it uses $(D_{i,t-1} - D_{i,t-2})$ and $(\Pi_{i,t-1} - \Pi_{i,t-2})$ as additional instruments in the levels eqn (6.15), under the assumption that these differences are uncorrelated with the firm-specific effect, η_i, even though the levels of the series are correlated with η_i. We call this technique GMM-in-systems.

We proceed as follows. We estimate the basic model, and other variations so to include other lag structures.[6] We report the main results relating to the models explained in Section 6.2, but also estimate a model based on eqn (6.9), showing that the coefficient of $D_{i,t-2}$ is neither individually nor jointly statistically significant. For all these specifications, we report the results of each of the four estimation techniques described above: OLS in levels, Within-Groups (WG), GMM-in-first-differences (GMM(DIF)) and GMM-in-systems (GMM(SYS)).[7] This procedure shows us how much the size of the speed of adjustment coefficient (i.e. $1 - \alpha$) and the one of the implicit target payout ratio (i.e. $\beta/(1 - \alpha)$) varies across the different estimation techniques. In addition, it will also be useful to compare our results with those of previous studies which have mainly used the basic OLS-estimation.

The fact that in 10 per cent of the cases we have zero dividend payouts in at least two consecutive years, and that in five firms no dividends are paid at all during the sample period, may suggest other estimation procedures. First, a Tobit or limited dependent variable model could be employed to address censoring problems (Maddala 1983). However, there is a high degree of persistence in the dividend per share time series (reflected in a high autoregressive parameter), which the literature on Tobit models has not adequately addressed. Another limitation of the Tobit model lies in its underlying assumption of homoskedastic error terms. Second, panel data estimation with sample selection bias could capture the dynamics of the time series while simultaneously controlling for the cases with no changes in the dividend (Amemiya 1973; Heckman 1979).[8] This approach also faces some problems. First, the estimated parameters obtained by the probit from the first-step

---

[5] Both one-step and two-step versions of GMM first-difference showed a downward finite sample bias.

[6] As discussed in Section 6.2, there is no a priori theoretical guide as to the lag structure of the dividend model.

[7] Our estimation procedure is implemented using the Dynamic Panel Data (DPD) programme (Arellano and Bond 1988) which operates under Gauss.

[8] Such an approach involves a two-step procedure. Essentially, in the first step, we obtain the expected values of the residuals that are subject to the truncation (i.e. the sample selection rule). These expected values involve unknown parameters, but they can be estimated by the probit method. In a second step, we introduce the estimated values of these variables into a panel data model similar to eqn (6.15), and estimate this model on the restricted sample (i.e. the sample which excludes the firms with zero dividend payout policies).

procedure which are incorporated in the panel regression, are most likely to be correlated with the disturbance term. Therefore, we would have to find valid instruments for these estimated parameters. Alternatively, the probit would incorporate the explanatory variables dated, for example, $t - 2$, so that the unknown parameter estimates are exogenous with respect to the current disturbance. The problem is that the probit would not be informative, on the grounds that, for example, earnings dated $t - 2$ are weak predictors of the current decision to change or not the dividend.

Considering the problems with our alternative estimation techniques (Tobit and sample selection models), we opt for the dynamic panel approach with GMM in-differences and in-systems described above.

6.4.2. *Results*

We discuss three sets of results: (i) those corresponding to the published earnings model; (ii) those obtained from the cash flow model; and (iii) those derived from a model which includes earnings and cash flows simultaneously.

The parameter estimates obtained from the published earnings model (eqn 6.16) are reported in Table 6.5. The coefficient on the lagged dividends, α, varies from 0.42, obtained in the WG estimation, to 0.79, when OLS in levels is used. Thus, the speed of adjustment $(1-\alpha)$ lies within a broad range, namely [0.21, 0.58]. Clearly, a speed of adjustment coefficient of a magnitude of 0.58 makes less economic sense than a coefficient of 0.25 (from GMM(SYS)) because, on average, 50 per cent of our sample firms do not change their dividends and, when they change it, the average percentage increases and decreases are modest (see Tables 6.3 and 6.4). This suggests that some estimation techniques yield incorrect results which may be the consequence of biases introduced by unobserved influences on the dividend behaviour of individual firms. Table 6.5 also shows that the GMM(DIF) and GMM(SYS) estimation procedures yield realistic speed of adjustment estimates, while the GMM(DIF)-estimates may be biased downward compared to the GMM(SYS)-estimates (inline with the econometric arguments above). The Sargan test on the validity of the instrument set consistently rejects instruments dated $t - 2$, possibly due to the fact that the measurement errors are serially uncorrelated.

Another useful statistic is the implicit target payout ratio $(\beta/(1 - \alpha))$, which can be calculated from Table 6.5. The target payout ratio varies from 15 per cent (specification (d)) to 41 per cent (specification (a)) and is significantly lower than the observed payout ratio which amounts to 86 per cent.[9] This is true irrespective of the technique used to obtain the estimators. In other terms, biases due to fixed-effects cannot account for the discrepancy between implicit and observed dividend payout ratios. Using GMM(SYS), which econometrically ought to give a parameter estimate closer to the true observed value, one obtains an implicit payout ratio of 28 per cent (specification (g)) and 25 per cent (specification (h)). Thus, it seems that for German firms the dividend decisions are not based on long-term target dividend payout ratios.

---

[9] Table 6.2 shows that the target payout ratio is 86%; dividends per share are DM12.3 and earnings per share amount to DM14.3.

Table 6.5. *Dividend model with published earnings*

Variables	OLS in levels		WG		GMM (DIF)		GMM (SYS)	
	(a)	(b)	(c)	(d)	(e)	(f)	(g)	(h)
Const.	1.598***	1.630***	—	—	—	—	—	—
	(0.472)	(0.457)						
$D_{i,t-1}$	0.776***	0.786***	0.437***	0.420***	0.584***	0.592***	0.682***	0.745***
	(0.047)	(0.049)	(0.041)	(0.043)	(0.080)	(0.083)	(0.070)	(0.082)
PP_{it}	0.090***	0.093***	0.098***	0.097***	0.077***	0.078***	0.088***	0.095***
	(0.011)	(0.012)	(0.011)	(0.011)	(0.017)	(0.017)	(0.017)	(0.019)
$PP_{i,t-1}$	—	−0.012	—	0.010**	—	−0.003	—	−0.034
		(0.008)		(0.005)		(0.010)		(0.023)
Time dummies	Yes	Yes	Yes	Yes	Yes	Yes	Yes	Yes
m_1	−1.994	−2.248	2.804	3.154	−4.142	−4.108	−4.220	−4.292
m_2	1.638	1.511	3.829	3.822	1.401	1.424	1.475	1.538
Sargan (d.f.)	—	—	—	—	71 (61)	69 (60)	72 (68)	77 (67)
Observations	1876	1876	1655	1655	1655	1655	1655	1655

Notes: D_{it} is the dependent variable and stands for dividends per share. PP are published earnings per share. Time dummies are included in all specifications. m_1 and m_2 are tests for the absence of first-order and second-order serial correlation in the residuals, asymptotically distributed as $N(0, 1)$ under the null of no serial correlation. The Sargan statistic is a test of the over-identifying restrictions, asymptotically distributed as $\chi^2(k)$ under the null of valid instruments, with degrees of freedom (k) reported in parentheses. OLS stands for Ordinary Least Squares. WG stands for Within-Group estimation: specifications (c) and (d) have variables expressed as deviations from the time mean. Variables in specifications (e) and (f) are expressed in first-differences. Specifications (g) and (h) are linear systems of first-differenced and levels equations. GMM(DIF) and GMM(SYS) are one-step estimators. Instruments: Specifications (e) and (f): $D_{t-3} \ldots D_1$ and $PP_{t-3} \ldots PP_1$. Specifications (g) and (h) $D_{t-3} \ldots D_1$ and ΔD_{t-2}, and $PP_{t-3} \ldots PP_1$ and ΔPP_{t-2}. Standard errors, asymptotically robust to heteroskedasticity, are reported in parentheses.

* stands for statistical significance at the 10% level.
** stands for statistical significance at the 5% level.
*** stands for statistical significance at the 1% level.

How do our estimates of the speed of adjustment and the implicit dividend payout ratio perform in comparison to the dividend literature? In previous studies, the estimated speed of adjustment is usually substantially lower than the observed one. For instance, Behm and Zimmermann (1993) test the partial adjustment model for a sample of thirty-two major German quoted firms during 1962 and 1988. Using an OLS regression on pooled data, the authors find that a specification based on current earnings only has a speed of adjustment of 0.26. Including lagged earnings into the model as well reduces the speed of adjustment coefficient to 0.13. The implicit target payout ratio of 48 per cent in the Behm and Zimmerman study is also lower than the observed ratio of 58 per cent (both figures are on a net basis). For US studies, the estimated average speed of adjustment is also lower than the observed one. For example, the one estimated by Lintner was approximately 30 per cent with a target payout ratio of 50 per cent of earnings. Lintner's implicit target payout ratio seems to be substantially higher than ours in specification (h). Fama and Babiak (1968) find that a specification, in which the constant term is suppressed and the level of earnings for $t - 1$ is added, provides the best prediction of dividends. Specification (h) includes such a lagged earnings variable but the coefficient is only statistically significant at the 15 per cent level. Note also that Fama and Babiak (1968) find an average speed of adjustment of approximately 0.37, slightly higher than Lintner's.

To summarize, the estimations of the published earnings model for German firms suggest that dividend decisions are not based on long-term target payouts, as originally hypothesized by Lintner (1956). This view is supported by implicit payout ratios that deviate substantially from observed payout ratios. An alternative explanation is that target payout ratios are expressed in another profitability measure, for example, cash flows. This would be consistent with the fact that the published earnings figure is likely to be conservative as German firms withhold part of their earnings to build up (legal) reserves. Moreover, it would also be consistent with the hypothesis that firms adjust slowly to cash flows rather than earnings. We investigate this alternative view by re-estimating our model using a cash flow basis.

Table 6.6 shows that a cash flow model yields parameter estimates which are much closer to reality. Specifications (g) and (h) based on the GMM(SYS) estimation technique give a speed of adjustment of 0.33 and 0.26, respectively, similar to the speed of adjustment obtained in the published earnings model. Unlike the earnings model, the cash flow model gives a more realistic (implicit) target payout ratio. This target payout is 19.6 per cent (specification (g)), which is comparable to the mean (or observed) payout ratio of 21.4 per cent.[10] Notice also, that the coefficient on the lagged cash flows variable is now statistically significant (at the 7 per cent level).

When inspecting the results obtained by simultaneously including published earnings and cash flows (see Table 6.7), we find that the explanatory power of the cash flow variables disappears, but that the one of published earnings remains. This result is true irrespective of the estimation technique. Therefore, although the cash flow model seems economically more meaningful (see Chapter 5 for the arguments involved) and is better at explaining the dividend policy of German firms, it is puzzling that earnings dominate in the combined model. One possible reason for this may be published earnings smoothing (relative to cash flow) as well as dividend smoothing. Consequently, the true correlation between dividends and cash flows that are not smoothed may be higher than that between dividends and smoothed earnings. We further investigate this issue by regressing current published earnings on lagged published earnings using GMM(SYS). We find a coefficient of persistence (i.e. the autoregressive parameter) of 0.682. We then replicate this experiment for cash flows and find a coefficient of 0.321. This suggests more persistence in published earnings than in cash flows, consistent with our descriptive statistics.

Regarding the speed of adjustment of dividends towards the long-term target payout ratio, Germany is somewhat in between two extremes. On the one hand, companies from Anglo-American countries only slowly adjust their dividend policy. For instance, the partial adjustment model by Short, Zhang, and Keasey (2002) shows that UK firms have a long-term target payout ratio, which is positively correlated to institutional ownership and negatively to managerial ownership. In contrast, 'emerging markets firms often have a target payout ratio but they are generally less concerned with volatility in dividends over

---

[10] In Table 6.2, the dividends per share are DM12.3 and the cash flow per share amounts to DM57.6, giving a cash flow payout ratio of 21.4%.

Table 6.6. *Dividend model with cash flows*

Variables	OLS in levels		WG		GMM (DIF)		GMM (SYS)	
	(a)	(b)	(c)	(d)	(e)	(f)	(g)	(h)
Const.	0.987**	1.259***	—	—	—	—	—	—
	(0.414)	(0.391)						
$D_{i,t-1}$	0.827***	0.841***	0.462***	0.465***	0.528***	0.553***	0.674***	0.737***
	(0.049)	(0.046)	(0.043)	(0.023)	(0.096)	(0.090)	(0.082)	(0.081)
CF_{it}	0.026***	0.045***	0.059***	0.060***	0.077***	0.080***	0.064***	0.088***
	(0.005)	(0.008)	(0.008)	(0.004)	(0.019)	(0.019)	(0.015)	(0.018)
$CF_{i,t-1}$	—	−0.026***	—	−0.002	—	−0.017	—	−0.035*
		(0.009)		(0.004)		(0.014)		(0.020)
Time dummies	Yes	Yes	Yes	Yes	Yes	Yes	Yes	Yes
m_1	−1.382	−1.872	3.469	8.381	−4.514	−4.643	−4.655	−4.899
m_2	1.959	1.437	3.996	6.421	1.130	1.250	1.339	1.431
Sargan (d.f.)	—	—	—	—	63 (61)	64 (60)	76 (68)	70 (67)
Observations	1876	1876	1655	1655	1434	1434	1434	1434

Notes: D_{it} is the dependent variable and stands for dividends per share. CF are cash flows per share. Time dummies are included in all specifications. m_1 and m_2 are tests for the absence of first-order and second-order serial correlation in the residuals, asymptotically distributed as $N(0, 1)$ under the null of no serial correlation. The Sargan statistic is a test of the overidentifying restrictions, asymptotically distributed as $\chi^2(k)$ under the null of valid instruments, with degrees of freedom (k) reported in parentheses. OLS stands for Ordinary Least Squares. WG stands for Within-Group estimation: specifications (c) and (d) have variables expressed as deviations from time mean. Variables in specifications (e) and (f) are expressed in first-differences. Specifications (g) and (h) are linear systems of first-differenced and levels equations. GMM(DIF) and GMM(SYS) are one-step estimators. Instruments: Specifications (e) and (f): $D_{t-3} \ldots D_1$ and $CF_{t-3} \ldots CF_1$. Specifications (g) and (h) $D_{t-3} \ldots D_1$, ΔD_{t-2} and $CF_{t-3} \ldots CF_1$, ΔCF_{t-2}. Standard errors, asymptotically robust to heteroskedasticity, are reported in parentheses.

* stands for statistical significance at the 10% level.

** stands for statistical significance at the 5% level.

*** stands for statistical significance at the 1% level.

time and, consequently, dividend smoothing over time is less important' (Glen et al. 1995: 24). For instance, Adaoglu (2000) shows that the companies listed on the Istanbul Stock Exchange still have unstable dividend policies even after the regulation that required that half of the earnings had to be distributed as cash dividends was abandoned.

6.4.3. *Alternative Specifications*

In order to verify the robustness of the above results, we first consider the impact of differences in dividend practice by industry. We estimate the earnings and cash flow models including nine industry dummies, but the Wald test of the joint significance of these industries is rejected. Moreover, the coefficients of all the other explanatory variables (cash flows, published earnings, or lagged dividends) remain nearly unchanged.

To control for inflation, we deflate all variables by the Consumer Price Index as reported in the monthly bulletin of the *Deutsche Bundesbank*. We compute dividends, published earnings,

Table 6.7. *Dividend model with published earnings and cash flows simultaneously*

Variables	OLS in levels	WG	GMM (DIF)	GMM (SYS)
	(a)	(b)	(c)	(d)
Const.	1.591***	—	—	—
	(0.409)			
$D_{i,t-1}$	0.787***	0.421***	0.522***	0.714***
	(0.050)	(0.044)	(0.086)	(0.086)
PP_{it}	0.103***	0.105***	0.074**	0.069*
	(0.017)	(0.018)	(0.034)	(0.036)
$PP_{i,t-1}$	−0.022	0.008	0.022	−0.007
	(0.015)	(0.012)	(0.030)	(0.038)
CF_{it}	−0.010	−0.008	0.005	0.032
	(0.013)	(0.014)	(0.033)	(0.034)
$CF_{i,t-1}$	0.011	0.001	−0.028	−0.016
	(0.012)	(0.010)	(0.027)	(0.031)
Time dummies	Yes	Yes	Yes	Yes
m_1	−2.248	−5.162	−4.755	−4.843
m_2	1.500	1.944	1.476	1.536
Sargan (d.f.)	—	—	97 (86)	116 (100)
Observations	1876	1655	1655	1655

Notes: D_{it} is the dependent variable in all specifications. It represents dividends per share, PP are published earnings per share and CF are cash flows per share. Time dummies are included in all specifications. m_1 and m_2 are tests for the absence of first-order and second-order serial correlation in the residuals, asymptotically distributed as $N(0, 1)$ under the null of no serial correlation. The Sargan statistic is a test of the overidentifying restrictions, asymptotically distributed as $\chi^2(k)$ under the null of valid instruments, with degrees of freedom (k) reported in parentheses. Specification (b) has variables expressed as deviations from time mean. OLS stands for Ordinary Least Squares. WG stands for Within-Group estimation: variables in specification (c) are expressed in first-differences. Specification (d) is a linear system of first-differenced and levels equations. GMM(DIF) and GMM(SYS) are one-step estimators. Instruments: Specifications (c): $D_{t-3} \ldots D_1$, $PP_{t-3} \ldots PP_1$ and $CF_{t-3} \ldots CF_1$. Specification (d) $D_{t-3} \ldots D_1$, ΔD_{t-2}, $PP_{t-3} \ldots PP_1$, ΔPP_{t-2} and $CF_{t-3} \ldots CF_1$, ΔCF_{t-2}. Standard errors, asymptotically robust to heteroskedasticity, are reported in parentheses.

* stands for statistical significance at the 10% level.
** stands for statistical significance at the 5% level.
*** stands for statistical significance at the 1% level.

and cash flows at constant prices of 1985 and re-estimate the models of Section 6.4.2. We conclude that the results do not alter substantially by correcting for inflation.[11] An inspection of the dividend per share time series in real and nominal terms shows that almost all firms change the real dividend per share, as opposed to the nominal dividend which is

---

[11] For example, the GMM(SYS) point estimates for model (h) in Table 6.5 are 0.761 for the coefficient of the lagged dividends, 0.084 for current earnings and −0.028 for the coefficient of lagged earnings, compared to 0.755, 0.095, and −0.034, respectively, obtained for the same model but at current prices. Similarly insignificant differences are found in the estimation of the cash flow model and the model that tests the joint inclusion of cash flows and published earnings.

characterized by a higher discreteness. However, in terms of cross-sectional variation there is not much further information added to the model by estimating it at constant prices. We conclude, therefore, that there is no strong case for using real instead of nominal dividend and earnings figures in the estimations.

Next, we scale our variables in line with the suggestion by Bond, Chennells, and Windmeijer (1996) who argue that the presence of firms with very different sizes may be a source of heteroskedasticity in the point estimates. There are several possible variables one can employ to scale dividends and earnings, for example, total assets, sales, and market capitalization. We use market capitalization at the beginning of the sample period and the basic empirically testable eqn (6.15) becomes:

$$\frac{TD_{it}}{MVE_{i0}} = \alpha\left(\frac{TD_{i,t-1}}{MVE_{i0}}\right) + \beta\left(\frac{T\Pi_{it}}{MVE_{i0}}\right) + YEAR_t + \eta_i + V_{it} \tag{6.17}$$

where TD stands for total dividends and TΠ is total published earnings or cash flows. Table 6.8 reports a summary of the results for the scaled model (6.17) and its variations including the use of lagged earnings and cash flows. The main observation from this table is that the patterns and the point estimates do not differ significantly from the non-scaled models. We still obtain a cash flow model that produces an implicit payout ratio that is close to the observed ratio, a published earnings model that yields implicit parameters that differ substantially from the observed figures and a high autoregressive parameter. Finally, a model with published earnings and cash flows simultaneously shows a similar pattern to the non-scaled model: cash flows are no longer statistically significant determinants of dividends. The two GMM techniques yield consistent estimators in the scaled model.

Bond, Chennells, and Windmeijer (1996) estimate a specification similar to (a) of Table 6.8 for a sample of 1,218 UK industrial and commercial quoted companies. They estimate a specification with lagged dividends and current and lagged earnings using a GMM(DIF) technique. They find an autoregressive parameter of the magnitude of 0.69, yielding a speed of adjustment of 0.31. This compares with the parameter of 0.71 that we obtain in specification (a), inducing a speed of adjustment of 0.29. In other words, we find a somewhat lower speed of adjustment for German firms compared to UK data. This result is also similar to the one we find for the non-scaled model (see Section 6.4.2). Bond, Chennells, and Windmeijer (1996) also report an implicit cash flow payout ratio of 33.2 per cent compared to ours of 28 per cent (specification (d)).

As the inclusion of the fourteen firms that are controlled by other listed German sample firms may create a bias due to double-counting (see Section 6.3.2), we eliminate these firms and re-estimate specifications (c) and (d) of Table 6.8 for a sample of 207 firms. We use the same instrument set and find no significant changes in the point estimates. For example, the autoregressive parameter was 0.708 in the cash flow model and 0.734 in the published earnings model. Moreover, current cash flows had a coefficient of 0.081 and lagged values a coefficient of -0.035.

Finally, we discuss the methodological problems related to the fact that we observe (*a*) a high volatility in the dividend per share time series (compared to that of Anglo-American companies), and (*b*) a high number of firms which do not change the dividend and have zero

Dividend Policy, Earnings, and Cash Flow

Table 6.8. *Summary results of the scaled estimations*

Variables	GMM(DIF)		GMM(SYS)		
	(a)	(b)	(c)	(d)	(e)
$TD_{i,t-1}$	0.710***	0.685***	0.722***	0.720***	0.661***
	(0.094)	(0.095)	(0.074)	(0.080)	(0.070)
TPP_{it}	0.069***	—	0.066***	—	0.056
	(0.020)		(0.018)		(0.050)
$TPP_{i,t-1}$	−0.040	—	−0.031	—	−0.010
	(0.031)		(0.027)		(0.044)
TCF_{it}	—	0.080***	—	0.079***	0.012
		(0.017)		(0.018)	(0.045)
$TCF_{i,t-1}$	—	−0.026	—	−0.031	−0.003
		(0.027)		(0.028)	(0.042)
m_1	−5.062	−5.005	−4.832	−4.931	−5.068
m_2	0.676	0.266	0.628	0.346	0.481
Sargan (d.f.)	64.0 (53)	55.5 (53)	77.6 (67)	73.9 (67)	110.8 (100)
Observations	1655	1655	1655	1655	1655

Notes: TD_{it} is the dependent variable in all specifications. It represents total dividends. TPP are total published earnings and TCF are total cash flows. Both variables are scaled by the market capitalization. Time dummies are included in all specifications. m_1 and m_2 are tests for the absence of first-order and second-order serial correlation in the residuals, asymptotically distributed as $N(0, 1)$ under the null of no serial correlation. The Sargan statistic is a test of the overidentifying restrictions, asymptotically distributed as $\chi^2(k)$ under the null of valid instruments, with degrees of freedom (k) reported in parentheses. Variables in specifications (a) and (b) are expressed in first-differences. Specifications (c), (d), and (e) are a linear system of first-differenced and levels equations. GMM(DIF) and GMM(SYS) are one-step estimators. Instruments: Specifications (a): $TD_{t-3} \ldots TD_1$, $TPP_{t-3} \ldots TPP_1$; (b) $TD_{t-3} \ldots TD_1$, $TCF_{t-3} \ldots TCF_1$. (c) $TD_{t-3} \ldots TD_1$, ΔTD_{t-2}, $TPP_{t-3} \ldots TPP_1$, ΔTPP_{t-2}; (d) $TD_{t-3} \ldots TD_1$, ΔTD_{t-2} and $TCF_{t-3} \ldots TCF_1$, ΔTCF_{t-2}. Standard-errors, asymptotically robust to heteroskedasticity, are reported in parentheses.

* stands for statistical significance at the 10% level.
** stands for statistical significance at the 5% level.
*** stands for statistical significance at the 1% level.

dividend payout policies in at least two consecutive years (see Section 6.3.3). To investigate the influence of these characteristics of the dividend per share series on the size of the autoregressive parameter, we estimate the basic model using the GMM(SYS) technique for a sample that excludes those firms which did not change the dividend per share in at least 75 per cent of the years in our sample period. Accordingly, we eliminate thirty-one firms, that is, 14 per cent of our entire sample. Re-estimating the model specifications using this smaller sample yields a larger autoregressive parameter.

6.5. CONCLUSIONS

The extensive literature on dividend policy of Anglo-American companies, which builds on Lintner (1956), shows that most firms set long-term target payout ratios. Changes in dividends are triggered by major unexpected and persistent changes in earnings, and dividend changes are avoided if a reversal to the previous dividend level is likely in the short run. Consequently, not the level of the dividend level but a change in dividends matters as a signal to the market. In this chapter, we examined whether these stylized facts also hold for German firms which operate in a totally different corporate governance regime which is characterized by concentrated control, ownership pyramids, and the representation of banks on the board (see Chapters 2 and 3). To this end, we fit micro models of dividend behaviour to a data set of German industrial and commercial quoted firms comprising more than half of all German quoted companies.

In contrast to the Anglo-American evidence, German dividends are more volatile, and dividend omissions and zero dividend payout policies occur more frequently. When we use a partial adjustment model to estimate the implicit target payout ratio and the speed of adjustment of dividends towards a long-run target payout ratio based on published earnings, we find that none of our model specifications gives results that are in line with the observed payout and speed of adjustment. Our results do not improve when we abandon the basic estimation techniques such as OLS or WG for more advanced ones such as GMM-in-differences or GMM-in-systems. The latter two estimation methodologies avoid the biases arising from the estimation of unbalanced dynamic panel data models with a small number of time periods, a large cross-section of firms and unobserved heterogeneity across firms. We find that our model specifications on the relation between dividends, and past dividend policy and published earnings show that the estimated speed of dividend adjustment is consistent with observed dividend patterns. Still, even the GMM estimation techniques yield an implicit target payout ratio based on public earnings of around 25 per cent, which is substantially lower than the observed payout of 86 per cent. Therefore, German firms do not base their dividend decisions on long-term target dividend payout ratios based on public earnings.

However, the published earnings figure may not correctly reflect corporate performance as German firms tend to retain a significant part of their earnings to build up legal reserves. Given the conservative nature of published earnings figures, the long-term payout ratio may be based on cash flows. We do indeed find that the Lintner partial adjustment model yields realistic estimation results when cash flows are substituted for published earnings. Both the speed of dividend adjustment and the implicit payout ratios are close to our observed results, and confirm our prediction that cash flows are economically more meaningful. The implicit target payout ratio of 20 per cent is comparable to the observed one of 21 per cent on a cash flow basis. Hence, we conclude that dividend payout ratios of German firms are based on cash flows rather than published earnings. The fact that our partial adjustment models provide better results with cash flows than with published earnings may result from a higher degree of smoothing of earnings than of cash flows. This is shown by the autocorrelation of published earnings which is substantially higher than that of cash flows.

APPENDIX

We provide a summary of the dynamic panel data estimation techniques employed in this chapter. We describe these in the context of an autoregressive specification of the form

$$y_{it} = \alpha y_{i,t-1} + \eta_i + v_{it}, \tag{6.18}$$

where

- η_i is a firm-specific effect
- v_{it} is a disturbance term
- for individual i in time t (whereby t is typically small and i large)
- $i = 1, \ldots, N; \qquad t = 1, \ldots, T$

An estimation of eqn (6.18) using Ordinary Least Squares regression may lead to inconsistent and biased estimators of α. The reason is that $\mathrm{cov}(y_{i,t-1}, \eta_i) \neq 0$, that is, the firm-specific effect may be correlated with the lagged dependent variable. As a result of this correlation, α is typically biased upwards (Hsiao 1986). To eliminate the firm-specific effect, one could use a Within-Groups estimator (WG). Essentially, it comes down to estimate eqn (6.19) using an OLS regression:

$$(y_{it} - y_{i.}) = \alpha(y_{i,t-1} - y_{i-1}) + (v_{it} - v_{i.}), \tag{6.19}$$

where

- $y_{i.} = (y_{i1} + y_{i2} + \cdots + y_{i,t-1} + y_{it} + \cdots + y_{iT})/T,$ (6.20)
- $v_{i.} = (v_{i1} + v_{i2} + \cdots + v_{i,t-1} + v_{it} + \cdots + v_{iT})/T,$ (6.21)

that is, $y_{i.}$ is the time mean of y_{it}, and $v_{i.}$ is the time mean of v_{it}.

However, unless T is high, this estimation technique also generates inconsistent estimates which are biased downwards if $\mathrm{cov}(y_{i,t-1}, v_{i.}) \neq 0$. If $\alpha > 0$, the bias is always negative and does not go to zero when α tends to zero. When exogenous variables are incorporated in eqn (6.18), the situation worsens (Nickell 1981).

To obtain consistent estimators of α we use an approach based on Instrumental Variable estimation methods. For that, we first-difference eqn (6.18) to obtain

$$(y_{it} - y_{i,t-1}) = \alpha(y_{i,t} - y_{i,t-1}) + (v_{it} - v_{i,t-1}), \tag{6.22}$$

which we denote more simply as

$$\overline{y}_{it} = \alpha(\overline{y}_{i,t-1}) + \overline{v}_{it} \tag{6.23}$$

Provided $E(v_{it}, v_{i,t-1}) = 0$, that is, there is no serial correlation in the disturbance v_{it},

$$\mathrm{cov}(y_{i,t-2}, (v_{it} - v_{i,t-1})) = 0. \tag{6.24}$$

Moreover,

$$\mathrm{cov}(y_{i,t-2}, (y_{i,t-1} - y_{i,t-2})) \neq 0. \tag{6.25}$$

From eqns (6.24) and (6.25), we conclude that $y_{i,t-1}$ can be used as an instrument in the estimation of eqns (6.22) or (6.23). In general, if v_{it} are serially uncorrelated, we can use all lagged values of y as instruments (Anderson and Hsiao 1981—AH). Arellano and Bond (1991) point out that the AH estimator is—although consistent—not efficient. Provided that $T > 3$, there exist further valid instruments in later cross-sections that can provide further information. The authors develop a Generalized Method of Moments (GMM) estimator that exploits all the moment restrictions that follow from the assumption of no serial correlation in the errors. More specifically, (B.6) leads to the overidentifying restrictions

(1) $\quad (y_{i3} - y_{i2}) = \alpha(y_{i2} - y_{i1}) + (v_{i3} - v_{i2})$

(2) $\quad (y_{i4} - y_{i3}) = \alpha(y_{i3} - y_{i2}) + (v_{i4} - v_{i3})$

$\vdots$

$(T - 2) \quad (y_{iT} - y_{i,T-1}) = \alpha(y_{i,T-1} - y_{i,T-2}) + (v_{iT} - v_{i,T-1})$

Assuming there is no serial correlation in v_{it}, the moment restrictions

$$E(Z_i' \bar{V}_i) = 0, \quad i = 1, ..., N, \tag{6.26}$$

where

$$Z_i = \begin{bmatrix} y_{i1} & 0 & \cdots & & 0 \\ 0 & y_{i1} y_{i2} & 0 & & \vdots \\ \vdots & 0 & \ddots & & 0 \\ 0 & \cdots & 0 & & y_{i1} \cdots y_{iT-2} \end{bmatrix},$$

Z_i being a matrix $(T - 2) \times n$, and

$$\bar{V}_i = \begin{bmatrix} \bar{v}_{i3} \\ \bar{v}_{i4} \\ \vdots \\ \bar{v}_{iT} \end{bmatrix}, \qquad \bar{V}_i = (T-2) \times 1,$$

can be used to form a GMM estimator. Put differently, the estimator technique consists of estimating the following equations

$$\begin{bmatrix} \bar{y}_{i3} \\ \bar{y}_{i4} \\ \vdots \\ \bar{y}_{iT} \end{bmatrix} = \alpha \begin{bmatrix} \bar{y}_{i2} \\ \bar{y}_{i3} \\ \vdots \\ \bar{y}_{i,T-1} \end{bmatrix} + \begin{bmatrix} \bar{v}_{i3} \\ \bar{v}_{i4} \\ \vdots \\ \bar{v}_{iT} \end{bmatrix}, \tag{6.27}$$

using the matrix Z_i of valid instruments.

Blundell and Bond (1998) and Arellano and Bover (1995) have refined the instrumental variable estimator. Their Monte Carlo analysis shows that in dynamic panel data models where the autoregressive parameter is moderately large and the number of time series observations is moderately small, the GMM-in-first-differences estimator is poorly behaved. Lagged levels of the series provide weak instruments for the first-differenced equation in this case. Arellano and Bover (1995) and Blundell and Bond (1998) propose a linear GMM estimator in a system of first-differences and levels-equation that offers an efficiency gain in situations where the GMM-in-differences performs poorly. Formally, starting from (6.18), the question the authors address relates to the conditions under which $\bar{y}_{i,t-1}$ is uncorrelated with η_i. Expanding the first-differences of (6.18):

$$\begin{aligned}
\bar{y}_{it} &= \alpha\,\bar{y}_{i,t-1} + \bar{v}_{it} \\
&= \alpha\left(\alpha\bar{y}_{i,t-2} + \bar{v}_{i,t-1}\right) + \bar{v}_{it} \\
&= \alpha\left[\alpha\left(\alpha\bar{y}_{i,t-3} + \bar{v}_{i,t-2}\right) + \bar{v}_{i,t-1}\right] + \bar{v}_{it} \\
&= \alpha^3\,\bar{y}_{i,t-3} + \alpha^2\,\bar{v}_{i,t-2} + \alpha\bar{v}_{i,t-1} + \bar{v}_{it} \\
&= \cdots\cdots\cdots\cdots
\end{aligned}$$

(6.28)

$$= \alpha^K\,\bar{y}_{i2} + \sum_{j=0}^{k-1}\alpha^j\bar{v}_{i,t-j}.$$

The key is that $\bar{y}_{i2}$ is uncorrelated with η_i. Hence, under stationarity conditions (essentially $\alpha < 1$), $\bar{y}_{i,t-1}$ can be used as an instrument in the level equation (6.18). The technique consists then of estimating

$$y^+_{it} = \alpha y^+_{i,t-1} + u^+_{it},$$

(6.29)

using Z^+_{it} as instruments, where

$$y^+_{it} = \begin{bmatrix} \bar{y}_3 \\ \vdots \\ \bar{y}_T \\ \cdots \\ y_3 \\ \vdots \\ y_T \end{bmatrix}, \qquad u^+_{it} = \begin{bmatrix} \bar{v}_3 \\ \vdots \\ \bar{v}_T \\ \cdots\cdots \\ \eta_i + v_3 \\ \vdots \\ \eta_i + v_T \end{bmatrix},$$

(6.30)

and

$$Z^+_{it} = \begin{bmatrix}
y_{i1} & 0 & \cdots & & 0 & 0 & \cdots & \cdots & 0 \\
0 & y_{i1}\ y_{i2} & 0 & & \vdots & \vdots & & \ddots & \vdots \\
\vdots & 0 & \ddots & & 0 & \vdots & & \ddots & \vdots \\
0 & \cdots & 0 & y_{i1}\cdots y_{i,T-2} & 0 & \cdots & \cdots & 0 \\
0 & \cdots & & & 0 & \bar{y}_2 & 0 & \cdots & 0 \\
\vdots & \ddots & & & \vdots & 0 & \bar{y}_3 & 0 & \vdots \\
\vdots & & \ddots & & \vdots & \vdots & 0 & \ddots & 0 \\
0 & \cdots & & \cdots & 0 & 0 & \cdots & 0 & \bar{y}_{T-1}
\end{bmatrix}.$$

(6.31)

7

When do Firms Change the Dividend Policy?*

7.1. INTRODUCTION

In the previous chapter we examined the decision *by how much* German firms change the dividend payout. In this chapter we study another interesting question regarding the dividend policy decision: we focus on *when* firms change the dividend. This question is important as a change in the dividend payout may have important repercussions on the share price (see Chapter 3). Given that the dividends per share time series of German firms are characterized by a high discreteness, that is, infrequent small changes, we will opt for a discrete choice modelling approach.

A qualitative analysis of the decision to change the dividend can be interpreted in the light of what Modigliani and Miller (1959) and Miller and Modigliani (1961) call the 'information content of dividends'. For example, Miller and Modigliani (1961: 430) argue that '. . . where a firm has adopted a policy of stabilization with a long-established and generally appreciated "target payout ratio", investors are likely to (and have a good reason to) interpret a change in the dividend rate as a change in management's views of future profit prospects for the firm'. Hence, changes in dividend policy may convey information not otherwise known to the market. This notion of signalling was formalized initially by, for example, Bhattacharya (1979); Miller and Rock (1985); and John and Williams (1985), and was tested empirically by others like Aharony and Swary (1980); Asquith and Mullins (1983); and Healy and Palepu (1988). The timing decision of dividend changes is also relevant in the context of Lintner's (1956) survey of management practices. Lintner's (1956: 99) survey points out that '. . . the belief on the part of many managements that most stockholders prefer a reasonably stable rate and that the market puts a premium on stability or gradual growth in the rate, was strong enough that most managements sought to avoid making changes in their dividend rates that might have to be reversed within a year or so'.

We will apply a discrete choice approach to address the following issues. First, we test whether bottom line net earnings are the key determinants of the decision to increase or decrease current dividends. Lintner (1956: 107) observes that '. . . net earnings were the predominant element which determines current changes in dividends . . .'. However, as DeAngelo, DeAngelo, and Skinner (1992) point out, Lintner's sample is mainly comprised of large and well-established firms which have a higher propensity for dividend increases.

---

* This chapter is loosely based on Goerg, Renneboog an da Silva (2003).

Consequently, DeAngelo, DeAngelo, and Skinner (1992) investigate whether bottom line net earnings also drive dividend reductions.

Whereas in Chapter 6, we reported that a panel data analysis of the Lintner model fits the German data well, we now conduct several experiments to test whether there is an asymmetry in the dividend behaviour of German firms. For example, anecdotal evidence suggests that German firms have more scope for decreasing their dividends in the case of temporary losses than Anglo-American firms (see, for example, Goergen and Renneboog 2003). Second, the question as to when firms omit the dividend—as opposed to just cut it to a strictly positive level—is a central issue in dividend policy. For instance, one can argue that managers are reluctant to omit the dividend (see, for example, DeAngelo and DeAngelo 1990: 1424) and instead may prefer dividends cuts reducing the chance of a necessary omission in the future. However, a dividend omission is a sensitive decision because '. . . although people might disagree over the proper level of positive dividends, it is more difficult to argue that a zero payout represents an adequate "reward" for stockholders' (p. 1425). Hence, we investigate the degree of flexibility in the dividend setting of German firms and the importance of current changes in profitability rather than that of permanent shifts in profits.

This chapter is structured in the following way. In Section 7.2, we concisely describe the estimation technique and the model. Section 7.3 uses an ordered probit approach to model the probability of decreasing, increasing, or maintaining the dividend on a panel of 221 German industrial and commercial firms during the period of 1984–93. We also perform robustness checks on subsamples to better analyse the impact of temporary changes in profitability on the likelihood of a shift in dividend policy. Section 7.4 addresses the question as to when German firms omit the dividend rather than reduce it only partially. We look at what happens to the dividend per share of firms which made losses after years of good performance. Section 7.5 considers the decision to increase the dividend in the aftermath of dividend cuts and omissions. We measure how many years it takes to re-establish the payout to the level of the period prior to the omission or cut. Section 7.6 summarizes the evidence and concludes the chapter.

7.2. THE BASIC ESTIMATION MODEL

The decision to decrease, maintain, or increase the dividend can be considered as a variable that is inherently ordered. Hence, a simple multinomial logit or probit models would fail to account for the ordinal nature of the variable. Likewise, an ordinary regression is not appropriate as it would treat the difference between increasing and maintaining the dividend in the same way as that between maintaining and decreasing the dividend. However, the variables should be seen as a ranking. Therefore, we use an ordered probit (McElvey and Zaviona 1975). Similarly to the binomial probit model, the ordered probit is built around a latent regression.[1] The underlying model is as follows:

$$y^\star = \beta' X + \varepsilon \tag{7.1}$$

[1] See Maddala (1983: 46–9) for a detailed account of this technique.

where y^* is an unobserved variable, X is a set of explanatory variables, and ε is the residual. Suppose the decision to decrease the dividend takes the value of 0, the decision to maintain takes the value of 1 and the decision to increase takes the value of 2. Although y^* is not observed, y is observed:

$$
\begin{aligned}
y &= 0 && \text{if } y^* \leq 0, \\
y &= 1 && \text{if } 0 < y^* \leq \mu, \\
y &= 2 && \text{if } \mu \leq y^*,
\end{aligned}
$$

where μ is an unknown parameter to be estimated with β. ε is assumed to be normally distributed across observations (as in the binomial probit model) with a mean of zero and a variance of one.[2] This gives us the following probabilities:

$$
\begin{aligned}
P(y = 0) &= \Phi(-\beta'X), \\
P(y = 1) &= \Phi(\mu - \beta'X) - \Phi(-\beta'X), \\
P(y = 2) &= 1 - \Phi(\mu - \beta'X),
\end{aligned}
$$

where Φ is the cumulative standard normal. The coefficients are estimated using the maximum likelihood function.

7.3. THE DECISION TO CHANGE THE DIVIDEND: THE GENERAL MODEL

In this section we look at the classic scenario in which managers have perfect knowledge of the past and current stream of cash flows and incomplete knowledge about the future. When do managers decide to increase the dividend conditional on the information they have? And when do they decide to decrease the dividend? How do these results compare with Lintner's findings? These are some of the questions we address in this section. To do so, we use the same data and sample described in Chapter 6: Panel data on 221 German industrial and commercial quoted companies, covering the period of 1984–93. The dividend-per-share time series is used at current prices and is grossed up to take taxes into account. Since 'specially designated dividends' represent, in a vast majority of cases, shifts in the dividend policy of German firms (see Chapter 6), we include these dividends in the series. The dependent variable of model (7.1) takes three values: it is equal to 0 if the dividend per share decreases from period $t-1$ to t, equal to 1 if the dividend is maintained from $t-1$ to t and equal to 2 if there is an increase. We estimate a variety of specifications based on model (6.1) and include the following explanatory variables: a lagged dependent variable (dD_{t-1}), indicating whether there was an increased, decreased, or unchanged dividend in period $t-2$ to $t-1$, the current level of net income (NI_t) or cash flow (CF_t), the level of past net income (NI_{t-1}) or cash flow (CF_{t-1}), and the change in net income from period $t-1$ to t (ΔNI_t) or change in cash flow (ΔCF_t). These variables were standardized by the book value of equity for

[2] As Greene (2003: 737) puts it, the model can also be estimated with a logistically distributed disturbance. In practice, this re-formulation makes virtually no difference.

[3] Throughout the whole period, there were 208 firm-year observations consisting of annual net earnings losses and eighty cash flow annual losses.

the previous period. Finally, we test the significance of a dummy variable that takes the value of one if a loss occurs in period t (NIloss$_t$, or CFloss$_t$).[3] We estimate the basic model with net earnings (or published profits, or net income) separately from the model with cash flows (defined as zero distribution profits gross of depreciation and changes in provisions). We also estimate a specification which includes both profit measures. Different specifications are formulated with further lags of these variables but they are neither individually nor jointly statistically significant.[4]

7.3.1. *The Net Earnings Model*

Table 7.1 reports the results of the estimation with net income (NI) as a proxy for profits. Not surprisingly, in all model specifications (a)–(f), the past dividend decision has a positive and statistically significant effect on the probability of changing the current dividend. If in the previous period, the dividend was increased (decreased), the probability of an increase in dividends in the current period is high (low). This confirms the robustness of the findings from Chapter 6, where we found a highly positive autoregressive parameter estimate in the panel data model. Specification (a) shows that current net income has a positive and statistically significant effect on the probability of a dividend increase ($t = 12.3$). Comparing specifications (a)–(c) of Table 7.1 allows us to study whether it is current rather than past levels of earnings which have an impact on the dividend policy decision. We can conclude that current earnings levels influence the change in dividends per share and not past earnings (which are either insignificant (see specification (b)) or have the wrong sign (specification (c)). Furthermore, including past levels of earnings gives a poorer fit. Specification (f) shows that not only earnings levels are important determinants of dividend changes, but so are changes in earnings. Thus, consistent with the seminal papers by Lintner (1956) and Fama and Babiak (1968), current levels and changes in earnings are key determinants of the decision to shift dividend policy.

Specifications (d) and (e) reveal an important result: including an earnings loss dummy improves the goodness of fit of the model. Both specifications show that the coefficient on the earnings loss variable is negative and statistically significant at less than 0.1 per cent. Moreover, both the pseudo R^2 and the R_p^2 (i.e. the percentage of correct predictions) are larger than in the other specifications. Thus, the level of earnings or the changes in earnings are not the only key factors affecting the decision to change the dividend. Negative earnings, irrespective of the size of the loss, are a significant determinant of the decision to change the dividend. In other words, firms that report an annual loss have a significantly higher probability of a dividend reduction. This finding is consistent with DeAngelo, DeAngelo, and Skinner (1992: 1845). In Section 7.4, we will re-examine this finding by focusing on firms that incur a loss after an established track record of positive earnings.

---

[4] We test the null hypothesis of homoskedasticity using a Lagrange Multiplier test (see Davidson and MacKinnon 1984). We reject the null hypothesis. Therefore, the models are estimated assuming multiplicative heteroskedasticity (i.e. var$[\varepsilon_i] = [\exp(\gamma' y_i^*)]^2$), essentially adding an additional parameter vector (see Greene 2003: 232–5) for an explanation of the procedure).

Table 7.1. *Ordered probit analysis of the decision to decrease, maintain, or increase the dividend: A model with net income (NI)*

	(a)	(b)	(c)	(d)	(e)	(f)
Panel I: Coefficients (standard errors)						
Const.	0.915***	0.863***	0.942***	1.167***	1.209***	0.938***
	(0.068)	(0.070)	(0.074)	(0.079)	(0.082)	(0.075)
dD_{t-1}	0.087*	0.232***	0.128***	0.093*	0.096*	0.137***
	(0.049)	(0.048)	(0.048)	(0.049)	(0.048)	(0.049)
NI_t	0.723***	—	0.968***	0.402***	—	0.360***
	(0.059)		(0.064)	(0.074)		(0.080)
NI_{t-1}	—	−0.013	−0.554***	—	—	—
		(0.082)	(0.083)			
ΔNI_t	—	—	—	—	0.659***	0.628***
					(0.073)	(0.094)
$NIloss_t$	—	—	—	−0.844***	−0.891***	—
				(0.142)	(0.134)	
Panel II: Goodness of fit						
Log-likel.	−1618.7	−1681.6	−1597.5	−1577.1	−1572.8	−1594.8
Pseudo R^2	4.7%	1.0%	6.0%	7.2%	7.4%	6.1%
R_p^2	50.6%	48.1%	50.4%	51%	51.9%	50.6%

Notes: The dependent variable equals 0 if the dividend is decreased, 1 if maintained and 2 if increased. The sample consists of 221 industrial and commercial firms and accounting data report to the period 1984–93. The sample size is 1655 firm-year observations in all regressions. Net income and the change in net income are standardized by the book value of equity for the previous year. All specifications assume multiplicative heteroskedasticity. All model specifications are significant with *p*-values <0.001. Pseudo R^2 follows McFadden (1974). R_p^2 stands for the percentage of correct predictions.

* stands for significance at 10% level.
** stands for significance at 5% level.
*** stands for significance at 1% level.

7.3.2. The Cash Flow Model

Table 7.2 reports the results obtained from estimating the same specifications as in the previous section, but using cash flows instead of net earnings. The table confirms the strong effect of past dividends and shows that current cash flows as well as changes in cash flows are key determinants of the decision to shift dividend policy. Past cash flows show the same patterns as past earnings, that is, they are weak predictors of shifts in today's dividend policy. However, there are two main differences. Although comparisons of goodness of fit in discrete choice models have several limitations,[5] it is nonetheless true that the pseudo R^2 and the percentage of correct predictions (R_p^2) of the net earnings model strictly dominate those of the cash flow model in almost all specifications. A second difference is the explanatory power of the cash flow loss dummy. Specification (d) shows that a cash flow loss dummy is statistically significant if it is included with the level of current cash flows. However, if one includes the change in cash flows instead of the level (specification (e)),

[5] See Aldrich and Nelson (1984) and Maddala (1983).

When do Firms Change the Dividend?

Table 7.2. *Ordered probit analysis of the decision to decrease, maintain, or increase the dividend: A model with cash flows (CF)*

	(a)	(b)	(c)	(d)	(e)	(f)
Panel I: Coefficients (standard errors)						
Const.	0.729***	0.889***	0.871***	0.853***	0.927***	0.891***
	(0.071)	(0.079)	(0.078)	(0.078)	(0.073)	(0.080)
dD_{t-1}	0.194***	0.234***	0.183***	0.173***	0.178***	0.188***
	(0.047)	(0.048)	(0.046)	(0.048)	(0.047)	(0.048)
CF_t	0.175***	—	0.551***	0.113***	—	0.011
	(0.034)		(0.047)	(0.037)		(0.039)
CF_{t-1}	—	−0.029	−0.499***	—	—	—
		(0.037)	(0.051)			
ΔCF_t	—	—	—	—	0.580***	0.613***
					(0.052)	(0.062)
$CFloss_t$	—	—	—	−0.645***	−0.270	—
				(0.215)	(0.199)	
Panel II: Goodness of fit						
Log-likel.	−1667.6	−1681.2	−1632.1	−1660.3	−1623.7	−1625.0
Pseudo R^2	1.9%	1.1%	3.9%	2.3%	4.4%	4.4%
R_p^2	49.2%	48.1%	49.6%	48.5%	50.2%	49.9%

Notes: The dependent variable equals 0 if the dividend is decreased, 1 if maintained and 2 if increased. The sample consists of 221 industrial and commercial firms and accounting data report to the period 1984–93. The sample size is 1655 firm-year observations in all regressions. Cash flows (zero distribution profits gross of depreciation and changes in provisions) and the change in cash flows are standardized by the book value of equity for the previous year. All specifications assume multiplicative heteroskedasticity. All model specifications are significant with p-values < 0.001. Pseudo R^2 follows McFadden (1974). R_p^2 stands for the percentage of correct predictions

* stands for statistical significance at the 10% level.
** stands for statistical significance at the 5% level.
*** stands for statistical significance at the 1% level.

the loss dummy is no longer statistically significant. We conclude that a zero cash flow is less indicative of a 'break point' in the relation between profitability (compare with Section 7.3.1).[6]

This section has provided preliminary evidence on how profits influence the decision to change the payout policy. Although it has confirmed Lintner's (1956) findings that current

---

[6] Although not reported in the tables, we also incorporate current net earnings in a specification with a lagged dependent variable and current cash flows. Similar to the findings of the previous chapter, the coefficients on the cash flow variables are no longer economically meaningful and statistically significant. For example, the effect of current cash flows (although not statistically significant) on the probability to decrease dividends, has the wrong sign—the higher the cash flows the higher the probability of reducing dividends, which is clearly contradictory with specification (b) of Table 6.2, although this may be explained by the correlation between both series (correlation coefficient of 0.48). The coefficients on the net earnings variable were similar to those of specification (a) in Table 6.1: they had the same sign and similar statistical significance.

earnings are key determinants of the dividend decision, it has also identified a significant departure from Lintner's results: The occurrence of an earnings loss has a substantial predictive power *over* and *above* current earnings and changes in current earnings. It might be argued that the above analysis suffers from a methodological problem. As Miller and Modigliani (1961: 430) point out, changes in dividend policy in firms that have adopted a policy of stable dividends with a long-established dividend record are likely to be interpreted as a change in managers' views of the future stream of the firm's cash flows. In other words, it might be argued that the analysis of the decision of when to shift dividend policy is more relevant in the context of firms with established past dividends and performance records. If managers have adopted a policy of stable dividends and then decide to shift it, this shift is likely to carry more valuable information than a shift in a firm with unstable track records. In Section 7.4 we incorporate the practical implications of this remark in the framework of a discrete choice modelling.

7.4. WHEN DO GERMAN FIRMS OMIT OR CUT THE DIVIDEND?

DeAngelo, DeAngelo, and Skinner (1992) focus on firms listed on the New York Stock Exchange (NYSE) with established track records of positive earnings and dividend payments and examine the impact of an annual earnings loss on the dividend policy of those firms. They choose annual earnings losses since '. . . a loss unambiguously represents a low earnings realization for such firms [with established track records]'. (p. 1840) Furthermore, '. . . dividend changes for such firms are more reliably viewed as deliberate policy shifts . . .' (p. 1840). In this section, we adopt a similar methodology.

7.4.1. *Dividend Omissions, Dividend Reductions, and Earnings Losses*

We first divide our sample period into two periods of 5 years: 1984–88 and 1989–93. Out of the sample of 221 German firms described above, 189 firms have track records of strictly positive earnings and dividends during 1984–88. The period 1984–93 is particularly well-suited for this kind of analysis as it is a period of economic prosperity followed by a period of economic slowdown. The German data confirm that in the period 1984–88, there are considerably fewer cases of firms with losses than in the subsequent five-year period. In particular, there is a significant number of firms suffering losses in the years 1991 and 1992. We partition this sample of 189 firms into two groups of firms. A first sample, N_1, consists of firms with at least one annual net earnings loss during 1989–93: Seventy-one firms fall under this category. A second sample, N_2, consists of 118 firms with strictly positive earnings and dividends during the same period.

Table 7.3 reports the frequency of dividend cuts, omissions, increases, and maintained dividends in the two samples, N_1 and N_2. In the loss sample (N_1), we look at what happens to the dividend per share in the year of the *first* annual loss during 1989–93; hence the Seventy-one observations. For the profit-making sample (N_2), the table reports the dividend per share of those firms for each of the years from 1989 to 1993 (there are 568 firm-year observations).

Table 7.3. *Dividend changes for (1) 71 firms with at least one annual loss during 1989–93 (N_1), and (2) 118 firms with strictly positive earnings through 1989–93 (N_2).*

	Number of firm-years	No. (%) of cases with dividend			
		Cuts	Omissions	Increases	Maintained
Loss-making firms	71	8 (11.3)	57 (80.3)	1 (1.4)	5 (7)
Profit-making firms	568	77 (13.6)	4 (0.7)	244 (43)	243 (42.8)

Notes: Both N_1 and N_2 had strictly positive earnings and dividends during the period 1984–88. Dividend cuts are partial reductions in the dividend and dividend omissions stand for 100% reductions. For N_1 we show the number of dividend cuts, omissions, increases, and dividends maintained in the year of the first earnings loss. Hence, we have 71 firm-years. For N_2 we give the frequency of dividend cuts, omissions, increases, and dividends maintained in the total number of firm-year observations during 1989–93.

The table reveals a striking fact: fifty-seven firms (80.3 per cent) in the N_1 sample omit the dividend in the initial year in which they make an earnings loss. Only eight firms cut the dividend partially and five maintain it. This can be contrasted with the profit-making sample where we find only four firms (0.7 per cent of N_2) that omitted the dividend per share and seventy-seven firms (13.6 per cent) that cut it. Therefore, an annual loss, irrespective of its magnitude, has considerable explanatory power on the decision to omit the dividend. We observe that managers do not hesitate to omit the dividend in the year where firms make losses for the first time after a period of at least five years of stable performance and strictly positive dividends.

Our results stand in marked contrast with those of two studies on US data. DeAngelo, DeAngelo, and Skinner (1992) find significantly different results for a sample of 167 loss-making and 440 profit-making NYSE firms. For the loss-making sample, they report 51 per cent of firms (i.e. eighty-five firms) which reduce the dividend, as opposed to only 15 per cent (twenty-five firms) which omit the dividend. DeAngelo and DeAngelo (1990) study the dividend policy adjustments of eighty NYSE firms which suffered at least three years of losses during 1980–85, but had a positive performance in the year preceding their initial loss. Their logit analysis of the decision to cut dividends versus omit dividends showed that '. . . managers of firms with long dividend histories are especially reluctant to omit dividends' (p. 1428). Thus, the downward flexibility of the dividend policy in German firms following losses seems substantially larger than that in US firms.

7.4.2. *Probit Analysis of the Decision to Omit the Dividend*

We now formally test the decision to omit the dividend under the scenario where firms have an established past performance of positive earnings and dividends and experience a negative shock that translates into a significant deterioration of net earnings. Do managers change the dividend policy in such a case? How much of the dividend change can be explained by the changes in earnings and their magnitude? We use an ordered probit analysis to examine these questions.

Table 7.4. *Ordered probit analysis of the decision to omit, cut, or maintain / increase the dividend in loss and non-loss firms during 1989–93: A model with net earnings*

	(a)	(b)	(c)	(d)
Panel I: Coefficients (standard errors)				
Const.	0.692***	1.175***	1.692***	1.686***
	(0.159)	(0.153)	(0.225)	(0.255)
NI_t	0.390**	—	—	0.277
	(0.185)			(0.250)
DNI_t	—	1.570***	—	0.619***
		(0.210)		(0.244)
$NIloss_t$	—	—	−2.355***	−1.890***
			(0.251)	(0.337)
Panel II: Goodness of fit				
Log-likel.	−163.7	−150.7	−116.3	−109.1
Pseudo R^2	10.3%	17.5%	36.3%	40.2%
R_p^2	55.6%	62.4%	76.4%	76.4%

Notes: The dependent variable dD equals 0 if the dividend is omitted, 1 if the dividend is cut to a strictly positive level and 2 if the dividend is increased or maintained. The sample consists of (1) 71 firms in which the event year corresponds to the initial year they made losses over the period 1989–93, and of (2) 107 firms in which the event year is the first year with an earnings decline but which have strictly positive earnings during 1989–93. There are, therefore, 178 observations. Earnings and changes in earnings are standardized by the book value of equity for the preceding year. All specifications assume multiplicative heteroskedasticity. All model specifications are significant with p-values <0.001. Pseudo R^2 follows McFadden (1974). R_p^2 stands for the percentage of correct predictions.

* stands for statistical significance at the 10% level.
** stands for statistical significance at the 5% level.
*** stands for statistical significance at the 1% level.

Table 7.4 reports the results of the ordered probit analysis of the decision to omit ($dD = 0$), cut ($dD = 1$), and increase/maintain ($dD = 2$). The table sheds further light on the validity of our findings from Section 7.4.1. Following DeAngelo, DeAngelo, and Skinner (1992), we focus on a sample of (1) seventy-one firms in which the event year corresponds to the first year with losses throughout the period 1989–93, and of (2) 107 firms in which the event year is the first year with an earnings decline that is followed by strictly positive earnings during the period 1989–93. Consequently, we have 178 observations. The independent variables are net earnings in period t, changes in net earnings from $t − 1$ to t and a loss dummy which equals one if there is a net earnings loss in period t. The first two variables are standardized by the book value of equity for the preceding period.

Specifications (a)–(c) in Table 7.4 report the univariate regression results. Taken separately, all three variables have a statistically significant effect on the probability to cut versus omit and maintain/increase versus omit. However, a comparison of the measures of goodness of fit shows that specification (c) with the earnings loss dummy has a fit that substantially dominates specifications (a) and (b). Furthermore, a specification with both net earnings and a loss dummy (not reported) does not provide a significant improvement in the regression results when compared to specification (c). In the unreported specification, the coefficient on the net earnings variable has a t-ratio of only 1.77, compared with the coefficient on the loss dummy which is highly statistical significant ($t = -5.9$). When we include changes in net earnings instead of the net earnings (not reported), we obtain a similar pattern. Our measures of goodness of fit suggest that such a specification hardly, if at all, improves the regression results relative to specification (c).[7] The slight increase in the pseudo R^2, in comparison to specification (c), reflects the fact that the pseudo R^2 does not incorporate a penalty for increasing the number of exogenous variables.[8] Finally, specification (d) includes all three variables. The loss dummy remains significant and net earnings is no longer statistically significant. However, changes in net earnings is still highly significant. Although not reported in Table 7.4, we estimate a model with net earnings and changes in net earnings only. Again we find that the coefficient of the changes-in-earnings variable is statistically significant whereas that on net earnings is not.

As a final robustness check on these results we re-run the ordered probit regressions on the same dependent variable but on a slightly different sample. The sample consists now of (1) seventy-one firms in which the event year corresponds to the initial year of the loss over the period 1989–93, and (2) 118 firms in which the event year is the first year there was either a net earnings or a cash flow decline, but strictly positive earnings and cash flows during 1989–93.[9] The estimations for this sample of various specifications, including one containing both cash flows and net earnings, are presented in Table 7.5.

The explanatory power of the earnings loss dummy remains intact across all three specifications, irrespective of whether we include cash flows, net earnings, or both. The lowest t-ratio for the coefficient of the loss dummy is $t = -2.13$ (specification (a)). When we include both cash flows and net earnings in the specification with the loss dummy (specification (c)), the coefficient on the loss dummy is highly significant with a t-ratio of -6.5. Specifications (a) and (c) show that, for the decision to cut versus omit, the magnitude of net earnings is not statistically significant. This contrasts with our result from Section 7.3.2, where we report stronger results for net earnings than for cash flow. One plausible explanation is that the inclusion of the loss dummy in this context extracts most of the explanatory power of the level of net earnings.

To conclude, there is overwhelming evidence on the explanatory power of annual earnings losses on the dividend policy of German firms. Annual losses have a substantial incremental effect on the decision to omit the dividend, over and above declining earnings and cash flows. The experiment set up in this section has served to corroborate the results from Section 7.3 and to establish that an annual loss leads to an omission of the dividend rather than to just a dividend cut.

---

[7] See Goergen and Renneboog (2003) for details on these alternative specifications.

[8] See Aldrich and Nelson (1984: 57).

[9] There are 221 observations as for some firms there are two event years as the year of the net earnings decline does not coincide with the year of the cash flows decline.

Table 7.5. *Ordered probit analysis of the decision to omit, cut, or maintain/increase the dividend in loss and non-loss firms during 1989–93: A model with cash flows and net earnings*

	(a)	(b)	(c)
Panel I: Coefficients (standard errors)			
Const.	0.928***	1.416***	1.394***
	(0.195)	(0.211)	(0.217)
NI$_t$	0.216	—	0.197
	(0.179)		(0.271)
CF$_t$	—	0.291***	0.247***
		(0.082)	(0.091)
NIloss$_t$	−0.601**	−2.140***	−2.010***
	(0.282)	(0.232)	(0.310)
Panel II: Goodness of fit			
Log-likel.	−179.1	−139.5	−139.3
Pseudo R^2	18%	36.1%	36.2%
R^2_p	63.8%	76.9%	76.9%

Notes: The dependent variable dD equals 0 if the dividend is omitted, 1 if the dividend is cut to a strictly positive level and 2 if the dividend is increased or maintained. The sample consists of (1) 71 firms in which the event year corresponds to the initial year of losses over the period 1989–93, and (2) 118 firms in which the event year is the first year with either a net earnings or a cash flow decline but strictly positive earnings/cash flows during 1989–93. There are 221 observations. Earnings and cash flows (zero distribution profits gross of depreciation and provisions) are standardized by the book value of equity for the previous year. All specifications assume multiplicative heteroskedasticity. All model specifications are significant with p-values <0.001. Pseudo-R^2 follows McFadden (1974). R^2_p stands for the percentage of correct predictions.

* stands for statistical significance at the 10% level.
** stands for statistical significance at the 5% level.
*** stands for statistical significance at the 1% level.

7.4.3. *Earnings Performance Around the Initial Loss Year and the Decision to Omit the Dividend*

Healy and Palepu (1988: 161) report that firms omitting the dividend have statistically significant earnings declines in the year of the dividend omission and the year before. In addition, they report an earnings improvement over the three years following the dividend omission. The authors (p. 163) argue that 'this finding is somewhat puzzling, given the large negative market reaction to the omission announcement'. Similarly, DeAngelo, DeAngelo, and Skinner (1992, table IV) find that loss-making firms that reduce their dividend have significantly lower losses in the year of the loss and the year before, than loss-making firms that do not reduce their dividends. They also find that for loss-making firms that reduce the dividends, statistically significant earnings improvements are made one year after the loss. DeAngelo, DeAngelo, and Skinner (1992) come up with a plausible explanation for Healy and Palepu's (1988) puzzle of the earnings improvement after the omission: '. . . dividend reduction decisions reflect the low level of current and expected future earnings, and not simply year-to-year earnings changes' (p. 1849). The high incidence of dividend omissions in our data could also reflect the fact that German managers are reacting to expected persistence of earnings problems. This hypothesis is consistent with Modigliani and Miller (1958: 288) who suggest '. . . the role of dividends as a proxy measure of long term earnings anticipations'.

Following this argument, we test the hypothesis that dividend omissions are associated with persistent past, present, and future bad performance. To do so, we perform a binomial probit analysis on the sample of seventy-one firms (i.e. N_1) whose event year is the initial year of annual loss during 1989–93, after five or more years of strictly positive earnings and dividend payments. As fifteen firms made annual losses in 1993, we also collected accounting information on future earnings and dividends (namely for 1994). Three firms went bankrupt within two years after the first annual loss.

Table 7.6 reports the estimation results of the probit whose dependent variable equals one if there is a dividend omission and zero otherwise. The explanatory variables are the level of net earnings in periods $t-2$, $t-1$, t, and $t+1$, where t stands for the year of the initial loss (noted NI_{t-2}, NI_{t-1}, NI_t and NI_{t+1}, respectively). Following DeAngelo, DeAngelo, and Skinner (1992), NI_{t+1} is used as a proxy for managers' expectations about future earnings in the year of the dividend decision. Note, however, that the inclusion of this variable may suffer from a serious endogeneity problem. In Section 6.2 (of Chapter 6), we argued that the Lintner (1956) equation (6.5) could also be obtained by using an 'adaptive expectations model'. The central assumption underlying this model is that current dividends are a function of long run expected earnings. If this formulation is correct, adding NI_{t+1} to our probit model will not add any extra information, as current dividends already account for managerial expectations of future earnings. There is no easy way of circumventing this endogeneity problem unless we would include information on, say, analysts' expectations of the future earnings of the firm, information which is not available for the sample period. Still, we include this variable with the aim of replicating the DeAngelo, DeAngelo, and Skinner (1992) analysis for the USA.

All the coefficients in Table 7.6 have a negative sign, meaning that a higher level in net earnings decreases the probability of a dividend omission. However, all specifications generally have a very low pseudo R^2, reflecting the low statistical significance of the parameter estimates. Net earnings in the years $t-2$ to $t-1$ are not significant, as reported in Section 7.3. Current net earnings have a statistically significant effect only at the 10 per cent level while net earnings one year after the annual loss are not significantly correlated with dividend omissions. Contrary to DeAngelo, DeAngelo, and Skinner (1992), we reject the null hypothesis that firms omitting the dividend have persistence in net earnings difficulties.

We estimate the same specifications but with cash flows instead of net earnings. We find a slightly different pattern: higher cash flows two years and one year prior to the loss year are significantly associated with a lower probability of dividend omissions. A similar pattern is uncovered for cash flows one year after the year of the loss. However, the effects are no longer significant when past, current, and future cash flows are jointly estimated, again suggesting a weak correlation between dividend omissions, and deep and persistent poor performance.

Table 7.6. *Binomial probit analysis of the relationship between the decision to omit the dividend and the persistence and depth of net earnings difficulties around the loss year*

	(a)	(b)	(c)	(d)	(e)
Panel I: Coefficients (standard errors)					
Const.	1.369***	1.326***	0.811**	1.158***	0.705
	(0.448)	(0.404)	(0.415)	(0.302)	(0.495)
NI_{t-2}	−0.145	—	—	—	—
	(0.953)				
NI_{t-1}	—	−0.377	—	—	−0.185
		(1.194)			(1.181)
NI_t	—	—	−1.303*	—	−1.073
			(0.791)		(0.729)
NI_{t+1}	—	—	—	−0.526	−0.663
				(0.357)	(0.457)
Panel II: Goodness of fit					
Log-likel	−36.6	−36.6	−34.5	−35.2	−33.7
Pseudo R^2	0.01%	0.01%	5.8%	3.9%	7.9%
R_p^2	78.9%	78.9%	78.9%	77.5%	78.9%
signif. level (%)	0.880	0.915	0.074	0.096	0.124

Notes: The dependent variable equals 1 if the dividend is omitted and 0 otherwise. The sample consists of 71 firms in which the event year corresponds to the initial year in which they made losses over the period 1989–93, after five or more years of strictly positive earnings and dividend payments. There are, therefore, 71 observations. Net earnings in periods $t-2$, $t-1$, t, and $t+1$, where t is the year of the annual loss, are standardized by the book value of equity for the previous year. Standard-errors are robust to heteroskedasticity following White (1980). Pseudo-R^2 follows McFadden (1974). R_p^2 stands for the percentage of correct predictions.

* stands for statistical significance at the 10% level.
** stands for statistical significance at the 5% level.
*** stands for statistical significance at the 1% level.

7.4.4. *How do These Results Compare with Lintner–Miller–Modigliani (L–M–M)?*

We have found evidence consistent with a fundamental fact: firms suffering an annual net earnings loss following good past performance omit their dividend in an overwhelming majority of the cases. Dividend omissions are not associated with higher and more persistent earnings problems and future worse performance. Our results are consistent with the Fischer, Jansen, and Meyer (1975) survey of the dividend practices of German firms which showed that dividends are not paid out of companies' reserves.

Our results stand in marked contrast to the predictions based on L–M–M, namely that dividends are downwards inflexible if earnings declines are not persistent. Moreover, the inclination of German firms to omit current dividends, when suffering current losses, suggests a weaker role of dividends as signalling devices in comparison to the USA. If dividends convey information about prospects, as suggested by Modigliani and Miller (1958, 1959), then a dividend omission would only take place if managers were pessimistic about the future value of the firm. In that framework, Healy and Palepu (1988) provide empirical evidence that the abnormal share price reaction to the announcement of a dividend omission is correlated with the firms' earnings changes in the year of and the year after the dividend announcements. Our results show that German firms do not hesitate to reduce dividends in cases of a *temporary* deterioration in performance. It is, therefore, interesting to establish to what extent the dividend payouts of German firms recover to the levels that were in place prior to the dividend omissions and cuts.

7.5. DIVIDEND REBOUNDS AFTER DIVIDEND OMISSIONS AND REDUCTIONS

In this section we analyse the decision to increase the dividend subsequent to omissions or cuts. It is likely that the downward flexibility in dividend changes, when earnings decline on a temporary basis, is matched by a similar upward flexibility once the earnings pick up again. Without a similar upward flexibility, one would expect a continual decrease in the long-term payout ratio of German firms. We focus on the aftermath of dividend reductions and omissions, and address two questions: (1) How many years does it take for firms to increase or initiate the dividend after a dividend reduction or omission, respectively, and (2) in case they increase or re-initiate, what is the average increase or initiation relative to the payout ratio that existed prior to the dividend reduction or omission.

We start by considering dividend behaviour surrounding dividend omissions. To this end, we construct a sample of all firms that omitted the dividend during the period of 1985–91, such that we can examine a five-year window, starting one year before the dividend omission and ending three years after the omission. Out of the 221 firms, we find sixty-one firms satisfying these criteria yielding sixty-three observations as two firms omitted the dividend twice during this period. The event year, t, is the year of the dividend omission. By definition, in year $t - 1$ the firms in this sample paid a strictly positive dividend.

Table 7.7 reports a number of remarkable facts. First, panel I shows that approximately 56 per cent of the firms initiate a strictly positive payout policy already within the two years after omitting the dividend, and 28.6 per cent of the firms initiate within only one year. Only 35 per cent of the firms take more than three years to initiate the dividend. Second, in the first two years after t, the majority of firms revert to the dividend levels in place prior to the dividend omission. Indeed, we can see from panel II that the average gross dividend per share paid when firms re-initiate the dividend in periods $t + 1$ and $t + 2$ is similar to the one paid in year $t - 1$. Third, these results are not driven by the fact that in period $t - 1$ the gross dividend per share was relatively low, as they are similar to the average gross dividend per share paid by 221 firms during 1984–93 is DM12.3 (Table 6.2, Chapter 6).

Next, we focus on dividend reductions to a still-positive level. We create a sample of all firms which reduce the dividend payout between 1985 and 1991, such that we can examine a five-year window around t, the year of the dividend reduction. Out of the 221 firms, we find sixty-two firms which satisfy these criteria.[10]

---

[10] The sample would have amounted to seventy firms if we had included eight cases of reductions where in year $t - 1$ there was a 'specially designated dividend' that was paid but that was not maintained in subsequent years.

Table 7.7. *Dividend rebounds after dividend omissions*

1 year after *t*	2 years after *t*	3 years after *t*	More than 3 years after *t*
Panel I: Number (proportion) of firms initiating the dividend			
18 (28.6%)	17 (27%)	6 (9.5%)	22 (34.9%)

	1 year after *t*	2 years after *t*	3 years after *t*
Panel II: Average (median) gross dividend (DM) around t of firms initiating the dividend			
t − 1	10.5 (8.2)	9.4 (9.4)	13.6 (11.7)
t	0 (0)	0 (0)	0 (0)
t + 1	8.8 (8.6)	0 (0)	0 (0)
t + 2	—	10.2 (6.3)	0 (0)
t + 3	—	—	16.05 (14.85)

Note: The sample consists of 61 firms. The event year is the first year during 1985–91 in which firms omitted the dividend per share. There are 63 observations as two firms omitted the dividend twice during the period of analysis. *t* stands for the first year of dividend omission after at least one year of strictly positive payouts.

Table 7.8. *Dividend rebounds after dividend reductions*

1 year after *t*	2 years after *t*	3 years or more after *t*
Panel I: Number (proportion) of firms increasing the dividend		
31 (50%)	16 (25.8%)	15 (24.2%)

	1 year after *t*	2 years after *t*
Panel II: Average (Median) gross dividend (DM) around t of firms increasing the dividend		
t − 1	17.6 (15.6)	18.0 (16.1)
t	11.1 (9.4)	11.9 (10.2)
t + 1	15.9 (12.1)	11.5 (9.4)
t + 2	—	14.0 (12.1)

Note: The sample consists of 62 firms and observations. The event year is the initial year during 1985–91 in which firms reduced the dividend to a still-positive level. *t* stands for the first year of dividend reduction after at least one year of strictly positive payouts.

Table 7.8 shows a similar pattern to the one observed for dividend rebounds after omissions, that is: a quick recovery of the dividend following a reduction. Panel I observes that 78 per cent of the firms increase the dividend within two years of the dividend reduction in year *t*. Only 24 per cent of the whole sample takes more than two years to increase the dividend per share. Panel II compares the average gross dividend prior and subsequent to the dividend reduction. Firms that increase the dividend in the year after the reduction, almost revert to the payout level of year *t* − 1. The ratio of new to former levels of dividend payouts is as high as 90 per cent.

In summary, we observe that for a majority of German firms, dividend omissions and partial reductions are associated with a fast re-establishment of the payout policy in those firms prior to the omission or reduction. Suppose that performance has improved significantly in year $t + 1$, after a year of bad performance leading to a dividend reduction or omission. Then, an increase or a re-initiation of the dividend can be expected. This shows that in German firms, dividend policy changes very quickly and closely follows earnings patterns. Our evidence contradicts Lintner's (1956: 103) predictions regarding firms' reluctance to decrease current dividends if earnings decline temporarily. It also contrasts with Modigliani and Miller's (1958: 288) hypothesis that dividends provide good proxies for earnings anticipations.

7.6. SUMMARY

In this chapter we propose a discrete choice approach to model the dividend decision of German firms. We focus on establishing how past, current, and future profits affect the timing of dividend changes rather than the amount of the dividend change. To this end, we use a discrete choice model that measures the probability that firms shift dividend policies upwards or downwards. The rationale for this modelling strategy is twofold: (1) we take into consideration the high incidence of discreteness in the dividends-per-share time series, suggesting perhaps that a dynamic panel data estimation of the Lintner type might not be an appropriate model of corporate dividend behaviour in Germany; and (2) to test the signalling theory of dividends for German firms.

We start by showing that bottom line earnings are key determinants of when to change the dividend in German firms, a finding consistent with Lintner (1956). Cash flows are used to correct for accounting conservatism in the earnings figure and to test a cash flow explanation for dividend changes. We find that cash flows are also important determinants of the decision to change the dividend.

This chapter also highlights two features of German dividend policy that are not captured by the Lintner (1956) and Miller and Modigliani (1961) framework. First, we observe that the *level* of net earnings is *not* the main determinant of a dividend reduction or omission. In fact, the occurrence of an annual loss has higher explanatory power than the magnitude of the loss itself. We find that 80 per cent of the firms with at least five years of positive earnings and dividends omit the dividend in the loss year, irrespective of the magnitude of the earnings loss and of the past and future earnings. Second, German firms quickly revert to the dividend level prior to the dividend omission or reduction. We find that more than half of the German firms which omitted the dividend, re-establish the dividend payout prior to the omission within merely two years. A similar pattern applies to dividend reductions. These findings contrast with the predictions of Lintner (1956) and Miller and Modigliani (1961) that dividends will only change if managers believe that these dividends will not have to be reversed in the short run.

Although we did not find sufficient evidence in Chapter 6 to reject Lintner's (1956) corporate dividend model, the discrete choice approach undertaken in this chapter has shown that the Lintner model is not entirely satisfactory. More specifically, the model does not capture the dividend behaviour of German firms with a temporary deterioration in profitability. The Lintner model describes the dividend policy of well-established, well performing (German) firms, but not that of firms facing sudden temporary falls in profitability. Our findings do not comply with DeAngelo, DeAngelo, and Skinner (1992) who report that US firms are more likely to reduce dividends when the current loss is higher and when persistent future earnings problems are expected (findings which are consistent with the predictions by Miller and Modigliani 1961).

These results can be interpreted in the light of signalling theories of dividend policy. The fact that German firms frequently omit and cut dividends and quickly revert to the payout prior to the omission or cut suggests that dividends do not convey (much) information about the value of the firm. This contrasts, for example, with Kalay (1980) who argues that the managerial reluctance to cut dividends is a necessary condition for a dividend policy to be informative.

8

Dividend Policy, Corporate Control, and Tax Clienteles

8.1. INTRODUCTION

In this chapter we examine the impact of levels of control and changes in control on dividend policy in Germany. Empirical evidence on the relation between dividend policy and ownership is scarce and focuses mainly on countries with diffuse ownership and control such as the USA or the UK. Hardly anything is known about the dividend policy of closely held public corporations. It is interesting to study German firms for two reasons. First, German dividend payout policy is substantially different from that of the UK or USA. For example, Chapter 6 showed that German firms pay out a smaller proportion of their cash flows as dividends. Moreover, Chapter 7 showed that they are less reluctant to cut and omit the dividend in the presence of a temporary deterioration in performance. Second, ownership and control is usually concentrated in the hands of a large shareholder. This raises an interesting question: do the dividend patterns reflect the control structures? The hypotheses addressed in this chapter (and summarized in Chapter 4) draw on the theme that dividends and concentration of ownership or control act as alternative monitoring and signalling devices. Therefore, different forms of control may give rise to the setting of different dividend payouts and different dividend policies.

We use two econometric tools described in previous chapters: a dividend model which controls for unobserved heterogeneity across firms, year-specific effects, and profits, and a qualitative model of the decision to change the dividend. The chapter is structured as follows. Section 8.2 describes the data and the methodology. We present summary statistics for the sample of 221 German industrial and commercial publicly quoted firms. As 'pyramiding' (i.e. the fact that voting shares in a company are controlled via intermediate investment companies throughout several layers) is a characteristic of the German system, we provide a set of descriptive statistics on first-tier control as well as ultimate control. Subsequently, we show dividend payout ratios across different patterns of control. Section 8.3 summarizes the regression results on the relation between dividends, earnings, and corporate control. We employ dynamic panel data models similar to those in Chapter 6, but include variables accounting for control. In Section 8.4, we examine *when* German firms with different forms of ultimate control change their dividend policies. We focus mainly on the firm's decision to omit the dividend as our results stand in marked contrast with those from US studies. In Section 8.5, we examine the issue of whether a bank's influence through proxy votes is an important determinant of dividends. In Section 8.6, we investigate whether the complexity of control structures influences dividend policy. We also test whether investors'

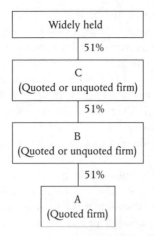

Figure 8.1. *Example of a 'pyramid' structure*

Note: Firm A is one of the firms in our sample. At the first-tier of the pyramid, it is controlled by firm B (which holds 51 per cent of its voting shares), which can be a quoted or unquoted firm. At the next layer, we find that firm B is controlled by firm C (which holds 51 per cent of its voting shares), which again can be quoted or unquoted, but is in this case widely held. *Ultimately*, firm C controls firm A.

tax considerations are influential determinants of dividend patterns. Section 8.7 summarizes the findings of the chapter.

8.2. DATA AND METHODOLOGY

8.2.1. *Data and Ownership Patterns*

We use the same sample as in Chapter 6 which consists of 221 German industrial and commercial quoted firms. We gather information on all the disclosed holdings of voting shares over the period 1984–93 from *Hoppenstedt—Saling Aktienführer*. Large shareholders controlling more than 25 per cent of the voting rights are classified into the following eight categories: families or individuals, German banks, German industrial or commercial corporations, German insurance companies, German (local or federal) state authorities, foreign institutions and companies, German industrial or financial holding companies, and foundations (*Stiftungen*). An important feature of the German structure of corporate ownership is the frequent occurrence of complex control structures (see, for example, Adams 1994; Franks and Mayer 1995, 2001; Becht and Boehmer 2001; Boehmer 2002).[1] Quoted firms can be controlled by other corporations and these, in turn, can be controlled by families or individuals, banks, state authorities, etc. or be widely held companies. In Fig. 8.1, the ultimate controlling shareholder is corporation C, which is a widely held firm.

[1] Franks and Mayer (1995); Renneboog (2000); and Nicodano (1998) record complex control structures in France, Belgium, and Italy, respectively. This suggests that complex, concentrated shareholding structures are a common feature of Continental European capital markets (see Barca and Becht 2001) whereas the simple, diffuse ownership structures are common in the UK (Goergen and Renneboog 2001) and the USA (La Porta et al. 2000).

We collect data on *first-tier* control as well as *ultimate* control. To complement the shareholder data from *Hoppenstedt—Saling Aktienführer*, we also use *Commerzbank—Wer gehört zu Wem*, a guide that is published every three years and which contains a survey of the equity cross-holdings between roughly 11,000 of the larger German firms with an equity capital amounting to at least €0.51 m (DM1 m.). This guide is particularly useful in cases where companies at intermediate layers are privately held, and are therefore not cited in *Hoppenstedt—Saling Aktienführer*. The drawback of the guide is that it does not capture the timing of the changes in ownership and control in between the publication dates. Therefore, to minimize this problem, we use lagged measures of control in our regressions (see Section 8.3.1).

The ultimate controlling shareholder of the quoted firm A in our sample is said to be at the first-tier if either (1) there is no shareholder holding at least 25 per cent of the voting shares of A or (2) the first-tier shareholder is a bank or insurance company, the German State, a foreign company or institution, or a family. In all other cases, the ultimate shareholder is situated at a higher tier which is reached when we arrive at a layer where one of these two criteria is satisfied or when we find a corporation which is widely held. If we reach such a widely held firm at a specific layer, we state that ultimate control lies with this corporation (and at this layer). Figure 8.1 serves to illustrate this point: we consider corporation C to be the ultimate shareholder of corporation A. We can claim that the parent company C controls its subsidiary A through different layers of the pyramid.

In Table 8.1 we examine the control structure of the firms in our sample for 1984, 1989, and 1993, respectively. The 221 firms are classified according to the category of the largest shareholder at both the first-tier and the ultimate levels. In addition, we use two voting equity thresholds: 25 and 50 per cent. For example, panel A describes control in 1984. It shows that, at the first layer, both families and corporations can be found to be the largest categories of shareholders with at least 25 per cent of the voting shares, in 25.8 per cent of our sample, that is, in forty-seven firms each. The table confirms what is now viewed as a well-known stylized fact of German corporate governance: a great majority of German publicly quoted companies are controlled by a single large shareholder and in most cases these large shareholders are other corporations or families (see Edwards and Fischer 1994; Franks and Mayer 1995, 2001; Gorton and Schmid 2000; and Köke 2003 for similar conclusions).

Table 8.1 shows that the power of families as largest shareholders both at the ultimate and first tiers has hardly changed in the ten-year period between 1984 and 1993, although within each category large share stakes may change hands (Jenkinson and Ljunqvist 2001). Control by banks suffers a slight decrease in importance. For example, in 1984, banks were the largest shareholders in 12.1 per cent of the firms compared to 7.7 per cent in 1993. A similar pattern holds when we look at ultimate control. The importance of corporations as largest shareholders at the first tier increases from 25.8 per cent in 1984 to 33.7 in 1993. Furthermore, the proportion of widely held firms is almost identical at the beginning, middle and end of our sample period.

Comparing control at the first tier with ultimate control over the ten-year period gives the perhaps most significant insight that can be derived from Table 8.1. We find that the importance of families and banks increases when ultimate control is considered. This shows that these

Table 8.1. *First-tier and ultimate control of 221 German industrial and commercial quoted firms in 1984, 1989, and 1993*

	First-tier control				Ultimate level control			
	≥25%		≥50%		≥25%		≥50%	
	%	Nr	%	Nr	%	Nr	%	Nr
Panel I: 1984								
A. *Widely held*	15.4	28	45.6	83	15.9	29	46.2	84
B. *Closely held, the largest shareholder with*:								
1. Family	25.8	47	19.8	36	33.0	60	24.7	45
2. Indust./commerc. firm	25.8	47	18.7	34	11.0	20	8.2	15
3. State	4.4	8	3.3	6	7.7	14	5.5	10
4. Bank	12.1	22	2.7	5	15.9	29	5.5	10
5. Insurer	0.5	1	0	0	1.1	2	0	0
6. Foreign firm/institution	6.0	11	4.9	9	8.2	15	7.1	13
7. Holding company	9.3	17	4.4	8	0	0	0	0
8. Foundation	0.5	1	0.5	1	1.6	3	1.1	2
9. Unknown	0	0	0	0	5.5	10	1.6	3
TOTAL	100	182	100	182	100	182	100	182
Panel II: 1989								
A. *Widely held*	15.8	35	41.2	91	16.3	36	41.6	92
B. *Closely held, the largest shareholder with*:								
1. Family	26.7	59	22.6	50	36.2	80	29.4	65
2. Indust./commerc. firm	27.6	61	19.5	43	10.0	22	7.2	16
3. State	3.6	8	3.2	7	6.3	14	5.0	11
4. Bank	8.6	19	2.7	6	12.2	27	5.0	11
5. Insurer	0.5	1	0	0	0.5	1	0	0
6. Foreign firm/institution	6.3	14	4.1	9	9.5	21	7.2	16
7. Holding company	9.5	21	5.4	12	0.9	2	0	0
8. Foundation	1.4	3	1.4	3	2.7	6	1.8	4
9. Unknown	0	0	0	0	5.4	12	2.7	6
TOTAL	100	221	100	221	100	221	100	221
Panel III: 1993								
A. *Widely held*	14.9	31	39.4	82	15.9	33	39.9	83
B. *Closely held, the largest shareholder with*:								
1. Family	22.1	46	16.3	34	32.7	68	25.0	52
2. Indust./commerc. firm	33.7	70	26.4	55	12.0	25	9.6	20
3. State	4.3	9	3.4	7	8.7	18	6.3	13
4. Bank	7.7	16	2.4	5	10.1	21	3.8	8
5. Insurer	1.9	4	0	0	1.9	4	0	0
6. Foreign firm/institution	5.3	11	5.3	11	10.6	22	10.6	22

Table 8.1. *(Continued)*

	First-tier control				Ultimate level control			
	≥25%		≥50%		≥25%		≥50%	
	%	Nr	%	Nr	%	Nr	%	Nr
7. Holding company	9.1	19	5.8	12	0.5	1	0.5	1
8. Foundation	1.0	2	1.0	2	1.9	4	1.4	3
9. Unknown	0	0	0	0	5.8	12	2.9	6
TOTAL	100	208	100	208	100	208	100	208

Note: Widely held firms are firms without a shareholder controlling at least 25% (or 50%) of the voting shares. Closely held firms are categorized according to the category of their controlling shareholder. The sample size varies over the ten-year period as some firms in our sample are not quoted during the whole period and some others go private or bankrupt (see Chapter 6 for further details).

types of shareholders are frequently using intermediate investment companies to control a firm. Consequently, a study that measures control merely at the first tier may suffer from a significant bias and come up with erroneous conclusions. For example, in 1984, families (banks) are the largest shareholders at the first tier in almost 25.8 (12.1) per cent of the cases. However, at the ultimate level, the figure increases to 33 (15.9) per cent. Corporations at the ultimate level are not an important category of controlling shareholders as they are only present in approximately 10–12 per cent of the sample, as opposed to approximately 26–34 per cent at the first tier.

Our observations are subject to the following remarks. First, bank control may be underestimated as this table does not take into account the proxy votes that banks can exercise on behalf of their customers (*Depotstimmrecht*). Gottschalk (1988) provides data on proxy votes held by the three largest banks for a sample of thirty-two major German firms at the annual general meetings in 1986. He shows that the three banks had a majority of the votes in almost half of his sample, and in a further ten cases the big banks controlled between 25 and 50 per cent of the votes exercised. Baums and Fraune (1995) provide data on proxy votes for a sample of twenty-four major firms for 1992 and find that in four cases, the three big banks control a majority of the votes cast, and in a further ten cases the big banks control between 25 and 50 per cent. There are several particular features on banks unveiled by these two studies. First, the proxy votes occur mainly in firms without a shareholder (with at least 25 per cent of the voting rights). Second, the concentration of proxy votes held by the three largest banks during the 1970s and 1980s slightly decreased, which is confirmed by Gorton and Schmid (2000: 9). Köke (2003) believes that the discrepancy between German banks' ownership rights and voting rights is probably small because a precondition for bank voting power based on proxy rights is widely held ownership, a rare phenomenon in German firms.

8.2.2. *Dividends and Control: Some Univariate Statistics*

In this section, we show univariate statistics on how dividend payout ratios vary across different patterns of ownership and control. Table 8.2 reports the average payout ratios in

Table 8.2. *Dividend payout ratios of firms without a control change over the period 1984–93*

Type of control	Average cash flow per share (DM)	Average gross dividend per share (DM)	Dividend payout ratio (%)	Nr. of firms
Widely held firms	71.99	13.70	19.03 (20.80)	23
Family-controlled firms	48.76	11.81	24.22 (31.50)	69
Company-controlled firms	61.77	11.41	18.50 (24.95)	19
Bank-controlled firms	72.80	12.37	16.99 (16.60)	22

Note: Cash flows are defined as zero distribution profits gross of depreciation and changes in long-term provisions. Dividends are gross of taxation on distributed earnings. Of the original sample of 221 German industrial and commercial firms, 133 were *ultimately* controlled either by a family, a bank, another industrial corporation or widely held (no large shareholder controlling more than 25% of the voting rights), over the whole period 1984–93. Firms in this sub-sample were not subject to changes in control over the sample period. We calculate two dividend payout ratios. A first definition is the ratio of the average gross dividend across all firms over the whole period 1984–93 over the average cash flow for all firms over the whole period 1984–93. The second definition (presented in parentheses in the table) is the average of all firms' dividend payout ratios.

widely held firms, in family-controlled firms, in firms controlled by other corporations and in bank-controlled firms, where the controlling shareholder did *not* change over the ten-year period 1984–93. Out of the total sample of 221 firms, 133 firms satisfy this criterion. Family-controlled firms have the highest dividend payout ratio across these four types of firms whereas bank-controlled firms have the lowest. Widely held firms also have a high payout ratio. When we calculate the dividend payout ratios on a published earnings basis (rather than on a cash flow basis), the ratios vary from a minimum of 77 per cent in widely held firms to a maximum of 81 per cent in firms controlled by other corporations.

Whereas Table 8.2 presented dividend payout ratios of listed firms with no change in control over a ten-year period, in Table 8.3 we focus on what happens to firms' dividend policies when there is a change, for example, when their control status changes from a situation of no large shareholder (widely held) to bank-control or family-control, and vice versa. We select a subsample of firms with substantial changes in control and with control and accounting data available in a window of five consecutive years around the event year (the year of the control change). Table 8.3 shows that there are twenty-three firms that initially have no controlling shareholder but become closely held. Of these twenty-three firms, sixteen firms become family-controlled, and in seven firms banks become the dominant shareholder. Additionally, twenty-three firms lose their controlling shareholder and end up being widely held. Out of these twenty-three firms, fourteen and nine, respectively, are family- and bank-controlled prior to the control change.

Table 8.3 reports the average payout ratios of the firms in these subsamples for a period spanning two years prior to the year of the control change to two years after the change. The fact that a firm becomes widely held or closely held does not seem to trigger significant changes in dividend policy (compare columns 1 and 2). However, this conclusion is not upheld if we consider the nature of the largest shareholder. The last two columns of the table report that a change in control from widely held to bank-controlled is associated with a decrease in the payout ratio and, vice versa, a firm that was previously bank-controlled and

Table 8.3. *Dividend payout ratios around the year of the control change*

Year		Widely held becomes closely held	Closely held becomes widely held	Widely held becomes family-controlled	Family-controlled becomes widely held	Widely held becomes bank-controlled	Bank-controlled becomes widely held
				Nature of control change			
−2	Div	6.1	7.9	4.2	6.8	9.3	9.2
	CF	33.0	54.2	40.4	34.6	28.8	78.6
	Div/CF	18.5	14.6	10.3	19.6	32.3	11.7
−1	Div	7.9	8.3	6.9	5.9	9.6	11.3
	CF	28.2	57.9	42.4	34.9	24.6	86.6
	Div/CF	28.1	14.3	16.3	16.8	39.0	13.0
0	Div	9.3	9.8	9.2	8.5	9.4	11.5
	CF	28.5	53.9	31.0	35.9	27.1	76.5
	Div/CF	32.6	18.2	29.6	23.7	34.7	15.0
1	Div	7.5	11.2	7.6	9.3	7.2	13.1
	CF	29.8	70.8	32.6	38.6	25.1	90.0
	Div/CF	25.2	15.8	23.4	24.0	28.7	14.6
2	Div	9.9	9.7	10.3	6.5	9.2	13.0
	CF	42.6	71	43.9	33.8	40.4	91.1
	Div/CF	23.2	13.7	23.5	19.2	22.8	14.3
Nr. of firms		23	23	16	14	7	9

Note: Widely held firms are firms without a large shareholder controlling at least 25% of the voting shares. Control is defined as control at the ultimate level. The sample consists of firms with a change in control during 1986–91, a period chosen in order to have five years of data around the year of the change in control. Cash flows (CF) and dividends (Div) are defined as in Table 8.2 and are expressed as DM per share figures. Dividend payout ratios (Div/CF) are expressed as percentages. The event year, $t = 0$, is the year of the change in control.

subsequently becomes widely held experiences a rise in its payout ratio after the control change. Somewhat mixed evidence is found when we consider the transition from family control to dispersed control, and vice versa. The latter is associated with increasing payout ratios whereas we cannot establish a pattern for the former.

In this section, we have described the cross-sectional variation in dividend payout ratios, with bank-controlled firms showing lower payout ratios than other types of closely held corporations and widely held firms. In the next section, we estimate a panel data model similar to that in Chapter 6, but including variables measuring control. We examine the extent to which firms with different control structures are inclined to omit dividends when published earnings or cash flows decline. We report the results on a cash flow basis because levels of ratios on that basis have a higher cross-sectional variation. However, we also estimate the same specifications using a published earnings basis to check the robustness of the results based on cash flows.

8.3. THE RELATION BETWEEN DIVIDENDS, PROFITS, AND OWNERSHIP AND CONTROL STRUCTURES

In this section, we discuss various specifications of a model relating dividends, profits (measured by cash flows), and ownership and control patterns using OLS in levels, GMM-in-differences (GMM(DIF)) and GMM-in-systems (GMM(SYS)) (see Chapter 6 for a discussion of these methodologies). For reasons of brevity, we only report the results relating to OLS in levels and GMM(SYS). We briefly refer to the results of the published earnings model and of the GMM(DIF) estimation when the results are different from those reported.

Out of the sample of 221 firms, described in Section 8.2.1, we exclude those firms that are subsidiaries of foreign companies, are controlled by state authorities or by foundations, as well as firms for which we cannot establish the nature of the ultimate largest shareholder. We obtain a sample of 191 firms that are controlled by a family, bank, or another corporation or are widely held.

We estimate the following model:

$$\frac{D_{it}}{\text{MVE}_{i0}} = \alpha \left(\frac{D_{i,t-1}}{\text{MVE}_{i0}} \right) + \beta \left(\frac{\Pi_{it}}{\text{MVE}_{i0}} \right) + \delta \left(\frac{\Pi_{i,t-1}}{\text{MVE}_{i0}} \right) + \rho C_{i,t-1} + \text{YEAR}_t + \eta_i + V_{it} \quad (8.1)$$

where D_{it} stands for the total dividends for firm i at time t, Π; represents total cash flow or published earnings, C is a measure for control concentration that we measure at time $t-1$, MVE_{i0} is a scaling measure (the market capitalization of firm i at the beginning of the period), YEAR stands for the time dummies, η_i are firm-specific effects and V_{it} is the disturbance term.

8.3.1. *Measures of Control*

We use different measures for the degree of control in individual firms. First, we consider the proportion of the voting shares owned by the largest shareholder at the ultimate level (L_1). A shareholder is labelled as the largest shareholder if he is the shareholder with the highest percentage of voting rights and if he owns at least 25 per cent of the votes. This shareholder may or may not be on the management board (*Vorstand*) or supervisory board (*Aufsichtsrat*) of the firm in which he holds shares. In the overwhelming majority of listed German firms, the large shareholders are represented on at least one of the boards. Legally, 50 per cent of the supervisory board seats, including that of the chairman, are reserved for the shareholder representatives. For example, Goergen (1998: 58–9) analyses the management and supervisory board representation of fifty-one firms whose major shareholder at the time of going public is a family. The author finds that 'members of the family hold on average 17 per cent of the shareholder seats on the supervisory board and hold on average almost half of the seats on the management board. [. . .] In 27.5 per cent of companies, members of the family sit on both boards. [. . .] in 88 per cent of the companies a family member is chairman of at least one of the two boards.' This is confirmed by Gerum, Steinmann, and Fees (1988) and Franks and Mayer (2001).

It should be pointed out that the agency costs are substantially different depending on the type of ultimate controlling shareholder. If the ultimate shareholder of a specific firm is a widely held corporation, that firm may suffer from a lack of shareholder monitoring and managers may have (too) much discretion to set corporate policy. Thus, such a control structure may give rise to agency costs that are more severe than if the firm is controlled by a family or individual. We construct a Herfindahl index (H) based on all the disclosed stakes of voting shares at the ultimate level.[2] However, there is a fundamental problem with the data when calculating this index. As stated above, shareholders did not have to disclose shareholdings below 25 per cent until after 1995 when the disclosure threshold was reduced to 5 per cent. Therefore, the Herfindahl index may be a noisy measure for control. WH_1 and WH_2 are dummy variables that equal one if there is no large shareholder with at least 25 or 50 per cent, respectively, of the voting capital, at the ultimate level. Finally, for each class of large shareholders we construct a variable measuring the percentage of voting rights held by the largest shareholder. We define $B_{i,t-1}$ as a variable that takes the value of the proportion of votes held by a bank, when a bank is the largest shareholder of firm i at time $t-1$ with at least 25 per cent of the voting shares, and is 0 otherwise. $F_{i,t-1}$ and $IC_{i,t-1}$ are variables measuring the concentration of votes held by families and corporations, respectively.[3]

The issue of whether control is exogenously determined deserves some discussion. Some authors argue that dividends, and ownership or control structures are simultaneously determined (e.g. Jensen, Solberg, and Zorn 1992). However, as described in Section 8.2, control patterns in Germany have not changed much over the 1980s and 1990s, whereas the dividend policies of our sample firms have undergone much more substantial changes. This suggests that ownership and control structures are exogenous with respect to dividends. We also include the control variables dated $t-1$ in our specifications. Still, in order to avoid the possible endogeneity problem of control, we use an instrumental variable estimation technique and verify the validity of our instruments (see below). We also estimate interactive terms of control and performance in all the specifications, but do not report the results here as all these interaction terms are individually and jointly statistically insignificant. For all specifications, we also estimate the effect of firm size, as measured by the market capitalization of the firm at time $t=0$. We exclude it on the grounds that the coefficient is statistically insignificant and that, as size does not change substantially over time, the effect of this variable is largely eliminated in a fixed-effects model.

As in Schooley and Barney (1994) and Hamid, Prakash, and Smyser (1995) we test for the presence of a parabolic relation between dividends, and ownership or control by adding two other variables to our model: the squared ultimate level of control (L_1^2) and the squared Herfindahl index (H^2). This methodology is also adopted by studies examining the relationship between control and performance (see chapter 2 of Goergen (1998) for an overview of these studies).

---

[2] The index is defined as $H_i = \sum_j s_{ij}^2$, where, s_{ij} is the stake of voting shares held by shareholder j in firm i.

[3] The results do not change substantially when we take the proportion of the voting shares held by each class of shareholders when they are the largest owners but control less than 25% of the voting rights.

8.3.2. *Dividends and Control*

Table 8.4 reports the results of the OLS in levels and GMM(SYS) estimation procedures. Prior to reporting the results, it is worth discussing the set of instruments used in the GMM(SYS) procedure. In Chapter 6, the panel data estimations revealed that instruments of the basic variables (dividends, cash flows, published earnings) dated $t - 2$ (levels) in the differenced equations and dated $t - 1$ (changes) in the levels equations, were rejected by the Sargan tests on the validity of instruments. We suggested that this reflects a (serially uncorrelated) measurement error in dividends and profits or cash flows. In this chapter, we expand the basic model using corporate control variables. The inclusion of these variables does not modify our earlier conclusions about the validity of the instruments for the basic variables. Therefore, the set of instruments used in the GMM(SYS)-instrumental variable procedure are levels of dividends and cash flows all dated $t - 3$ to $t - 5$ in the differenced equations, and first-differences dated $t - 2$ in the levels equations.[4]

Specifications (a), (d), and (e) reveal that there is no linear relation between dividend payout and control. The result is valid irrespective of the estimation technique and the measure of control. Although not reported in the table, the GMM(DIF) estimation technique yields the same result. We conclude that there is no evidence supporting hypothesis 2. Specification (b), allowing for a quadratic relation between dividend payouts and the fraction of voting shares held by the concentrated owner (L_1), produces a statistically significant result using GMM(SYS), within the 10 per cent significance level. The linear term is negative and marginally significant (with a t-ratio of -1.68) whereas the quadratic term is positive (t-ratio of 1.82). This suggests that the largest voting stake in the firm is negatively related to dividend payouts at low levels of control, while the relation becomes positive when the stake is large. Note, however, that the Wald test of joint significance of the linear and quadratic term reveals a p-value of only 18 per cent. To locate the minimum, we differentiate dividends with respect to L_1 and we set the derivative equal to 0:

$$\frac{d(DIV)}{d(L_1)} = -0.086 + 2(0.098)(L_1) = 0,$$

to obtain

$$L_{1\,min} = 43.9\%.$$

We also estimate specification (b) using GMM(DIF). The linear term has a negative coefficient with a p-value of 11 per cent and the quadratic term has a positive coefficient with a p-value of 9 per cent, implying that there is a somewhat weaker parabolic effect but confirming the GMM(SYS) results. Finally, the same specification is estimated using published earnings. The patterns are the same: OLS does not produce a statistically significant

---

[4] The reader should note that we have reduced the number of instruments used for the basic variables, compared to the set used in Chapter 6. The reason for this is that by adding the control variables, extra instruments are added to the estimation. As a result, the number of instruments becomes large with respect to the sample size, causing deterioration in the performance of the estimation procedure. This is sometimes called the 'small sample size bias'. Therefore, we have reduced the number of instruments used for the basic variables.

Table 8.4. *Panel data estimation of the relation between dividends, cash flows, and different measures of control*

	(a)		(b)		(c)		(d)		(e)	
	OLS (1)	GMM (2)	OLS (3)	GMM (4)	OLS (5)	GMM (6)	OLS (7)	GMM (8)	OLS (9)	GMM (10)
Const.	0.006***	0.005*	0.006***	0.014	0.006***	0.004	0.006***	0.004**	0.006***	0.005***
	(0.001)	(0.003)	(0.002)	(0.009)	(0.001)	(0.006)	(0.001)	(0.002)	(0.001)	(0.002)
$D_{i,t-1}$	0.764***	0.741***	0.764***	0.738***	0.763***	0.725***	0.764***	0.723***	0.764***	0.757***
	(0.037)	(0.067)	(0.037)	(0.070)	(0.037)	(0.066)	(0.037)	(0.069)	(0.037)	(0.076)
CF_{it}	0.047***	0.047***	0.047***	0.048***	0.047***	0.048***	0.047***	0.052***	0.047***	0.047***
	(0.006)	(0.015)	(0.006)	(0.015)	(0.006)	(0.015)	(0.006)	(0.015)	(0.006)	(0.012)
$CF_{i,t-1}$	−0.024***	−0.012	−0.024***	−0.011	−0.024***	−0.011	−0.024***	−0.014	−0.024***	−0.021
	(0.007)	(0.018)	(0.007)	(0.018)	(0.007)	(0.018)	(0.007)	(0.021)	(0.007)	(0.020)
$L_{1i,t-1}$	−0.001	−0.001	−0.001	−0.086*	—	—	—	—	—	—
	(0.002)	(0.002)	(0.004)	(0.051)						
$L^2_{1i,t-1}$	—	—	−0.001	0.098*	—	—	—	—	—	—
			(0.004)	(0.054)						
$H_{i,t-1}$	—	—	—	—	0.01	0.003	—	—	—	—
					(0.004)	(0.037)				
$H^2_{i,t-1}$	—	—	—	—	−0.002	−0.005	—	—	—	—
					(0.005)	(0.044)				
$WH_{1i,t-1}$	—	—	—	—	—	—	0.001	−0.001	—	—
							(0.001)	(0.001)		
$WH_{2i,t-1}$	—	—	—	—	—	—	—	—	−0.001	−0.001
									(0.001)	(0.001)

Table 8.4. (Continued)

	(a)		(b)		(c)		(d)		(e)	
	OLS (1)	GMM (2)	OLS (3)	GMM (4)	OLS (5)	GMM (6)	OLS (7)	GMM (8)	OLS (9)	GMM (10)
m_1	0.410	−5.128	0.411	−5.137	0.398	−5.235	0.416	−5.108	0.415	−5.460
m_2	1.192	1.219	1.190	1.272	1.171	1.227	1.197	1.265	1.197	1.279
Sargan	—	85.54	—	81.02	—	84.61	—	95.50	—	89.96
(p-values)		(0.34)		(0.45)		(0.22)		(0.04)		(0.12)
No. of observation	1612	1421	1612	1421	1612	1421	1612	1421	1612	1421

Notes: The sample size is 191 firms and is obtained by excluding the firms, out of the original sample of 221 firms, that are subsidiaries of foreign companies, state-owned, owned by foundations or owned by an unknown shareholder. D_{it} is the dependent variable in the specifications. It represents total dividends scaled by the market value of equity at the beginning of the period. CF are total cash flows similarly scaled. L_1 is the proportion of voting shares held by the largest shareholder at the ultimate level. H is a Herfindahl index of all the disclosed shareholdings. WH_1 and WH_2 are dummy variables which equal one if there is no large shareholder with at least 25% and 50% of the voting shares, respectively. Time dummies are included in all models. m_1 and m_2 are tests for the absence of first-order and second-order serial correlation in the residuals, asymptotically distributed as $N(0,1)$ under the null of no serial correlation. Sargan is a test of the validity of the instruments, asymptotically distributed as χ^2 under the null of valid instruments. The p-values show the probability of generating the reported statistic under the null of valid instruments. Specifications (2), (4), (6), (8), and (10) are GMM-instrumental variable estimators based on a GMM-in-systems procedure, which consists of linear systems of first-differenced and levels equations. The set of instruments used are levels of dividends and cash flows variables dated $t − 3$ to $t − 5$ in the differenced equations, and first-differences dated $t − 2$ in the levels equations throughout all specifications. Moreover, the specifications use levels of control variables dated $t − 2$ to $t − 5$ for the differenced equations and levels of control variables dated $t − 1$ in the levels equations. Standard-errors, asymptotically robust to heteroskedasticity, are reported in parentheses.

*Represents statistical significance at the 10% level.

**Represents statistical significance at the 5% level.

***Represents statistical significance at the 1% level.

relation, but both GMM(SYS) and GMM(DIF) yield a statistically significant non-monotonic relation between dividends and the largest proportion of voting shares held in the firm.

Our results are consistent with hypothesis 3 and the findings of Schooley and Barney (1994) and Hamid, Prakash, and Smyser (1995). The point at which dividends reach a global minimum may be the point of entrenchment. For the USA, Schooley and Barney (1994) report that the dividend yield falls as CEO share ownership increases to 14.9 per cent, and the dividend yield increases thereafter. This proportion is considerably smaller than the one we find for German firms: 43.9 per cent. The lower percentage for US firms reflects the fact that publicly quoted firms in the USA have a more dispersed ownership structure than German firms. The non-linearity in the relation between control and dividends implies that dividends and shareholder control may be substitute monitoring mechanisms up to a specific level of control concentration but, beyond that level of control, strong shareholders prefer high dividends.[5,6]

To some extent, our results differ from Rozeff (1982), and Eckbo and Verma (1994). Rozeff (1982) finds a negative linear relation between dividend payout ratios and the proportion held by insiders in a sample of 1,000 US firms.[7] Eckbo and Verma (1994) examine the relation between managerial share ownership, voting power and cash dividend policy of 308 Canadian firms quoted on the Toronto Stock Exchange. They find that cash dividends decrease as the voting power of owner–managers increases, and are almost zero when owner–managers have absolute control over the firm.

8.3.3. *Dividends and the Type of Controlling Shareholder*

Whereas Table 8.4 examines the relation between dividend payouts and control without distinguishing between different types of controlling shareholder, the nature of control may be important as it may give rise to different forms of agency relations. In this subsection, we investigate the relation between dividends, cash flows and control exerted by different blockholder categories. The sample comprises 191 firms and for each year we partition the firms into four categories: widely held firms, bank-controlled firms, family-controlled firms, and firms controlled by other corporations. As before, control is measured as ultimate control. We estimate the coefficients on $F_{i,t-1}$, $IC_{i,t-1}$, and $B_{i,t-1}$ while excluding

---

[5] In Schooley and Barney (1994), CEO share ownership ranges from 0 to 30.55 per cent. The mean value of CEO share ownership is 2.5 per cent and the median is 0.42 per cent. This is clearly lower than the concentration of ownership and control in German firms as described in Table 8.1.

[6] As a robustness check of the above results we estimate a specification in which we allow for a higher order functional form between dividends and ownership. We add a cubic term to regression (4) of Table 8.4 and we find that the coefficients (*t*-statistic) of the linear control term, the quadratic term and the cubic term are −0.20 (−1.88), 0.44 (1.98) and −0.26 (−1.87), respectively. In other words, several minima may exist. However, in the literature no theoretical foundation is formulated to relate dividends with ownership or control in cubic or higher order. The previous studies that have reported evidence of a quadratic form have not explored further orders in the functional form of the relation between dividends and ownership/control (Schooley and Barney 1994; Hamid, Prakash, and Smyser 1995) and performance and ownership/control (e.g. McConnell and Servaes 1990).

[7] Note that in Rozeff's study, the choice of the ratio of dividends to published earnings as a dependent variable is subject to some criticism: the ratio can take astronomical values when profits are close to zero.

the variable $WH_{1i,t-1}$ from the regression, such that all the parameter estimates of the other variables are expressed in relation to the benchmark of widely held firms. Table 8.5 reports the main results: column (a) gives the OLS and GMM(SYS) estimates of the general model which includes the control variables by category of shareholder.[8]

It emerges from all the specifications that bank control has a strongly negative impact on the dividend payout ratio (with the t-values of the GMM(SYS) parameter estimates varying between -2.0 in specification (6) and -2.23 in specification (2)).[9] Companies controlled by other corporations also have lower payout ratios than widely held firms, but the coefficient is not statistically significant. Family-controlled firms have the highest payouts, as shown by the positive coefficient obtained in all the regressions, although the coefficient is not statistically significant (such that there is no statistical support for hypothesis 5).

In specification (c), we estimate the relation between bank control and dividends allowing for a non-linear relation between control, as measured by the voting stake held by the largest shareholder (L_1), and dividends. Bank control is still statistically significant at the 5 per cent level. However, if we compare the results obtained in regression (4) in Table 8.4 with the results obtained in regression (6) in Table 8.5, we observe that the statistical significance of the non-linear relation between dividends and control has decreased when the bank control variable is included. Table 8.5 also reveals that the statistical significance of these results is reduced when we include all control variables (specification (d)).[10] However,

---

[8] The set of instruments used in the GMM(SYS) procedure is the levels of dividends and cash flows all dated $t-3$ to $t-5$ in the differenced equations, and first-differences dated $t-2$ in the levels equations. The set of instruments used for the control variables varies depending on the significance of the Sargan test. The Sargan test accepted in some specifications the validity of later time periods. Therefore, the instrument set used is levels of ownership dated $t-2$ to $t-5$ in the differenced equations and levels *or* first-differences dated $t-1$ in the levels equations. The levels of the variables can be used as instruments if they are uncorrelated with the fixed effect (η_i); otherwise, we use first differences. The Sargan test reveals that past levels of two of the variables, F and IC, are uncorrelated with the firm-specific effects and therefore we use those instead of first differences. However, for bank control, the test discloses that the inclusion of levels instead of first-differences dated $t-1$ reduces the p-values of the test substantially (it drops to values within the range of 15–20 per cent). Therefore, we include first differences as instruments for the bank control in the levels equation.

[9] Note that due to the legal disclosure threshold, there is a discontinuity at the 25 per cent level of control. From 0 to 25 (exc.) per cent, firms are defined as widely held and the variables of classes of shareholders all equal zero. From 25 (incl.) to 100 per cent, the variables take the proportion of the voting stake held by each shareholder in case they are the largest owners. This calls for two remarks. First, to control for this one could include a set of three dummy variables that take the value of 1 if a particular class is the largest shareholder. However, because there is hardly any time-variation in these dummies, this is essentially a firm-specific effect that is eliminated when first-differenced. Second, since bank control is linearly and negatively associated with dividends, we need to check whether at the point of discontinuity (i.e. 25 per cent) bank-controlled firms have lower dividend payouts than widely held firms. For that, we examine the observed dividend payout ratios in two different ranges of bank control at any given point in time: [25%, 50%] and [50%, 100%]. The ratios obtained for each range are 16.8 and 17.1 per cent, respectively. These are lower than the payout ratios that we find for widely held firms and that are reported in Table 8.2, supporting the evidence that bank-controlled firms have the lowest dividend payouts.

[10] Unfortunately, this result is not comparable to previous studies as these only explore linear and quadratic specifications of the functional form of the relation between dividends and ownership or control (Schooley and Barney 1994; Hamid, Prakash, and Smyser 1995) and performance and ownership or control (e.g. McConnell and Servaes 1990).

Table 8.5. *Panel data estimation of the relation between dividends, cash flows, and control by banks, families, and corporations*

	(a)		(b)		(c)		(d)	
	OLS (1)	GMM (2)	OLS (3)	GMM (4)	OLS (5)	GMM (6)	OLS (7)	GMM (8)
Const.	0.0065***	0.0091***	0.0066***	0.0072**	0.0065***	0.0128*	0.0069***	0.0099***
	(0.0014)	(0.0035)	(0.0012)	(0.0036)	(0.0016)	(0.0071)	(0.0015)	(0.0061)
$D_{i,t-1}$	0.7621***	0.7214***	0.7633***	0.7189***	0.7621***	0.7256***	0.7714***	0.7387***
	(0.0369)	(0.0664)	(0.0367)	(0.0670)	(0.0367)	(0.0637)	(0.0378)	(0.0568)
CF_{it}	0.0483***	0.0458***	0.0460***	0.0481***	0.0472***	0.0492***	0.0561***	0.0613***
	(0.0075)	(0.0137)	(0.0063)	(0.0149)	(0.0059)	(0.0141)	(0.0051)	(0.0135)
$CF_{i,t-1}$	-0.0241***	-0.0143	-0.0239***	-0.0202	-0.0243***	-0.0155	-0.0234***	-0.0266
	(0.0075)	(0.0171)	(0.0074)	(0.0202)	(0.0073)	(0.0171)	(0.0073)	(0.0175)
$B_{i,t-1}$	-0.0047*	-0.0230***	-0.0049**	-0.0193**	-0.0035*	-0.0164**	-0.0039	-0.0133
	(0.0028)	(0.0103)	(0.0025)	(0.0092)	(0.0020)	(0.0082)	(0.0025)	(0.0098)
$IC_{i,t-1}$	-0.0027	-0.0046	—	—	—	—	-0.0022	-0.0046
	(0.0038)	(0.0035)					(0.0035)	(0.0065)
$F_{i,t-1}$	0.0013	0.0041	—	—	—	—	-0.0004	-0.0037
	(0.0019)	(0.0028)					(0.0031)	(0.0064)
$L_{i,t-1}$	—	—	—	—	0.0005	-0.0570	0.0018	-0.0241
					(0.0044)	(0.0388)	(0.0045)	(0.0328)
$L^2_{i,t-1}$	—	—	—	—	-0.0010	0.0601	-0.0014	0.0296
					(0.0046)	(0.0410)	(0.0050)	(0.0349)

Table 8.5. *(Continued)*

	(a)		(b)		(c)		(d)	
	OLS (1)	GMM (2)	OLS (3)	GMM (4)	OLS (5)	GMM (6)	OLS (7)	GMM (8)
m_1	0.379	−5.089	0.410	−5.088	0.433	−5.118	0.413	−5.044
m_2	1.166	1.255	1.185	1.337	1.182	1.222	1.172	1.355
Sargan	—	132.16	—	87.72	—	109.35	—	145.3
(p-value)		(0.359)		(0.260)		(0.446)		(0.257)
No. of observation	1612	1421	1612	1421	1612	1421	1612	1421

Notes: D_{it} is the dependent variable in all the specifications. $D_{i,t-1}$, $L_{i,t-1}$, $L_{i,t-1}^2$ and CF are defined as in Table 8.4. $F_{i,t-1}$ is the proportion of voting shares held by a family, when a family is the largest shareholder of the firm at the ultimate level at time $t-1$. It equals zero otherwise. Variables $B_{i,t-1}$ and $IC_{i,t-1}$ are similarly defined, but relate to the case when the largest shareholder is a bank or another corporation, respectively. Time dummies are included in all the specifications. m_1 and m_2 are tests for the absence of first-order and second-order serial correlation in the residuals, asymptotically distributed as $N(0,1)$ under the null of no serial correlation. The Sargan test is a test of the validity of the instruments, asymptotically distributed as χ^2 under the null of valid instruments. The p-values show the probability of generating the reported statistic under the null of valid instruments. Specifications (2), (4), (6), and (8) are GMM-instrumental variable estimators based on a GMM(SYS) procedure which consists of linear systems of first-differenced and levels equations. The set of instruments used are: levels of dividends, cash flows dated $t-3$ to $t-5$ for the differenced equations and first-differences dated $t-2$ for the levels equations. For bank control the instrument set is levels dated $t-2$ to $t-5$ in the differenced equations and first-differences dated $t-1$ in the levels equations. For family control the instrument set is levels dated $t-2$ to $t-5$ in the differenced equations and levels dated $t-1$ in the levels equations. For control by industrial corporations the instrument set is levels dated $t-4$ to $t-5$ for the differenced equations and levels dated $t-3$ in the levels equations. In specification (d) we reduce the number of instruments by eliminating instruments dated $t-5$. Standard errors, asymptotically robust to heteroskedasticity, are reported in parentheses.

*Represents statistical significance at the 10% level.

**Represents statistical significance at the 5% level.

***Represents statistical significance at the 1% level.

when we estimate the effect of higher order functional forms between dividends and control, we still find that the control pattern persists.[11] Gugler (2002) investigates the relation between control and dividends for Austrian firms and reaches somewhat different conclusions: state-controlled firms have the highest dividend payout (provided investment prospects are good) and practise dividend smoothing whereas family-controlled firms have lower ratios and do not engage in dividend smoothing. The dividend policy of bank-controlled and foreign-controlled firms is somewhere in between.

To verify the robustness of these results, we conduct further estimations using published earnings rather than cash flows. The results do not differ substantially from those reported above. For example, the coefficient on bank control in a specification similar to specification (c) of Table 8.5 has a *t*-ratio of −1.80 using OLS and −1.62 using GMM(SYS).

To summarize, bank control is related to significantly lower dividend payouts than dispersed ownership or family control. These results are consistent with the argument that bank control acts as a monitoring device and is a substitute for dividends (hypothesis 6). Our conclusion is in line with the findings by Cable (1985) and Gorton and Schmid (2000), who report that there is a positive influence of bank control on firm profitability. However, our finding contradicts Edwards and Fischer (1994) who state that German banks are not nearly as active in corporate governance as might be expected from their lending and equity voting power. Similarly, Franks and Mayer (2001) argue that banks do not in general exercise a high degree of control in German corporations where there is a non-bank blockholder.

Still, our findings are consistent with the literature on the investment decision of Japanese firms, which suggests that liquidity constraints resulting from asymmetric information are less important when firm belongs to a *keiretsu* group that also comprises a bank (see Hoshi, Kashyap, and Scharfstein 1991; Dewenter and Warther 1998; Gul 1999*b*). Bank control may reduce the need for high dividends as a monitoring device because this type of control may reduce asymmetric information between the major shareholders and the management, and thus reduce underinvestment due to potential liquidity constraints. Similarly, for the UK, Goergen and Renneboog (2001) report that large institutional holdings reduce suboptimal investment policies.

Note, however, that so far we have analysed bank control based on the directly and indirectly owned voting rights (measured as ultimate control) but without taking into account proxy votes. We will address this issue in Section 8.6. We also find that family-controlled firms have the largest payouts but that control by families or individuals does not seem to have an impact on dividend policy. This implies that, even though specific dividend payout policies may play a monitoring and signalling role, family control is not a substitute monitoring device for dividends. Our findings are consistent with the proposition that controlling families or individuals pay themselves higher dividends, presumably because these parties' investment portfolios are not well diversified.

---

[11] Adding a cubic term to regression 8 of Table 8.5 (not shown), we discover that the coefficient (*t*-statistic) of the linear term is −0.20 (−1.88), of the quadratic term is 0.44 (1.98), and of the cubic term is −0.26 (−1.87). In other words, there is some evidence pointing to the existence of several minima.

8.4. ANNUAL EARNINGS LOSSES, DIVIDEND OMISSIONS, AND CONTROL

In Chapter 7 we used a qualitative regression approach to model the dividend behaviour of German firms. We found that annual net earnings losses in firms with good records of past performance (defined as firms with at least five years of strictly positive earnings and dividend payouts) cause dividend omissions in 80 per cent of the cases in the year of the annual loss. We also showed that, whereas dividend omissions in the USA or UK are related to serious and persistent earnings problems, dividends in Germany are omitted when the earnings decline is only transitory. Dividends quickly revert to the levels prior to the decline once earnings start increasing. This flexible dividend behaviour of German firms contrasts with the dividend policy of US firms which seems more rigid and 'sticky'. Consequently, in Germany, dividends play a weaker role as signalling devices.

The purpose of this section is to establish to what extent the results reported in Chapter 7 can be explained by different patterns of control in German firms. The high control concentration that we observe in Germany (see Table 8.1) may be responsible for the flexibility in dividend policy as strong control may reduce agency concerns. Furthermore, controlling shareholders with board representation may have good access to corporate information which cuts down any signalling needs (hypothesis 1). The nature of the controlling shareholder may also be an important factor. Well-informed shareholders such as banks may reduce the need for costly dividend signalling. Hence, we may expect that bank-controlled firms are more likely to cut or even omit the dividend than other firms, even when the deterioration in performance is only transitory. A higher willingness to cut or omit the dividend is also consistent with the agency costs argument, if we are to believe that informational advantages permit banks to adopt a more effective monitoring role (hypothesis 6).

We create a set of dummy variables. WH_{1i} and WH_{2i} that equal 1 if there is no shareholder with at least 25 and 50 per cent, respectively, of the voting equity of firm i, and equal 0 otherwise. B_i, F_i, and IC_i equal 1 if a bank, a family or a corporation, respectively, are the controlling shareholders of firm i with at least 25 per cent of the voting equity, and are 0 otherwise. We also create a set of interactive terms that equal 1 if there is an earnings loss and if control is exerted by a bank, a family, or a corporation, respectively. As before, all control variables are measured at the ultimate level and at time $t-1$.

We re-estimate the same specifications as those in Tables 7.1 and 7.2 of Chapter 7, but add the set of dummy control variables described above. We report the results of an ordered probit analysis of the decision to decrease, maintain or increase the dividend in our sample of 191 German firms.[12] Our results show no evidence that any of the control dummies improve the fit of the specifications from Tables 7.1 and 7.2. The control variables are individually and jointly insignificant, and therefore do not explain the decision to decrease, maintain, or increase the dividend payout ratio. This result is valid for both cash flows and published earnings. However, a stronger test of the signalling theory consists in estimating the effect of a significant deterioration in performance—such as an earnings loss after a period of established performance of strictly positive profits and dividends—on dividends.

---

[12] We exclude thirty firms that are controlled either by foreign companies or foreign governments, foundations or have undisclosed control structures.

Table 8.6. *Ordered probit analysis of the relation between dividend omissions, earnings losses, and control structures*

	(a)	(b)	(c)	(d)	(e)	(f)
Panel I: Coefficients (standard errors)						
Const.	1.844***	2.044***	2.005***	1.673***	1.737***	1.664***
	(0.490)	(0.349)	(0.339)	(0.229)	(0.240)	(0.239)
NI_{it}	0.213	0.209	0.220	0.198	0.167	0.189
	(0.196)	(0.190)	(0.185)	(0.166)	(0.247)	(0.180)
$NILOSS_{it}$	−2.258***	−2.292***	−2.299***	−2.162***	−2.261***	−2.143***
	(0.399)	(0.394)	(0.382)	(0.343)	(0.328)	(0.314)
$B_{i,t-1}$	−0.794	−0.968***	−0.927***	—	—	—
	(0.501)	(0.384)	(0.368)			
$F_{i,t-1}$	0.111	−0.076	—	0.190	—	—
	(0.443)	(0.272)		(0.259)		
$WH_{1i,t-1}$	0.304	—	—	—	−0.007	—
	(0.474)				(0.386)	
$WHLOSS_{1i,t-1}$	—	—	—	—	1.027	—
					(0.659)	
$WH_{2i,t-1}$	—	—	—	—	—	0.154
						(0.254)
Panel II: Goodness of fit						
Log-likel.	−86.125	−86.409	−86.453	−95.385	−90.723	−92.165
Pseudo R^2	35.74%	35.53%	35.50%	28.83%	32.30%	31.24%
R^2_P	73.6%	73.6%	73.6%	71.3%	71.5%	72.0%

Notes: The dependent variable equals 0 if the dividend is omitted, 1 if the dividend is cut to a strictly positive level and 2 if the dividend is increased or maintained. The original sample consists of (1) 71 firms in which the event year corresponds to the initial year of losses in the period 1989–93 and (2) 107 firms in which the event year is the first year with an earnings decline but still strictly positive earnings during 1989–93. There are, therefore, 178 observations. Of these we exclude firms controlled by a foreign company, state authorities or foundations. The final sample of 129 firm-year observations serves as the basis for our estimations. Earnings (NI_{it}) are standardized by the book value of equity of the previous year. $NILOSS_{it}$ is a dummy variable that equals 1 if there is an annual earnings loss in year t. $B_{i,t-1}$ and $F_{i,t-1}$ are dummy variables which equal 1 if a bank or a family, respectively, are the controlling shareholders of firm i at time $t-1$, and zero otherwise. $WH_{1i,t-1}$ and $WH_{2i,t-1}$ are dummy variables that equal 1 if there is no large shareholder controlling at least 25% or 50%, respectively, of the voting shares of firm i at time $t-1$, and 0 otherwise. $WHLOSS_{1i,t-1}$ is an interactive term of the state of being widely held at 25% level and the presence of an annual earnings loss. All other interactive terms of control and performance are not shown as they are insignificant. All models assume multiplicative heteroskedasticity. All model specifications are significant with p-values < 0.001. Pseudo R^2 follows McFadden (1974). R^2_P stands for the percentage of correct predictions.

*Represents statistical significance at the 10% level.
**Represents statistical significance at the 5% level.
***Represents statistical significance at the 1% level.

Table 8.6 summarizes the results of such a model in which the dependent variable equals 0 if the dividend is omitted, 1 if the dividend is cut to a strictly positive level and 2 if the dividend is increased or maintained. The sample consists of 178 firms: Seventy-one companies for which the event year corresponds to the initial year with losses in the period 1989–93, and 107 firms for which the event year is the first year with an earnings decline but still strictly positive earnings during 1989–93.

The net earnings loss has a statistically significant effect on the decision to change the dividend policy.[13] Specifications (a)–(c) indicate that bank control increases the likelihood of a dividend omission, which is not inconsistent with the argument that the presence of banks reduces the need for dividends as signalling and monitoring devices (hypothesis 6). This result is consistent with other evidence on bank control on Japanese firms. Dewenter and Warther (1998) show that *keiretsu* firms cut and omit dividends more often than other Japanese firms.

None of the other control variables (control by families or by other corporations, and lack of control in widely held firms) or interaction terms of control with earnings are statistically significant. Given that coefficients on the dummy variables $WH_{1i,t-1}$, $WH_{2i,t-1}$ are not significant, there is no support for the argument that control acts as a substitute for dividends as signalling and monitoring devices.[14]

8.5. PROXY VOTES AND DIVIDENDS

The previous sections reveal that bank-controlled firms (1) exhibit lower dividend payouts and (2) omit the dividend more frequently than any other type of firms (controlled by different types of owners) in Germany when performance is poor. Still, our previous analysis does not consider the fact that German banks can act as delegated exercisers of voting rights on behalf of small individual shareholders who deposit their shares with the bank. As described in Section 8.2.1, the proportion of proxy votes is very high in widely held firms, but smaller in closely held firms and in firms not controlled by banks. In this section, we examine the effect of proxy votes held by banks on the dividend policy of German firms.

We test the influence of proxy votes on dividends by expanding our basic model with the following two variables: (1) BPROX, the voting rights controlled directly and indirectly (through intermediate layers) by banks (provided the control stake amounts to at least 25 per cent of the voting rights), *including* proxy votes and (2) PROXY, the size of the proxy votes held by the three main banks (*Deutsche Bank*, *Dresdner Bank*, and *Commerzbank*). Both variables are constructed using the data published in Gottschalk (1988) and Baums and Fraune (1995). The average proportion of proxy votes held by the three large banks in the firms cited in Gottschalk (1988) is 49.9 per cent with a standard deviation of 20.2 per cent.

---

[13] Note that the results do not change significantly if we include cash flows and changes in net earnings instead of levels of earnings.

[14] Although not reported in Table 8.6, we re-estimated the same model with a dummy variable equal to 1 for control by corporations, as well as an interactive term that equals 1 if there is an earnings loss and control by corporations. The results were not statistically significant.

In Baums and Fraune (1995), the average proportion of proxy votes held by the three banks is 37.5 per cent and the standard deviation amounts to 16 per cent. The percentages of proxy votes held in the firms incorporated in both studies remain stable (they are almost the same over the years 1986–92). This creates a methodological problem: in a fixed-effects regression model, a constant variable will be eliminated when the equation is first-differenced. Consequently, we estimate the model using OLS in levels. In a second step, we check the dynamics in our equation using GMM(SYS) and verify whether the OLS estimation creates biases in the bank control variables. We assume that bank control is uncorrelated with the firm-specific effect such that we can use the levels of these variables as instruments in the levels equation of the linear system of equations. This experiment is reported in column (e) of Table 8.7.

Specifications (a) and (b) in Table 8.7 indicate that bank control (i.e. ownership of voting rights plus proxy votes) is negatively related to dividend payouts but the coefficient is not statistically different from 0. In other terms, when we add proxy votes to the voting equity held directly by banks, the negative impact of bank control on dividends is no longer significant. When we estimate the dynamics using GMM(SYS) in specification (e), the lack of significance does not alter.

Specifications (c) and (d) reveal why the negative relation between the voting rights controlled by the bank disappears when we include the percentage of proxy votes held by the banks: the percentage of proxy votes is positively correlated with dividends (at the 10 per cent level of statistical significance in specification (c)). This positive correlation may result from the fact that, for instance, the percentage of proxy votes may be a proxy for the control structure of the firm. When many proxy votes are given to the bank, it may be that there are many small individual shareholders who may have a preference for high dividends. We will investigate whether taxation creates clienteles for specific dividend payout policies in Section 8.6.

Next, we estimate an ordered probit regression of the decision to omit the dividend, similar to the estimations in Table 8.6. Instead of a variable capturing the percentage of voting rights the bank controls directly or indirectly, we now estimate the influence of all the voting rights controlled by the bank including the proxy votes the bank can cast on behalf of it's customers. Whereas the coefficient of $B_{i,t-1}$ (voting rights controlled by banks excluding proxy votes) indicates a strongly significant negative relation between bank control and dividends (with a t-statistic of -2.52, similar to specification (c) of Table 8.6), this relation disappears when we substitute the percentage of all voting rights plus proxy votes controlled by banks (BPROX$_{i,t-1}$) for $B_{i,t-1}$ (the t-ratio is now only -0.98).

As a robustness check, we partition the widely held firms into a group of firms in which the banks do not exercise a large amount of proxy votes for their clients, and a group of widely held firms in which banks do control many proxy votes such that these firms may become *de facto* bank controlled. We estimate whether widely held firms without proxies are more reluctant to omit the dividend than the *de facto* bank controlled firms, but no statistically significant result emerges. Thus, this evidence is consistent with the findings reported in this section, but contradicts hypothesis 7. In summary, there is no evidence that proxy votes held by banks strengthen the relation between bank control (derived from ownership of votes) and dividends.

Table 8.7. *Panel data estimations of the relation between dividends, cash flows, and bank voting control*

	(a)	(b)	(c)	(d)	(e)
Const.	0.0064***	0.0063***	0.0060***	0.0062***	0.0049*
	(0.0012)	(0.0011)	(0.0011)	(0.0011)	(0.0026)
$D_{i,t-1}$	0.7741***	0.7736***	0.7834***	0.7840***	0.7356***
	(0.0367)	(0.0368)	(0.0371)	(0.0370)	(0.0729)
CF_{it}	0.0465***	0.0474***	0.0476***	0.0470**	0.0435*
	(0.0064)	(0.0058)	(0.0060)	(0.0059)	(0.0232)
$CF_{i,t-1}$	−0.0241***	−0.0242***	−0.0244***	−0.0245***	−0.0128
	(0.0074)	(0.0074)	(0.0074)	(0.0074)	(0.0303)
$BPROX_{i,t-1}$	−0.0023	−0.0012	—	—	−0.0018
	(0.0022)	(0.0017)			(0.0025)
$PROXY_i$	—	—	0.0045*	0.0023	—
			(0.0027)	(0.0022)	
$IBPROX_{i,t-1}$	0.0061	—	—	—	—
	(0.0118)				
$IPROXY_{it}$	—	—	−0.0109	—	—
			(0.0101)		
m_1	0.417	0.425	0.412	0.414	−5.049
m_2	—	—	—	—	1.265
Sargan (*p*-value)	—	—	—	—	62.96 (0.216)
Nr. of observation	1612	1612	1612	1612	1421

Notes: The sample size is 191 firms. D_{it} is the dependent variable in all models, CF are cash flows, $BPROX_{i,t-1}$ stands for the percentage of voting rights plus the percentage of proxy votes for firm i at time $t-1$, $PROXY_i$ stands for the size of the proxy votes held by the three large banks in firm i, held constant over the whole period, and $IBPROX_{i,t-1}$ and $IPROXY_{it}$ are interactive terms of cash flows, and the percentage of voting rights (own voting rights and proxy votes) controlled by banks and amount of proxy votes, respectively. Time dummies are included in all specifications. m_1 and m_2 are tests of first- and second-order serial correlation in the residuals, asymptotically distributed as $N(0,1)$ under the null of no serial correlation. Sargan is a test of the validity of the instruments, asymptotically distributed as χ^2 under the null of valid instruments. The *p*-values show the probability of generating the reported statistic under the null of valid instruments. Specifications (a), (b), (c), and (d) are OLS estimations. Specification (e) is estimated using the GMM-instrumental variable estimation technique (GMM(SYS)), which consists of a linear system of first-differenced and levels equations. The set of instruments used are: levels of dividends, cash flows dated $t-3$ to $t-5$ for the differenced equations, and first-differences dated $t-2$ for the levels equations. For bank control the instrument set is levels dated $t-1$ in the levels equations. Standard errors, asymptotically robust to heteroskedasticity, are reported in parentheses.

*Represents statistical significance at the 10% level.
**Represents statistical significance at the 5% level.
***Represents statistical significance at the 1% level.

8.6. FIRST-TIER CONTROL, TAXES, AND DIVIDENDS

In the previous sections we have investigated ultimate control and its impact on dividends. We now focus on the origin of the controlling shareholder at the first layer of the pyramid. This methodology serves two purposes. First, the analysis answers the question as to whether first-tier control has a similar impact on dividends as ultimate control. Essentially, we relax the assumption used in previous sections that control resides at the ultimate level. For example, it may be argued that control is diluted when an additional tier is added between the listed target firm and the ultimate shareholder. Therefore, it is possible that the dividend policy is set by the large shareholder at the first tier rather than by the ultimate controlling shareholder. In a study of the impact of performance and control on management and supervisory board turnover, Franks and Mayer (2001) show that pyramiding leads to less board turnover. The only exception is firms that are ultimately family-controlled, as families seem to be able to exercise more control throughout different layers.

Second, the tax status of shareholders at the first tier may have an impact on the dividend policy of the firm. We investigate whether firms adopt dividend policies that are fine-tuned towards the tax status of the controlling shareholder. Bond, Chennells, and Windmeijer (1996*b*), Eckbo and Verma (1994); and Lasfer (1996) examine the relation between the tax status of different shareholders and the dividend policy of their firms. Bond, Chennells, and Windmeijer (1996*b*) use an econometric approach similar to ours to estimate the impact of ownership and control by institutional investors (pension funds, insurers, etc.) on the dividend policy of UK firms. In the UK, until 1997,[15] these investors had a tax preference for dividends relative to capital gains, and therefore the authors predict a positive correlation between institutional share ownership and dividend payouts during their sample period. The results support their hypothesis. Lasfer (1996) constructs a tax discrimination variable which is defined as the degree of tax preference of different UK shareholders for dividends compared to capital gains. The author estimates a dividend model similar to Lintner's (1956) model, but adds a tax discrimination variable to it. He reports that a 1 per cent reduction in the average marginal income tax rate results in a 0.015 per cent increase in dividends and in a 0.09 per cent rise in the long-run optimal level of dividends. Eckbo and Verma (1994) test this relation on Canadian firms over the period 1977–88. Canadian citizens suffer a relative tax penalty on cash dividends compared to capital gains, whereas the opposite is the case for corporate/institutional shareholders whose dividend income is completely tax exempt. The findings confirm their hypothesis that taxation is a significant determinant of corporate dividend policy.

This section is structured as follows. We start by describing the tax treatment of dividends in Germany. Next, we report the summary statistics of the main first-tier control variables and explain how the tax discrimination variables are constructed. In Section 8.6.3, we report the results on the relation between first-tier control and dividends and compare them with the results based on ultimate control. Finally, in Section 8.6.4, we test the proposition that the tax status of different classes of shareholders in Germany significantly influences the dividend policy of firms.

8.6.1. *The Tax Treatment of Dividends in Germany*

This section describes the German tax system from 1977 until 1993. Subsequent changes in the German tax code are summarized below. During our sample period (and up to 2000), Germany operated a split-rate corporate tax system in which retained profits were taxed

---

[15] See Bell and Jenkinson (2002) for more details on the 1997 UK tax reform.

Table 8.8. *Corporation tax rates on retentions and dividends in Germany*

	Retentions [a,b] (%)	Distributions (%)
1977–89	56	36
1990–93	50	36

Notes:

[a] Because of tax exemptions and reductions, the tax charge for parts of the profit may vary from 0 to 50% between 1990 and 1993.

[b] It is, therefore, necessary to differentiate retained profits and reserves according to the rate of tax that they incur, because when they are distributed they must bear a uniform tax rate of 36%. When the firm distributes profits which have already been taxed at 56% (prior to 1990) or 50% (between 1990 and 1993), it can reclaim a reduction in its current tax bill or even a tax refund. For example, until December 1993, by distributing profits that had been retained before 1990, firms could receive a tax refund of 6%. As a consequence, a few companies that had accumulated comfortable levels of reserves before 1990 have paid extra dividends during this period.

more heavily than distributed profits (see Table 8.8). Still, there was an additional tax on distributed profits (i.e. dividends): a 25 per cent withholding tax was deducted at source from the dividends paid to shareholders. However, both the corporate tax rate on distributed profits and the withholding tax could be *fully* claimed by shareholders as a tax credit against their income tax liabilities. Hence, Germany operated a full imputation system of taxation.

Formally, a dividend payment of DM1 was worth

$$\frac{(1-t_s)}{(1-t_d)(1-t_h)},\qquad(8.2)$$

to the shareholder, where t_s stands for the shareholder's income tax rate, t_d for the corporate tax on distributed earnings, t_h for the withholding tax deducted at source by the company and paid to the fiscal authorities as the shareholder's income tax deducted at source. The shareholder has a preference for dividends versus capital gains if

$$\frac{(1-t_s)}{(1-t_d)(1-t_h)} > (1-t_g),\qquad(8.3)$$

where t_g stands for the capital gains tax rate.

This relative tax preference for dividends over capital gains depended on the tax status of each individual shareholder. It is worthwhile examining the tax status of three categories of large shareholders in Germany: (i) German citizens, (ii) German corporations (i.e. industrial and commercial firms, banks, and insurers), and (iii) foreign individuals and companies.

(i) *German citizens.* The corporation tax rate on distributed earnings, t_d, amounted to 36 per cent during our sample period and the withholding tax, t_h, was 25 per cent. The personal income tax (i.e. t_s) in Germany varied within the range of [0%, 53%]. There was no personal capital gains tax (i.e. $t_g = 0$) provided that shares were held for longer periods of time (i.e. at least 6 months). Short-term capital gains of more than DM1,000 were added to an individual's taxable income. Thus, the tax preference for dividends to capital gains depended on the marginal income tax bracket of the shareholder. We should consider three categories of individual domestic investors:

(a) The investor was in the [0%, 52%] marginal income tax bracket. When a shareholder's income tax, t_s, is 37 per cent, the strict inequality in eqn (8.3) always holds irrespective of whether the shareholder realized capital gains over short (less than 6 months) or long-term periods such that this type of investor preferred dividends to capital gains.

(b) The investor was taxed at the 52 per cent tax rate. In this case, he was indifferent between dividends and long-term capital gains, but had a tax preference for dividends to short-term capital gains.

(c) When the investor had a marginal income tax rate of 53 per cent, he had a tax preference for long-term capital gains.

(ii) *German corporations and institutions.* If the shareholder is a company or a financial institution the income tax t_s was equal to t_d or t_c, depending on whether the earnings of the target company were distributed or retained. In the first case (when t_s equals t_d), inequality (8.3) is always satisfied even if the tax on capital gains was equal to 0. In the second case (when t_s equals t_c), inequality (8.3) also always holds such that domestic corporations and financial institutions always preferred dividends to capital gains.

(iii) *Foreign individuals and corporations.* This category of investors was not entitled to a tax credit by the German fiscal authorities[16] and might, therefore, have been subjected to double taxation: corporate tax on the earnings of the German firm and withholding tax on dividends as well as income tax in the home country of the foreign investor. The inequality (8.3) is then reduced to

$$(1 - t_s) > (1 - t_g). \tag{8.4}$$

Double taxation of dividend income in most cases violated inequality (8.4) as t_s was usually higher than t_g. This implies that foreign investors preferred capital gains to dividends. Still, the preference might also have depended on double taxation treaties between the home country of the foreign investor and Germany.

In summary, the above analysis suggests an overall tax advantage of dividends for German individuals and corporations (unless German citizens are taxed at the highest marginal income rate). Foreign investors predominantly preferred capital gains to dividend income. Amihud and Murgia (1997: 4) argue that 'the dividend puzzle in Germany is quite the reverse of the puzzle in the USA: why do German companies not set higher dividend payouts, and then raise in the capital market the funds they need for investment?' As can be deduced from the above, this statement should be interpreted with greater care than the authors suggest. Although it is unambiguously true that the German tax system, relative to

---

[16] The withholding tax of 25 per cent may be reduced by German double taxation treaties with other countries.

the US system, discriminates considerably less against dividends,[17] the statement ignores one very important feature of the German corporate control system: a family is very often the controlling shareholder of German publicly quoted corporations. Indeed, as reported in Chapter 5, this is the case in 37.6 per cent of the German listed industrial and commercial companies. These families were likely to be in the highest marginal income tax bracket of 53 per cent when the taxable income was over DM120,042 (the limit valid at the end of our sample period), in which case they did not have a tax preference for dividends. It should be noted that, over our sample period, the German stock exchanges were less well developed than their Anglo-American counterparts and that the average German citizen did not directly (or indirectly via investment funds) invest in shares. According to a survey conducted by the Börse Online, a German magazine specialized in stock exchange analysis, there were 170,000 private investors in the German stock market in 1994.[18] If we assume that it is predominantly the more wealthy individuals who invest in shares, it is plausible to envisage a scenario where, apart from the controlling shareholders, a large proportion of the free float consists of individual shareholders who may prefer capital gains to dividends. In addition, as pointed out above, foreign investors, an important shareholder category, may also prefer capital gains. Therefore, Amihud and Murgia's (1997) claim regarding the German dividend puzzle claim is only unambiguously true when most of the shares are held by domestic corporations.

Evolution of Tax Regime in Germany since 1994

In 1994, the corporate tax on retentions was reduced to 45 per cent and that on distributions to 30 per cent (see also Table 8.8). From 1995, corporate tax on distributions was increased by 7.5 per cent, a 'solidarity surcharge' which resulted in a corporation tax rate of 48.375 per cent. In 1998, the surcharge was reduced to 5.5 per cent. McDonald (2001) shows that the German imputation system which creates a tax credit for the German shareholder but not for a foreign shareholder, the dividend is worth 42.86 per cent more to a taxable German shareholder (over the period 1994–98) than to a tax-exempt or foreign shareholder. The existence of the tax credit for German residents may induce tax arbitrage opportunities whereby foreign holders of German shares lend German shares to German residents to bridge the ex-dividend date. The share price on the ex-dividend day drops by more than the net dividend, namely by an amount that exceeds the tax dividend by more than half of the tax credit. Thus, the market value of the dividend tax credit exceeds half the credit as the price of a share that pays out a DM1 dividend drops by DM1.26. This implies that a foreign investor incurs a cost of 26 per cent of the value of the dividend from holding a share across the ex-dividend date. The paper also demonstrates that it is more tax efficient for foreign investors to hold derivatives (options, futures, swaps) rather than to invest directly in German shares. The empirical findings are consistent with costly tax arbitrage activity by German investors.

---

[17] In 2003, the US top tax rate for dividends was reduced to 15%, which is below the top rate of 20% for capital gains.

[18] Börse Online, vol. 29, 1994.

The full imputation system of taxation whereby the withholding tax on dividends could be fully claimed as a tax credit against income tax liabilities was abolished in the tax reform of October 2000. For profit distributions from 2001 onwards, the new so-called half-income method (*Halbeinkunftsverfahren*) is applied. The reduced corporation tax of 25 per cent (since 2001) is levied at the corporation level and the crediting or reimbursement of corporation tax paid by the corporation is no longer possible at the level of the shareholder receiving the dividend. The withholding tax for German citizens was reduced from 25 to 20 per cent in 2001. The withholding tax for shareholders residing in a foreign country is lowered to 15 per cent if there is a double taxation agreement between Germany and the home country of the foreign investor. In the case of German shareholders who are not subject to corporation tax, only 50 per cent of the dividends are included in the basis for income assessment.

Prior to 1999, the capital gains tax was zero for investments in equity held for longer than 6 months. From 1999 onwards, this rate only applied to shares held for at least 12 months. Whereas under the old system (prior to 2001) short-term capital gains were taxed at the income tax rate, under the current system only 50 per cent is now included in the taxable income base.

8.6.2. *First-Tier Ownership and Control and Tax Variables*

We consider ownership and control structures at the *first-tier* of the pyramid, and construct a new set of variables. We partition our sample of 191 companies into four categories: (i) firms with a domestic industrial or commercial corporation as largest shareholder which directly controls at least 25 per cent of the voting equity (variable $ICNP_{i,t-1}$ captures the percentage of voting rights by this class), (ii) firms controlled by domestic banks ($BNP_{i,t-1}$ includes the percentage voting rights owned by banks), (iii) firms controlled by families ($FNP_{i,t-1}$ is the percentage rights held by families), and (iv) widely held firms, that is, defined as firms without a shareholder owning at least 25 per cent the voting equity. All these variables are defined at the first ownership tier of the pyramid.

To examine the tax argument we calculate the following tax discrimination variable:

$$TAX = \frac{(1-t_s)}{(1-t_d)(1-t_h)(1-t_g)}, \tag{8.5}$$

where

- t_s is the income tax rate (for domestic individuals and domestic corporations);
- t_d is the corporation tax rate on dividends distributed, constant at 36 per cent during the years of our sample period;
- t_h is the withholding tax rate deducted at source from the dividends paid to shareholders, constant at the rate of 25 per cent over our time window;
- t_g is the capital gains tax rate.

If $TAX > 1$, then the shareholder has a tax preference for dividends to capital gains. If $TAX < 1$, the shareholder prefers capital gains. To establish a shareholder's tax status in terms of a preference for dividends to capital gains, we need to make some assumptions regarding t_s and t_g. The controlling shareholders are partitioned into three categories, according to their tax status: (*i*) *German citizens* (called families or individuals in previous sections), (*ii*) *domestic corporations* (financial and non-financial firms), and (*iii*) *foreign individuals or corporations*. Another category for which we need to calculate a tax discrimination variable consists of *widely held* firms (i.e. no controlling blockholder with at least 25 per cent of the voting equity).

(*i*)   German citizens are assumed to be taxed at the highest income tax rate. Until the end of the year 1989, the top income tax rate in Germany was 56 per cent (OECD 1989). In 1990, the top income tax rate decreased to 53 per cent, a rate still applicable in 1993. Furthermore, we assume that individuals hold large share stakes for a long period of time (at least 6 months) such that capital gains tax, t_g, is zero. Plugging these values into eqn (8.5), we obtain that the tax discrimination variable (TAX) for this category of investor amounted to 0.917 until 1989 (inclusive), and equalled 0.979 between 1990 and 1993. Hence, domestic individuals preferred long-term capital gains.

(*ii*) Domestic corporations are taxed at the corporate income tax rate. If all profits in the listed German sample firm were distributed as dividends, a tax rate on distributed earnings of 36 per cent (over the sample period) was applied. If all profits were retained, the corporation tax on retained earnings, t_c, was adopted. As shown in Table 8.8, the corporation tax on retained earnings was 56 per cent until 1989 (inclusive) and reduced to 50 per cent between 1990 and 1993. We assume that the average firm had a dividend payout ratio of 80 per cent, roughly equal to the proportion of published earnings that German firms pay out as gross dividends (see Chapter 5). Thus, the effective corporate income tax of the average firm was 40 per cent in the period up to 1989 [36%(80%) + 56%(20%)] and was reduced to 38.8 per cent for the period 1990–93 [36%(80%) + 50%(20%)]. The capital gains tax rate for corporations was the same as the effective corporate income tax rate. Plugging these values into eqn (8.5), we obtain a tax discrimination variable for domestic corporations and institutions of 2.08 for the period 1984–93. Thus, domestic corporations and institutions had a strong tax preference for dividends.

(*iii*) For foreign investors, the tax discrimination variable depended on the relative size of the income or corporation tax in the home country compared to the capital gains tax in the home country and on whether the withholding tax was deductible from the taxation in the home country. As specified above, the tax discrimination variable TAX for foreign investors was likely to be below 1, expressing a tax preference for capital gains. Still, as this outcome might not have applied to all foreign investors as a consequence of double taxation treaties, we set the tax variable equal to 1.

(*iv*) For widely held firms, we require a further set of assumptions. As we do not have information on the ownership structures of these firms, except that they do not have any shareholders with at least 25 per cent of the voting equity, we use the *aggregate weighted average tax rates* for each class of shareholders. To compute the aggregate weights we use a German survey on share ownership (*Deutsche Bundesbank* 1991) for the year 1990 and assume these aggregate weights remain unchanged over the period 1984–93. According to this source, 17 per cent of all the shares listed on the German Stock Exchanges in 1990 were in the hands of German citizens, 42 per cent in the hands of domestic enterprises, 5 per cent were owned by public authorities, 14 per cent owned by non-residents, 10 per cent by banks, and 12 per cent by insurance companies.[19] If domestic individuals, as specified above, had a tax discrimination variable of 0.917 until 1989 and 0.979 subsequently, if the foreign shareholders' tax variable is assumed to equal 1, and if domestic enterprises, public authorities, banks, and insurers had the same tax preference for dividends with a tax discrimination variable equal to 2.08 during 1984–93, the tax variable TAX for this type of firms amounts to 1.731 until 1989, resulting from [(42% + 5% + 10% + 12%)*2.08 + 17%*0.917 + 14%*1], and equals 1.741, subsequently.

From the above analysis and assumptions, we deduce that individuals had a tax preference for long-term capital gains and corporations had a strong tax preference for dividends. Furthermore, the tax discrimination variable calculated for widely held firms implies a tax preference for dividends. In Section 8.6.3, we will test the hypothesis (hypothesis 8) that the tax treatment of dividends influences the dividend policy using GMM techniques with instrumental variables.

8.6.3. Results

Table 8.9 summarizes the main results of the GMM(SYS) estimations. Specifications (a) and (b) show the impact on dividends of first-tier control by banks, families, and domestic corporations. The two estimations reveal a similar pattern to the ones found in previous sections: bank control is associated with significantly lower dividend payouts whereas no significant pattern is found for the other categories of controlling shareholders. Adding variables allowing for a quadratic relation with control (not shown) does not yield significant results, which is different from the results reports in Section 8.4. In relation to hypothesis 9, these results imply that there is no strong evidence that control is diluted at intermediary levels of the pyramid. The results in Sections 8.4 on the decision to omit, cut or hold/increase the dividend within a framework of ultimate control are confirmed when we estimate an ordered probit model using first-tier control. We find that (*a*) bank-controlled firms are more prone to omit the dividend in case of poor performance, although bank control only influences dividends when control is based on the banks' own direct share stakes and not on proxy votes, (*b*) there is no significant difference in the dividend behaviour of widely held and closely held (non-bank-controlled) firms.

Specification (c) deals with the issue whether controlling shareholders, with a supposedly different tax status, impose their preferences for cash dividends. For that, we estimate the impact of the tax discrimination variable ($TAX_{i,t}$) on dividends. The table reveals that the higher the tax advantage of receiving dividends, the lower is the dividend payout of

---

[19] A slightly different share ownership is given by the Deutsche Bundesbank (1995: 67) for 1994: 20.8% of the shares are held by households, 34.3% by non-financial firms, 4.3% by the public sector, 18.9% by institutional investors, and 21.7% by foreign holdings. Edwards and Fisher (1994) estimate that 20% of the German shares are held by foreigners.

Table 8.9. *Panel data estimations of the relation between dividends, cash flows, tax discrimination, and control structures at the first-tier level*

	(a)	(b)	(c)	(d)
Const.	0.0064*	0.0055	0.0224***	−0.0023
	(0.0033)	(0.0034)	(0.0093)	(0.0346)
$D_{i,t-1}$	0.7345***	0.7849***	0.7514***	0.7886***
	(0.0696)	(0.0691)	(0.0710)	(0.0691)
CF_{it}	0.0611***	0.0660***	0.0536***	0.0659***
	(0.0168)	(0.0203)	(0.0135)	(0.0151)
$CF_{i,t-1}$	−0.0333	−0.0436	−0.0169	−0.0414*
	(0.0264)	(0.0312)	(0.0225)	(0.0232)
$BNP_{i,t-1}$	−0.0050**	−0.0036*	—	−0.0116
	(0.0025)	(0.0021)		(0.0145)
$FNP_{i,t-1}$	0.0001	—	—	0.0058
	(0.0020)			(0.0226)
$ICNP_{i,t-1}$	−0.0018	—	—	−0.0044
	(0.0019)			(0.0115)
$TAX_{i,t}$	—	—	−0.0111*	0.0048
			(0.0058)	(0.0197)
m_1	−4.806	−4.890	−4.989	−4.912
m_2	1.394	1.451	1.356	1.461
Sargan (*p*-values)	105.56 (0.260)	65.24 (0.212)	88.04 (0.252)	129.04 (0.249)
Nr of observations	1421	1421	1421	1421

Notes: The sample size is 191 firms. D_{it} is the dependent variable in all models and CF are cash flows, both scaled. $TAX_{i,t}$ is a tax discrimination variable (see Section 8.6.2 for details on the calculation). $FNP_{i,t-1}$, $BNP_{i,t-1}$, and $ICNP_{i,t-1}$ represent first-tier control (in percentage points) by domestic families, banks, and industrial and commercial corporations variables, respectively. Specifications (a) and (b) test the influence of control at the first-tier influences dividend policy. Specification (c) estimates the impact of the tax status of shareholders in Germany on the dividend policy. Time dummies are included in all specifications. m_1 and m_2 are tests for the absence of first-order and second-order serial correlation in the residuals, asymptotically distributed as $N(0,1)$ under the null of no serial correlation. Sargan is a test of the validity of the instruments, asymptotically distributed as χ^2 under the null of valid instruments. The *p*-values show the probability of generating the reported statistic under the null of valid instruments. All specifications are estimated using a GMM-instrumental variable techniques, GMM(SYS) which consists of linear systems of first-differenced and levels equations. The set of instruments used in models (A) and (B) are: Levels of dividends and cash flows dated $t-3$ to $t-4$, and first-differences dated $t-2$. For the control variables, the set of instruments is: Levels dated $t-3$ to $t-4$, and levels dated $t-2$. Model (c): levels of dividends and cash flows dated $t-3$ to $t-5$, and first-differences dated $t-2$. For the tax variable: levels dated $t-2$ to $t-5$, and first-differences dated $t-1$. Standard errors, asymptotically robust to heteroskedasticity, are reported in parentheses.

*Represents statistical significance at the 10% level.
**Represents statistical significance at the 5% level.
***Represents statistical significance at the 1% level.

the firm. That is because control and ownership by corporations (banks and others) is associated with lower dividends, as we saw above. Specification (c) assumes that the tax variable is the only determinant of dividends. If we estimate a model where we allow for the control and ownership patterns to be determinants of dividends, we find that the tax variable is now positive although not statistically significant (specification (d)). In other words, there is no evidence that supports the argument that controlling shareholders with a different tax status impose their preferences on the minority shareholders. Our evidence is not consistent with what Lasfer (1996) and Bond, Chennells, and Windmeijer (1996*b*) find for the UK, and what Eckbo and Verma (1994) find for Canada.

In summary, evidence provided by this analysis (1) confirms that bank control at the first tier is associated with lower payout ratios and (2) does not support the argument that the tax status of controlling shareholders is an influential determinant of dividends in Germany. German corporations do not seem to own subsidiaries with the purpose of earning higher dividends because they can receive 100 per cent of the cash dividend tax free. In addition, firms that are controlled by individuals do not exhibit lower payout ratios because this may be tax inefficient for their main investors.

8.7. CONCLUSIONS

In this chapter, we investigate the impact of the cross-sectional and inter-temporal variation in control on dividends paid by German corporations. We utilize a panel data estimation technique, GMM(SYS), which controls for the potential endogeneity problems of control. We also examine the impact of different control structures on the willingness of German firms to omit the dividend following a significant deterioration in earnings performance.

We report a U-shaped relation between the proportion of the voting equity held by the largest shareholder and dividend payouts. We argue that this result is consistent with agency costs arguments for dividend policy. For low levels of insider control the observed negative relation between dividends and the largest shareholder's stake is consistent with Rozeff (1982) and with the argument that at this level of control, an increase in control tends to reduce agency costs. However, at high levels of control concentration, the level of dividends increases implying that there is a point beyond which control no longer acts as a substitute for dividends. This result has another implication. Shleifer and Vishny (1997), for example, argue that a governance structure with high concentration of ownership and control, such as the German market may deal with the problem of controlling managers, but it may be at the expense of minority investors, since, in such an environment, there are fewer measures protecting these investors from expropriation. Our results suggest that if there is expropriation of small investors by controlling shareholders in Germany this is not achieved via the payment of lower dividends (and retaining funds to use at their discretion) as their voting power increases and the power of small shareholders decreases. This result somewhat contradicts La Porte et al.'s (2000) argument. However, we also express some concern about the robustness of our result as, when we allow for a higher order function form of control, the estimations point to several local minima.

It should be noted that the proportion of voting shares held by the largest shareholder or the percentage of voting rights held by all blockholders (>25 per cent) does not accurately capture the impact of control on dividend policy. In effect, it is important to consider in this discussion the different classes of shareholders, as each class may give rise to different agency relations and costs. A central result that emerges from our analysis is that bank ownership of voting equity is associated with lower dividend payouts and a stronger propensity to omit the dividend. This result is true across different specifications and irrespective of whether we focus on first-tier control or ultimate control. This suggests that control is not gradually diluted across the pyramid. Our results are consistent with the argument that direct bank control mitigates asymmetries of information and agency costs. However, our evidence suggests that proxy votes and bank control are not alternative monitoring devices.

The result on the importance of bank control also corroborates the theories on corporate investment decisions. When a firm experiences liquidity constraints but has an investment project with a positive NPV, it may have to resort to the capital markets to attract funds to finance its investment project. The management may be convinced that the project is of high quality and hence should be assigned an appropriate (low) cost of capital. Still, the markets, who are at an informational disadvantage, may value the project as an average quality project, and hence may only be willing to fund the project at an average cost of capital. The result may be underinvestment if the positive NPV project cannot be undertaken. If the firm has a house bank the underinvestment may be reduced because this house bank may not be an informational disadvantage compared to the market as a result of the bank's knowledge of the firm's credit history, the bank's control stake with possible board representation. Thus, bank control may lead to a lower cost of capital and may reduce the (costly) need to signal firm quality to the market by use of the dividend policy. Elston (1993) finds evidence on German firms consistent with this idea.

Finally, we estimate the impact of the tax status of shareholders on the dividend policy of German firms. Our evidence does not support the proposition that different controlling shareholders with different tax preferences of dividends to long-term capital gains impose their preferences on other shareholders. In that respect, we find conflicting evidence with Eckbo and Verma (1994). When we include both the impact of bank control and a tax variable capturing the relative preference for dividends (relative to capital gains) into one dividend regression, the negative relation between bank control and dividends disappears. This suggests that preference for a low dividend payout ratio in bank-controlled firms is offset by a preference for high dividends from a taxation standpoint.

9

Conclusion

As little empirical research has been undertaken on the dividend policy of firms outside the Anglo-American corporate governance system, this book attempts to close this gap. In the first part of this book, we provide the reader with a description of the various corporate governance regimes that may shape dividend policy. This is followed by a survey of the— mostly Anglo-American—literature on dividend policy. In the second part of the book, the empirical part, we ask the question whether the dividend policy in a blockholder-based corporate governance regime has a different role from in a market-based system. In particular, we want to determine whether there is a negative relation between the level of dividends and the level of concentration of control. If this is the case, then dividends and control may be substitute monitoring mechanisms. Another interesting question is whether large shareholders are able to impose a dividend policy which is optimal for their tax status. For Germany in particular, often labelled as a bank-based economy, it is worthwhile to study whether bank control—based on equity ownership and proxy votes—is associated with lower dividends and less reluctance to cut and omit the dividend.

9.1. CORPORATE GOVERNANCE MECHANISMS AND THE DIVIDEND POLICY LITERATURE

We broadly define a corporate governance regime as the amalgam of mechanisms which ensure that the agent (the management of a corporation) runs the firm for the benefit of one or multiple principals (shareholders, creditors, suppliers, clients, employees, and other parties with whom the firm conducts its business). Roughly speaking, there are two generic corporate governance regimes: the market-based and the blockholder-based regime. The former is characterized by a high number of companies listed on the stock exchange, diffuse ownership, the one-share-one-vote rule, an active market for corporate control, and strong shareholder and creditor rights. The UK and the USA are the prototypes of this system. The blockholder system can be described by a small number of listed companies, the presence of large blockholders, complex ownership structures (shareholder pyramids and cross-ownership), frequent violations of the one-share-one-vote rule and weak shareholder protection. The Continental European countries are part of this regime. Our description of corporate governance regimes also highlights that not only does the control concentration differ across regimes, but so does its nature. In the UK and the USA, financial institutions hold most of the shares, although the size of their holdings is modest. A second important category of shareholder in these countries is directors. Their significant ownership has been documented to be potentially harmful in situations of poor performance as it may lead to entrenchment. In Continental Europe, the main shareholder categories are families or individuals, and corporations. Moreover, in Germany, the banks are an important source of finance. First, they frequently act as house banks by being the main provider of debt capital to companies. Second, they frequently hold substantial voting stakes and their control tends to be strengthened by proxy votes.

If the one-share-one-vote principle applies, having control over a firm requires a large investment. Still, in most European countries, mechanisms exist to deviate from the one-share-one-vote principle. As a consequence, it is possible to combine a high degree of control with a limited percentage of cash flow rights. These mechanisms are ownership pyramids or cascades, multiple voting rights, non-voting shares, and proxy votes. The combination of strong control with limited investment may lead to the expropriation of the minority shareholders by the large shareholder. In contrast, in the Anglo-American system where the principle of one-share-one-vote is normally upheld and ownership tends to be diffuse, the major agency problem is between managers and shareholders.

We focus on those corporate governance devices which may have a direct or indirect impact on dividend policy and distinguish between internal and external governance mechanisms. The internal mechanisms consist of the board of directors and the blockholders whereas the main external ones comprise the market for corporate control, the market for block trades, and creditor monitoring. We also show the importance of the regulatory framework (legislation, self-regulation, and stock exchange rules), such as investor and creditor protection, mandatory bid rules, and legal origin.

The role of dividends in terms of corporate control can be twofold. First, the dividend payout may be a bonding mechanism precommitting managers to pursue value maximization. A high dividend payout ensures that managers focus on generating sufficiently high levels of cash flows and that these are not invested into projects with returns below the cost of capital. As such, a tight dividend policy allows corporate monitors to reduce their monitoring efforts. Dividend policy may, thus, be a substitute corporate governance device to several internal monitoring mechanisms such as the board of directors or the blockholders. Second, dividend policy may also constitute an important signal, as dividend cuts are interpreted by the market as powerful signals of bad news both about the firm's current situation and its prospects. Consequently, the failure to meet the anticipated dividend level or payout may activate alternative corporate governance mechanisms which are better suited to deal with poor performance or financial distress. Given that (industry-corrected) underperformance may not only be caused by the management, but may also be due to the failure of the internal monitors (such as the board or the blockholders), external corporate governance mechanisms (such as the market for corporate control) may be activated to start board and/or asset restructuring of the firm.

It is important to note that a pre-condition for dividends is a signal of failing performance and corporate control is dividend 'stickiness'. In Anglo-American companies, there is ample evidence that managers are reluctant to reduce dividends, but it is questionable whether the same reluctance applies to Continental European companies, frequently controlled by one single dominant investor group. For example, as dividends of German firms are more volatile, they may be more in line with current earnings rather than with the long-term prospects of the firm. Dividends are then no longer a strong signal of poor management and governance.

9.2. DIVIDEND PAYOUT RATIOS IN GERMANY AND THE UK

This book provides important, new insights into the dividend policy of companies from a corporate governance system—the German system—which is not characterized by the separation of ownership and control à la Berle–Means (1932). We show that German firms pay out a lower proportion of their cash flows than UK or US firms. However, on a published profits basis, the conventional wisdom that German firms have significantly lower dividend payout ratios than UK or US firms is no longer true, as we find the exact inverse. The company law provisions on profit reporting and on profit transfers between a company and its parent, as well as accounting rules largely account for these two conflicting patterns. The most important legal provisions which influence the payout ratio are the following ones. First, some corporations have control agreements with their parent companies, whereby they transfer the profit and/or loss to their parent companies. These transfers are not dividends *per se*, but can be an opportunity for the parent company to benefit from tax losses at the subsidiary level. In our analysis, we exclude firms with control agreements from our dataset in order to avoid double counting of dividends. Second, German corporations are usually required to pay out at least 50 per cent of their published profits as dividends, although there may be stipulations in a firm's articles of association that mitigate the impact of this provision. Finally, German firms are usually not allowed to buy back their own shares over the time period of our empirical studies such that if they want to return funds to the shareholders, they have to resort to increasing the dividend payout. This is in marked contrast to the USA where share buybacks are a frequent occurrence.

Another reason why German firms pay out higher dividends (on a profit basis) than their Anglo-American counterparts can be found in the accounting rules. German accounting rules are often considered to be deficient in the information disclosed to investors relative to the Anglo-American financial reporting. Under the German system, managers have incentives to report modest profits, especially in the light of the requirement to pay out at least 50 per cent of the published profits. In addition, pension and other provisions may also account for a certain downward bias in the published profit figure.

We also document that not only are the payout levels different between German and UK or US firms, but so are the dividend policies. Dividends-per-shares of UK and US firms are relatively smooth over time and are characterized by frequent small adjustments. Conversely, dividends-per-share of German firms show less frequent but larger discrete jumps. Therefore, it seems that German dividend policy is more flexible compared to that of the UK or the USA, because German dividend changes follow earnings and cash flow changes more closely.

We also find that the dividend payout is related to the degree of control in German firms. In general, widely held firms have lower payout ratios than closely held firms. However, within the closely held firms, we report that the nature of control (the type of blockholder) has an important impact on dividend policy. First, firms controlled by other corporations have the highest payout ratios. Second, firms controlled by banks have dividend payout ratios which are significantly lower than the sample average. Finally, firms controlled by foreign companies, families, the state and holding companies are somewhat in the middle, all with virtually identical payout ratios.

9.3. THE DIVIDEND ADJUSTMENT PROCESS TO EARNINGS CHANGES

The seminal work by Lintner (1956) and Fama and Babiak (1968) on US dividend policy suggests that managers change dividends primarily in response to unanticipated and non-transitory changes in their firm's earnings. Moreover, firms have well-defined dividend policies: They usually have a long-run target payout ratio and also set the speed with which they adjust dividends towards this target. We estimate whether the empirical relations between dividends and earnings documented for Anglo-American firms also hold for Germany by applying Lintner's partial adjustment model. The study in this book improves on earlier research by using a more appropriate estimation methodology (an approach with instrumental variables based on the Generalized Method of Moments), a larger and more representative sample (our sample represents about 80 per cent of the market capitalization of the commercial and industrial firms listed on the German stock exchanges), a longer time window (10 years) and two different proxies for profitability (published earnings versus cash flow). Our time period from 1984 to 1993 is chosen to encompass a five-year economic boom followed by a recession. We find an implicit target dividend payout ratio of 25 per cent (of published earnings), which is substantially lower than the observed payout of 86 per cent. This implies that German firms do not base their dividend decisions on long-term target payout ratios expressed in terms of public earnings. As the published earnings figure may not correctly reflect corporate performance given that German firms tend to retain a significant part of their earnings to build up legal reserves, and given that the published earnings figures are conservative, we perform some robustness tests defining the payout ratio in terms of cash flows. Our estimations are closer to the observed dividend policy. This implies that the payout ratios of German firms are based on cash flows rather than published earnings.

9.4. WHEN DO GERMAN FIRMS CHANGE THEIR DIVIDEND?

Given that the dividends per share time series of German firms are characterized by a high discreteness, that is, frequent large changes, we opt for a discrete choice modelling approach. We analyse how past, current, and future profits affect the timing of dividend changes rather than the amount of the dividend change. We find that bottom line earnings are key determinants of dividend changes, a finding which is consistent with Lintner (1956). We also use cash flows to correct for accounting conservatism in the earnings figure and find that cash flows are also important determinants of the decision to change the dividend.

We highlight two features of German dividend policy that are not captured by the Lintner model. First, we observe that the *level* of net earnings is *not* the main determinant of a dividend reduction or omission. In fact, the occurrence of an annual loss has higher explanatory power than the magnitude of the loss itself. We find that 80 per cent of the firms with at least five years of positive earnings and dividends omit the dividend in the loss year, irrespective of the magnitude of the earnings loss and of the past and future earnings. Second, German firms quickly revert to the dividend level prior to the dividend omission or reduction. We find that more than half of the German firms, which omitted the dividend, return to the dividend payout prior to the omission within merely two years. A similar pattern applies to dividend reductions. These findings contrast with the predictions of Lintner (1956) and Miller and Modigliani (1961) that dividends will only change if managers believe that the dividends will not have to be reversed in the short run. Therefore, these models do not capture the dividend behaviour of German firms with a temporary deterioration in profitability. The Lintner model describes the dividend policy of well performing firms, but not that of firms facing sudden and temporary falls in profitability. Our findings also contradict those of DeAngelo, DeAngelo, and Skinner (1992) who report that US firms are more likely to reduce dividends when the current loss is higher and when persistent future earnings problems are expected.

Our findings can be interpreted in the light of signalling theories of dividend policy. The fact that German firms frequently omit and cut dividends and quickly revert to the payout prior to the omission or cut suggests that dividends do not convey (much) information about the future value of the firm.

9.5. CONTROL CONCENTRATION AND TAX CLIENTELES

We also examine the impact of the cross-sectional and inter-temporal variation in control on dividends paid by German corporations. As control is usually concentrated in the hands of a large shareholder, we investigate whether dividend patterns reflect this. Different forms of control may indeed give rise to the setting of different dividend payouts and dividend policies. We also examine the impact of different control structures on the willingness of German firms to omit the dividend following a significant deterioration in earnings.

We report a U-shaped relation between the proportion of the voting equity held by the largest shareholder and dividend payouts. This result seems consistent with agency costs arguments for dividend policy. For low levels of control, an increase in control by the largest shareholder is negatively related to the dividend payout ratio. This is consistent with the argument that an increase in control tends to reduce agency costs between managers and shareholders. At high levels of control, the payout ratio then increases. This implies that there is a point beyond which control no longer acts as a substitute for dividends. High concentration of control may deal with the agency problem of controlling managers, but it may be at the expense of minority investors, who face a higher risk of expropriation in a system with weak investor rights. Our results suggest that, if there is expropriation of small investors by the controlling shareholder, this is not achieved via the payment of lower dividends.

It is important to consider not only the degree of control but also the type of the controlling shareholder, as each type may give rise to different agency relations and costs. A central result that emerges from our analysis is that bank ownership of voting equity is associated with lower dividend payouts and a stronger propensity to omit the dividend. Our results are consistent with the argument that direct bank control mitigates asymmetries of information and agency costs. However, the exercise (of a sometimes large percentage) of proxy votes does not constitute an alternative to direct bank control.

Finally, we estimate the impact of the tax status of shareholders on the dividend policy of German firms. We examine whether taxation on dividends (relative to taxation on capital gains) creates tax clienteles. Our evidence does not support the proposition that controlling shareholders with different tax preferences for dividends impose their preferences on minority shareholders. We also find that a preference for a low dividend payout ratio in bank-controlled firms is somewhat offset by a preference for high dividends from a taxation standpoint.

The stylized facts and other empirical results uncovered by this book contribute to the ongoing discussion on corporate governance and the optimal system of corporate governance. Our results show that, although the Anglo-American system has a clear advantage in the form of higher investor protection, the German or Continental European system also has a major advantage as it provides firms with a higher flexibility in terms of their dividend policy.

References

Adams, M. (1994). 'Die Usurpation von Aktionärsbefugnissen mittels Ringverflechtung in der "Deutschland AG"'. *Die Aktienrechtsreform und Unternehmensverfassung* (April): 148–58.

Adaoglu, C. (2000). 'Instability in the dividend policy of the Istanbul Stock Exchange (ISE) corporations: Evidence from an emerging market'. *Emerging Markets Review* 1: 252–70.

Admati, R. A., Pfleiderer, P., and Zechner, J. (1994). 'Large shareholder activism, risk sharing, and financial markets equilibrium'. *Journal of Political Economy* 102: 1097–130.

Aghion, P. and Bolton, P. (1992). 'An incomplete contracts approach to financial contracting'. *Review of Economic Studies* 59: 473–94.

Agrawal, A. and Knoeber, C. (1996). 'Firm performance and mechanisms to control agency problems between managers and shareholders'. *Journal of Financial and Quantitative Analysis* 31: 377–97.

Aharony, J. and Swary, I. (1980). 'Quarterly dividend and earnings announcements and stockholders' returns: An empirical analysis'. *Journal of Finance* 35: 1–12.

Aldrich, J. and Nelson, F. (1984). *Linear Probability, Logit, and Probit Models*. New York: Sage Publications.

Allen, F. and Santomero, A. (2001). 'What do financial intermediaries do?' *Journal of Banking and Finance* 25: 271–94.

Ambarish, R., John, K., and Williams, J. (1987). 'Efficient signalling with dividends and investments'. *Journal of Finance* 42: 321–43.

Amemiya, T. (1973). 'Regression analysis when the dependent variable is truncated normal'. *Econometrica* 41: 997–1016.

Amihud, Y. and Murgia, M. (1997). 'Dividends, taxes and signaling: Evidence from Germany'. *Journal of Finance* 52: 397–408.

Anderson, T. and Hsiao, C. (1981). 'Estimation of dynamic models with error components'. *Journal of the American Statistical Association* 76: 598–606.

Arellano, M. and Bond, S. (1988). 'Dynamic panel data estimation using DPD—A guide for users'. Working paper, Institute of Fiscal Studies.

————— (1991). 'Some tests of specification for panel data: Monte Carlo evidence and an application to employment equations'. *Review of Economic Studies* 58: 277–97.

—— and Bover, O. (1995). 'Another look at the instrumental-variable estimation of error-component models'. *Journal of Econometrics* 68: 29–52.

Asquith, P. and Mullins, D. (1983). 'The impact of initiating dividend payments on shareholders wealth'. *Journal of Business* 56: 77–95.

————— (1986). 'Signaling with dividends, stock repurchases, and equity issues'. *Financial Management* 15: 27–44.

Bagwell, L. and Shoven, J. (1989). 'Cash distributions to shareholders'. *Journal of Economic Perspectives* 3: 129–40.

Baker, M. and Gompers, P. (2000). 'The determinants of board structure and function in entrepreneurial firms'. Working paper, Harvard Business School.

Banerjee, S., Leleux, B., and Vermaelen, T. (1997). 'Large shareholders and corporate control: An analysis of stake purchases by French holding companies'. *European Financial Management* 3: 23–43.

Bar-Yosef, S. and Huffman, L. (1986). 'The information content of dividends: A signalling approach'. *Journal of Financial and Quantitative Analysis* 21: 47–58.

Barca, F. and Becht, M. (2001). *The Control of Corporate Europe*. Oxford: Oxford University Press.

Barclay, M. J. and Holderness, C. G. (1989). 'Private benefits from control of public corporations'. *Journal of Financial Economics* 25: 371–95.

Barclay, M. J. and Holderness, C. G. (1991). 'Negotiated block trades and corporate control'. *Journal of Finance* 46: 861–78.

—— —— (1992). 'The law and large-block trades'. *Journal of Law and Economics* 35: 265–94.

Barro, J. and Barro, R. (1990). 'Pay, performance and turnover of bank CEOs'. *Journal of Labor Economics* 8: 448–81.

Baums, T. (2000). 'Corporate governance in Germany—System and current developments'. Working paper, University of Osnabrück.

—— and Fraune, M. (1995). 'Institutionelle Anleger and Publikumsgeselllschaft: Eine Empirische Untersuchung'. *Die Aktiengesellschaft* 40: 97–112.

Bebchuk, L. (1998). 'A theory of the choice between concentrated and dispersed ownership of corporate shares and votes'. Working paper, Harvard Law School.

—— and Roe, M. (2000). 'A theory of path dependence of corporate ownership and governance'. *Stanford Law Review* 52: 775–808.

—— Coates IV, J. C., and Subramanian, G. (2002). 'The powerful antitakeover force of staggered boards: Theory, evidence, and policy'. *Stanford Law Review* 54: 887–924.

Becht, M. and Boehmer, E. (2001). 'Ownership and voting power in Germany'. In F. Barca and M. Becht (eds.), *The Control of Corporate Europe*. Oxford: Oxford University Press, pp. 128–53.

——, Bolton, P., and Röell, A. (2002). 'Corporate governance and control'. Working paper, European Corporate Governance Institute.

——, Chapelle, A., and Renneboog, L. (2001). 'Shareholding cascades: Separation of ownership and control in Belgium'. In F. Barca and M. Becht (eds.), *The Control of Corporate Europe*. Oxford: Oxford University Press, pp. 71–105.

Beck, T., Demirgüç-Kunt, A., and Levine, R. (2002). 'Law and finance: Why does legal origin matter?' *Journal of Comparative Economics*, forthcoming.

——, Levine, R., and Loayza, N. (2000). 'Finance and the sources of growth'. *Journal of Financial Economics* 58: 261–300.

Behm, U. and Zimmermann, H. (1993). 'The empirical relationship between dividends and earnings in Germany'. *Zeitschrift für Wirtschafts- und Sozialwissenschaften* 113: 225–54.

Bell, L. and Jenkinson, T. (2002). 'New evidence of the impact of dividend taxation and on the identity of the marginal investor'. *Journal of Finance* 57: 1321–46.

Bennedsen, M. and Nielsen, K. (2002). 'The impact of break-through rule on European firms'. Working paper, Copenhagen School of Economics.

Berglöf, E. and Burkart, M. (2002). 'Break-through in European takeover regulation?' Working paper, Stockholm School of Economics.

—— and Perotti, E. (1994). 'The governance structure of the Japanese financial Keiretsu'. *Journal of Financial Economics* 36: 259–84.

—— and von Thadden, E.-L. (1999). 'The changing corporate governance paradigm'. SITE Working Paper No 99/03, Stockholm School of Economics.

Berkovitch, E., Ronen, I., and Zender, J. (1997). 'Optimal bankruptcy law and firm-specific investments'. *European Economic Review* 41: 487–97.

Berle, A. and Means G. (1932). *The Modern Corporation and Private Property*. New York: Macmillan.

Bertrand, M. and Mullainathan, S. (2003). 'Enjoying the quiet life? Managerial behavior following anti-takeover legislation'. *Journal of Political Economy*, forthcoming.

Bethel, J. E., Liebeskind, J. P., and Opler, T. (1998). 'Block share purchases and corporate performance'. *Journal of Finance* 53: 605–34.

Bhagat, S. and Black, B. (2000). 'Board independence and long-term firm performance'. Working paper, University of Colorado.

Bhattacharya, S. (1979). 'Imperfect information, dividend policy and the "bird in hand" fallacy'. *Bell Journal of Economics* 10: 259–70.

Bianchi, M., Bianco, M., and Enriques, L. (2001). 'Pyramidal groups and the separation between ownership and control in Italy'. In F. Barca and M. Becht (eds.), *The Control of Corporate Europe*. Oxford: Oxford University Press, pp. 154–87.

Black, F. and Scholes, M. (1974). 'The effects of dividend yield and dividend policy on common stock prices and returns'. *Journal of Financial Economics* 1: 1–22.

—— (1976). 'The dividend puzzle'. *Journal of Portfolio Management* 2: 5–8.

Blackwell, D., Brickley, J., and Weisbach, M. (1994). 'Accounting information and internal performance evaluation: Evidence from Texas banks'. *Journal of Accounting and Economics* 17: 331–58.

Bloch, L. and Kremp, E. (2001). 'Ownership and voting power in France'. In F. Barca and M. Becht (eds.), *The Control of Corporate Europe*. Oxford: Oxford University Press, pp. 106–27.

Blundell, R. and Bond, S. (1998). 'Initial conditions and moment restrictions in dynamic panel data models'. *Journal of Econometrics* 87: 115–43.

Boehmer, E. (2002). 'Who controls German corporations?' In J. McCahery, P. Moerland, T. Raaijmakers, and L. Renneboog (eds.), *Corporate Governance Regimes: Convergence and Diversity*. Oxford: Oxford University Press, pp. 268–86.

Bolton, P. and von Thadden, E.-L. (1998). 'Blocks, liquidity and corporate control'. *Journal of Finance* 53: 1–25.

Bond, S., Chennells, L., and Devereux, M. (1995). 'Company dividends and taxes in the UK'. *Fiscal Studies* 16: 1–18.

—— —— —— (1996a), 'Taxes and company dividends: A microeconometric investigation exploiting cross-section variation in taxes'. *Economic Journal* 106: 320–33.

—— ——, and Windmeijer, E. F. (1996b). 'Shareholder status and company dividend behaviour'. Mimeo, Institute of Fiscal Studies.

Born, J. and Rimbey, J. (1993). 'A test of the Easterbrook hypothesis regarding dividend payments and agency costs'. *Journal of Financial Research* 46: 251–60.

—— (1988). 'Insider ownership and signals: Evidence from dividend initiation announcements effects'. *Financial Management* 17: 38–45.

Borokhovich, K., Brunarski, K., and Parrino, R. (1997). 'CEO contracting and anti-takeover amendments'. *Journal of Finance* 52: 1495–517.

Börsch-Supan, A. and Köke, J. (2000). 'An applied econometricians' view of empirical corporate finance studies'. Working paper, Center for European Economic Research (ZEW), University of Mannheim.

Bratton, W. and McCahery, J. A. (1999). 'Comparative corporate governance and the theory of the firm: The case against global cross reference'. *Columbia Journal of Transnational Law* 38: 213–97.

Brealey, R. and Myers, S. (2003). *Principles of Corporate Finance,* 7th edn. London: McGraw-Hill.

Brennan, M. (1970). 'Taxes, market valuation and corporate financial policy'. *National Tax Journal* 23: 417–27.

Brickley, J. and Van Horn, R. L. (2000). 'Incentives in nonprofit organizations: Evidence from hospitals'. Working paper, University of Rochester.

—— (1983). 'Shareholder wealth, information signalling and the specially designated dividend: An empirical study'. *Journal of Financial Economics* 12: 187–209.

Brunello, G., Graziano, C., and Parigi, B. (2003). 'CEO turnover in insider-dominated boards: The Italian case'. *Journal of Banking and Finance* 27: 1027–51.

Burkart, M. (1999). 'The economics of takeover regulation'. SITE Working Paper 99/06, Stockholm School of Economics.

—— Gromb, D., and Panunzi, F. (1997). 'Large shareholders, monitoring, and the value of the firm'. *Quarterly Journal of Economics* 112: 693–728.

—— —— —— (2000). 'Agency conflicts in public and negotiated transfers of corporate control'. *Journal of Finance* 55: 647–77.

Cable, J. (1985). 'Capital market information and industrial performance: The role of West German banks'. *Economic Journal* 95: 118–32.

Carlin, W. and Mayer, C. (2002). 'Financial markets and corporate governance'. In J. McCahery, P. Moerland, T. Raaijmakers, and L. Renneboog (eds.), Corporate Governance Regimes: Convergence and Diversity. Oxford: Oxford University Press.

Chen, C. and Steiner, T. (1999). 'Managerial ownership and agency conflicts: A nonlinear simultaneous equation analysis of managerial ownership, risk taking, debt policy, and dividend policy'. *Financial Review* 34: 119–346.

Chirinko, R. and Elston, J. (1996). 'Banking relationships in Germany; what should regulators do?' In Federal Reserve Bank of Chicago (ed.), *Rethinking Bank Regulation: What Should Regulators Do?* Chicago: Federal Reserve Bank of Chicago, pp. 239–55.

—— —— (2000). 'Finance, control, and profitability: An evaluation of German bank influence'. Working paper, Emory University.

Christie, W. (1994). 'Are dividend omissions truly the cruellest cut of all?' *Journal of Financial and Quantitative Analysis* 29: 459–80.

Coffee, J. C. (1991). 'Liquidity versus control: The institutional investor as corporate monitor'. *Columbia Law Review* 91: 1277–368.

Coles, J., Lemmon, M., and Meschke, F. (2002). 'Endogeneity in corporate finance'. Working paper, Arizona State University.

Comment, R. and Schwert, G. W. (1995). 'Poison pill or placebo? Evidence on the deterrence and wealth effects of modern antitakeover measures'. *Journal of Financial Economics* 39: 3–43.

Copeland, T. E. and Weston, J. F. (1988). *Financial Theory and Corporate Policy*, 3rd edn. New York: Addison Wesley, 946p.

Corbett, J. and Jenkinson, T. (1996). 'The financing of industry, 1970–89: An international comparison'. *Journal of the Japanese and International Economies* 10: 71–96.

Core, J., Guay, W., and D. Larcker (2001). 'Executive equity compensation and incentives: A survey'. Working paper, Wharton School, University of Pennsylvania.

Coughlan, A. and Schmidt, R. (1985). 'Executive compensation, managerial turnover, and firm performance: An empirical investigation', *Journal of Accounting and Economics* 7: 43–66.

Crespí-Cladera, R. and García-Cestona, M. (2001). 'Ownership and control of Spanish listed firms'. In F. Barca and M. Becht (eds.), *The Control of Corporate Europe*. Oxford: Oxford University Press, pp. 207–27.

—— and Renneboog, L. (2002). 'Coalition formation and shareholder monitoring in the UK'. Discussion paper CentER, Tilburg University.

——, Gispert, C., and Renneboog, L. (2002). 'Cash-based executive compensation in Spain and UK'. In J. McCahery, P. Moerland, T. Raaijmakers, and L. Renneboog (eds.), *Corporate Governance Regimes: Convergence and Diversity*. Oxford: Oxford University Press, pp. 647–67.

Crutchley, C. and Hansen, R. (1989). 'A test of the agency theory of managerial ownership, corporate leverage and corporate dividends'. *Financial Management* 18: 36–76.

——, Jensen, M., Jahera, J., and Raymond, J. (1999). 'Agency problems and the simultaneity of financial decision making—The role of institutional ownership'. *International Review of Financial Analysis* 8: 177–97.

Dann, L. (1981). 'Common stock repurchases: An analysis of the returns to bondholders and stock-holders'. *Journal of Financial Economics* 9: 113–38.

Davidson, R. and MacKinnon, J. (1984). 'Convenient specification tests for logit and probit models'. *Journal of Econometrics* 25: 241–62.

De Jong, A., Kabir, R., Marra, T., and Roell, A. (2001). 'Ownership and control in the Netherlands'. In F. Barca and M. Becht (eds.), *The Control of Corporate Europe*. Oxford: Oxford University Press.

DeAngelo, H. and DeAngelo, L. (1985). 'Managerial ownership of voting rights: A study of public corporations with dual classes of common stock'. *Journal of Finance* 14: 33–69.

—— —— (1990). 'Dividend policy and financial distress: An empirical investigation of troubled NYSE firms'. *Journal of Finance* 45: 1415–31.

—— —— and Skinner, D. (1992). 'Dividends and losses'. *Journal of Finance* 47: 1837–63.

—— —— —— (1996). 'Reversal of fortune dividend signaling and the disappearance of sustained earnings growth'. *Journal of Financial Economics* 40: 341–71.

Dempsey, S. and Laber, G. (1992). 'Effects of agency and transactions costs on dividend payout ratios: Further evidence of the agency-transaction cost hypothesis'. *Journal of Financial Research* 15: 317–21.

Demsetz, H. (1983). 'The structure of ownership and the theory of the firm'. *Journal of Law and Economics* 26: 375–90.

—— and Lehn, K. (1985). 'The structure of corporate ownership: Causes and consequences'. *Journal of Political Economy* 93: 1155–77.

Denis, D. and Denis, D. (1995). 'Performance changes following top management dismissals'. *Journal of Finance* 50: 1029–55.

Deutsche Bundesbank (1995). 'Securities ownership in Germany since 1989'. *Monthly Report of the Deutsche Bundesbank* (1995/8): 55–68.

—— (1991). 'The significance of shares as financing instruments'. *Monthly Report of the Deutsche Bundesbank* (1991/10): 21–8.

Devereux, M. and Schiantarelli, F. (1990). 'Investment, financial factors, and cash flow: Evidence from UK panel data'. In R. Glenn Hubbard (ed.), *Asymmetric Information, Corporate Finance and Investment*. Chicago: University of Chicago Press, pp. 279–306.

Dewenter, K. and Warther, V. (1998). 'Dividends, asymmetric information, and agency conflicts: Evidence from a comparison of the dividend policies of Japanese and US firms'. *Journal of Finance* 53: 879–904.

Dherment, I. and Renneboog, L (2002). 'Share price reactions to CEO resignations and large share-holder monitoring in listed French companies'. In J. McCahery, P. Moerland, T. Raaijmakers, and L. Renneboog (eds.), *Corporate Governance Regimes: Convergence and Diversity*. Oxford: Oxford University Press.

Diamond, D. W. (1984). 'Financial intermediation and delegated monitoring'. *Review of Economic Studies* 51: 393–414.

Dickerson, A., Gibson, H., and Tsakalotos, E. (1998). 'Takeover risk and dividend strategy: A study of UK firms'. *Journal of Industrial Economics* 46: 281–300.

Dong, M., Robinson, C., and Veld, C. (2002). 'Why individual investors want dividends'. Discussion paper CentER, Tilburg University.

Downes, D. and Heinkel, R. (1982). 'Signaling and the valuation of unseasoned new issues'. *Journal of Finance* 37: 1–10.

Drobetz, W., Schillhofer, A., and Zimmermann, H. (2003). 'Corporate governance and expected stock returns: Evidence from Germany'. Working paper, University of Basel.

Dyck, A. and Zingales, L. (2002). 'Private benefits of control: An international comparison'. *Journal of Finance*, forthcoming.

Easterbrook, F. (1984). 'Two agency-cost explanations of dividends'. *American Economic Review* 74: 650–9.

Eckbo, B. E. and Verma, S. (1994). 'Managerial share ownership, voting power, and cash dividend policy'. *Journal of Corporate Finance* 1: 33–62.

The Economist (1994). A survey of corporate governance, 29 Jan. 1994.

Edwards, J. and Fischer, K. (1994). *Banks, Finance and Investment in Germany.* London and Cambridge: CEPR and Cambridge University Press.

—— (1987). 'Recent developments in the theory of corporate finance'. *Oxford Review of Economic Policy* 3: 1–11.

—— and Mayer, C. (1986). 'An investigation into the dividend and the new equity issue practices of firms: Evidence from survey information'. Working paper No. 80, Institute of Fiscal Studies.

——, Mayer, C., Pashardes, B., and Poterba, J. (1986). 'The effects of taxation on corporate dividend policy in the UK'. Working Paper No. 96, Institute of Fiscal Studies.

Elston, J. (1993). 'Firm ownership structure and investment theory and evidence from German panel data'. Discussion Paper FS IV 93-28, Wissenschaftszentrum Berlin (WZB).

Elton, E. and Gruber, M. (1970). 'Marginal stockholder tax rates and clientele effect'. *Review of Economics and Statistics* 52: 68–74.

Espenlaub, S., Goergen, M., and Khurshed, A. (2001). 'IPO lock-in agreements in the UK'. *Journal of Business Finance and Accounting* 28: 1235–78.

Faccio, M. and Lang, L. (2002). 'The ultimative ownership of Western European companies'. *Journal of Financial Economics* 65: 365–95.

—— ——, and Young, L. (2001). 'Dividends and expropriation'. *American Economic Review* 91: 54–78.

Fama, E. and Jensen, M. (1983). 'Separation of ownership and control'. *Journal of Law and Economics* 26: 301–25.

—— (1980). 'Agency problems and the theory of the firm'. *Journal of Political Economy* 88: 288–307.

—— and Babiak, H. (1968). 'Dividend policy: An empirical analysis'. *American Statistical Association Journal* 63: 1132–61.

Filbeck, G. and Mullineaux, D. (1999). 'Agency costs and dividend payments—The case of bank holding companies'. *Quarterly Review of Economics and Finance* 39: 409–18.

Financial Times (1994). 'MPs urge flexibility in dividend payments', 29 April 1994: 9.

—— (1994). 'Daimler consider Anglo-US policy on dividends', 8 July 1994: 19.

—— (2002). 'M & G stresses need to maintain dividend', 8 October 2002: 1.

Fischer, O., Jansen, H., and Meyer, W. (1975). Langfristige Finanzplanung Deutscher Unternehmen, Hamburg.

Franks, J. and Mayer, C. (1996). 'Hostile takeovers and the correction of managerial failure'. *Journal of Financial Economics* 40: 163–81.

—— —— (1998). 'Bank Control, takeovers and corporate governance in Germany'. *Journal of Banking and Finance* 22: 1385–403.

—— —— (2001). 'Ownership and control in Germany'. *Review of Financial Studies* 14: 943–77.

—— —— (1995). 'Ownership and control'. In H. Sibert (ed.), *Trends in Business Organisation: Do Participation and Cooperation Increase Competitiveness?* Tübingen: Mohr, pp. 171–95.

—— ——, and Renneboog, L. (2001). 'Who disciplines management of poorly performing companies?' *Journal of Financial Intermediation* 10: 209–48.

Garvey, G. and Hanka, G. (1999). 'Capital structure and corporate control: The effect of anti-takeover statutes on firm leverage'. *Journal of Finance* 54: 519–46.

Gertner, R. and Kaplan, S. (1996). 'The value-maximizing board'. Working paper, University of Chicago.

Gerum, E., Steinmann, H., and Fees, W. (1988). Der Mitbestimmte Aufsichtsrat—eine Empirische Untersuchung, Stuttgart: Poeschel Verlag.

Glen, J., Karmokolias, Y., Miller, R., and Shah, S. (1995). 'Dividend policy and behavior in emerging markets: To pay or not to pay'. IFC Discussion paper 26.

Glen, J., Lee, K., and Singh, A. (2000). 'Competition, corporate governance and financing of corporate growth in emerging markets'. Discussion paper AF46, Department of Applied Economics, University of Cambridge.

Goergen, M. (1998). *Corporate governance and financial performance—A study of German and UK initial public offerings.* Cheltenham: Edward Elgar.

—— and Renneboog, L. (2000). 'The role of large shareholders in disciplining poor performance: Corporate governance in listed Belgian companies'. *Managerial Finance* 26: 22–41.

—— —— (2001). 'Strong managers and passive institutional investors in the UK'. In F. Barca and M. Becht (eds.), *The Control of Corporate Europe.* Oxford: Oxford University Press, pp. 258–84.

—— —— (2003*a*), 'Why are the levels of control (so) different in German and UK companies? Evidence from initial public offerings'. *Journal of Law, Economics and Organization* 19: 141–75.

—— —— (2003*b*), 'Shareholder wealth effects of European domestic and cross-border wealth effects'. *European Financial Management*, forthcoming.

—— —— and Correia da Silva, L. (2003). 'When do German firms change their dividends?' *Journal of Corporate Finance*, forthcoming.

Gompers, P., Ishii, J., and Metrick, A. (2003). 'Corporate governance and equity prices'. *Quarterly Journal of Economics* 118: 107–55.

Gonedes, N. (1978). 'Corporate signaling, external accounting, and capital market equilibrium: Evidence on dividends, income, and extraordinary items'. *Journal of Accounting Research* 16: 26–79.

Gorton, G. and Schmid, F. (2000). 'Universal banking and the performance of German firms'. *Journal of Financial Economics* 58: 29–80.

Gottschalk, A. (1988). 'Der Stimmrechtseinfluβ der banken in den Aktionärsvesammlungen der Groβunternehmen'. *WSI-Mitteilungen* 5: 294–8.

Greene, W. (2003). *Econometric Analysis*, 5th edn. New York: Prentice Hall.

—— —— (1980). 'Takeover bids, the free-rider problem, and the theory of the corporation'. *Bell Journal of Economics* 11: 42–64.

—— —— (1988). 'One share-one-vote and the market for corporate control'. *Journal of Financial Economics* 20: 175–202.

Gugler, K. (2003). 'Corporate governance, dividend payout policy, and the interrelation between dividends, and capital investment'. *Journal of Banking and Finance,* 27: 1297–321.

—— and Yurtoglu, B. (2003). 'Corporate governance and dividend pay-out policy in Germany'. *European Economic Review,* 47: 731–58.

—— Kalls, S., Stomper, A., and Zechner, J. (2001). 'The separation of ownership and control in Austria'. In F. Barca and M. Becht (eds.), *The Control of Corporate Europe.* Oxford: Oxford University Press.

Gul, F. (1999*a*), 'Government share ownership, investment opportunity set and corporate policy choices in China'. *Pacific-Basin Finance Journal* 7: 157–72.

—— (1999*b*), 'Growth opportunities, capital structure and dividend policies in Japan'. *Journal of Corporate Finance* 5: 141–68.

—— and Kealey, B. (1999). 'Chaebol, investment opportunity set and corporate debt and dividend policies of Korean companies'. *Review of Quantitative Finance and Accounting* 13: 401–16.

Hakansson, N. (1982). 'To pay or not to pay dividends'. *Journal of Finance* 37: 415–28.

Hallock, K. (1997). 'Reciprocally interlocking boards of directors and executive compensation'. *Journal of Financial and Quantitative Analysis* 32: 331–4.

—— (1999). 'Dual agency: Corporate boards with reciprocally interlocking relationships'. In J. Carpenter and D. Yermack (eds.), *Executive Compensation and Shareholder Value*. Amsterdam: Kluwer Academic Publishers, pp. 55–75.

Hamid, S., Prakash, A., and Smyser, M. (1995). 'The role of managerial demand and ownership in the determination of dividend and debt policies of mature corporations'. Unpublished paper, Florida International University.

Hansen, R., Kumar, R., and Shome, D. (1994). 'Dividend policy and corporate monitoring: Evidence from the regulation of the electric utility industry'. *Financial Management* 23: 16–22.

Harris, T. S., Lang, M., and Möller, H. P. (1994). 'The value relevance of German accounting measures: An empirical analysis'. *Journal of Accounting Research* 32: 187–209.

Hart, O. (1995). 'Corporate governance: Some theory and implications'. *Economic Journal* 105: 678–89.

Healy, P. and Palepu, K. (1988). 'Earnings information conveyed by dividend initiations and omissions'. *Journal of Financial Economics* 21: 149–75.

Heckman, J. (1979). 'Sample selection bias as a specification error'. *Econometrica* 47: 153–61.

Hellwig, M. (2000). 'Financial intermediation with risk aversion'. *Review of Economic Studies* 67: 719–42.

Hermalin, B. and Weisbach, M. (1991). 'The effects of board composition and direct incentives on firm performance'. *Financial Management* 20: 101–12.

—— —— (1998). 'Endogenously chosen boards of directors and their monitoring of the CEO'. *American Economic Review* 88: 96–118.

—— —— (2001). 'Boards of directors as an endogenously determined institution: A survey of the economic literature'. Working paper, University of Berkeley.

Himmelberg, C, Hubbard, R., and Palia, D. (1999). 'Understanding the determinants of managerial ownership and the link between ownership and performance'. *Journal of Financial Economics* 53: 353–84.

Holderness, C. G. and Sheehan, D. P. (1988). 'The role of majority shareholders in publicly held corporations: An explanatory analysis'. *Journal of Financial Economics* 20: 317–46.

Hort, H. (1984). 'Zur Dividendenpolitik der Aktiengesellschaften des Verarbeitenden Gewerbes der Bundesrepublik Deutschland—Ein Empirischer Beitrag'. Doctoral Dissertation, Saarbrücken, p. 260.

Hoshi, T., Kashyap, A., and Scharfstein, D. (1990). 'The role of banks in reducing the costs of financial distress in Japan'. *Journal of Financial Economics* 27: 67–88.

—— —— —— (1991). 'Corporate structure, liquidity, and investment: Evidence from Japanese industrial groups'. *Quarterly Journal of Economics* 106: 33–60.

Hsiao, C. (1986). *Analysis of Panel Data*. Cambridge: Cambridge University Press.

Hubbard, J. and Michaely, R. (1997). 'Do investors ignore dividend taxation? A reexamination of the citizens utilities case'. *Journal of Financial and Quantitative Analysis* 32: 117–35.

Huson, M., Parrino, R., and Starks, L. (2000). 'Internal monitoring and CEO turnover: A long-term perspective'. Working paper, University of Texas.

Jarrell, G. and Poulsen, A. (1989). 'The returns to acquiring firms in tender offers: Evidence from three decades'. *Financial Management* 18: 12–19.

Jenkinson, T. and Ljungqvist, A. (2001*e*). 'The role of hostile stakes in German corporate governance.' *Journal of Corporate Finance* 7: 397–446.

—— and Mayer, C. (1994). *Hostile Takeovers: Defence, Attack and Corporate Governance*. London: McGraw-Hill.

Jensen, G., Solberg, D., and Zorn, T. (1992). 'Simultaneous determination of insider ownership, debt, and dividend policies'. *Journal of Financial and Quantitative Analysis* 27: 247–63.

Jensen, M. (1993). 'The modern industrial revolution, exit, and the failure of internal control systems'. *Journal of Finance* 48: 831–80.

—— and Murphy, K. (1990). 'Performance pay and top-management incentives'. *Journal of Political Economy* 98: 225–64.

Jensen, M. C. and Meckling, W. H. (1986). 'Agency costs of free cash flow, corporate finance and takeovers'. *American Economic Review* 76: 323–9.

—— —— (1976). 'Theory of the firm: Managerial behaviour, agency costs, and ownership structure'. *Journal of Financial Economics* 3: 305–60.

John, K. and Lang, L. (1991). 'Insider trading around dividend announcements: Theory and evidence'. *Journal of Finance* 46: 1361–89.

—— and Williams, J. (1985). 'Dividends, dilution, and taxes: A signalling equilibrium'. *Journal of Finance* 40: 1053–70.

Johnson S., La Porta, R., Lopez-de-Silanes, F., and Shleifer, A. (2000). 'Tunnelling'. *American Economic Review* 90: 22–7.

Kahn, C. and Winton, A. (1998). 'Ownership structure, speculation, and shareholder intervention'. *Journal of Finance* 53: 99–129.

Kalay, A. (1980). 'Signaling, information content, and the reluctance to cut dividends'. *Journal of Financial and Quantitative Analysis* 15: 855–67.

Kane, A., Lee, Y., and Marcus, A. (1984). 'Earnings and dividend announcements: Is there a corroboration effect?' *Journal of Finance* 39: 1091–9.

Kaplan, S. (1994*a*). 'Top executive rewards and firm performance: A comparison of Japan and the US'. *Journal of Political Economy* 102: 510–46.

—— (1994*b*). 'Top executives, turnover and firm performance in Germany'. *Journal of Law, Economics and Organization* 10: 142–159.

—— and Minton, B. (1994). 'Appointments of outsiders to Japanese boards: Determinants and implications for managers'. *Journal of Financial Economics* 36: 225–58.

Karpoff, J. and Malatesta, P. (1989). 'The wealth effect of second generation state takeover legislation'. *Journal of Financial Economics* 25: 291–322.

Keim, D. B. and Madhavan, A. (1996). 'Large block transactions: Analysis and measurement of price effects'. *Review of Financial Studies* 9: 1–36.

Kester, W. (1986). 'Capital and ownership structure: A comparison of United States and Japanese manufacturing corporations'. *Financial Management* 15: 5–16.

Klein, A. (1998). 'Firm performance and board committee structure'. *Journal of Law and Economics* 41: 275–99.

Köke, J. (2003). 'The market for corporate control in a bank-based economy: A governance device?' *Journal of Corporate Finance*, forthcoming.

Kole, S. (1996). 'Managerial ownership and firm performance: Incentives or rewards?' In *Advances in Financial Economics* 2. London: JAI Press, pp. 119–49.

König, V. (1991). 'Dividende und Jahresüberschuß'. *Zeitschrift für Betriebswirtschaft*, 1149–55.

Krasa, S. and Villamil, A. (1992). 'Monitoring the monitor: An incentive structure for a financial intermediary'. *Journal of Economic Theory* 57: 197–221.

Kumar, P. (1988). 'Shareholder-manager conflict and the information content of dividends'. *Review of Financial Studies* 1: 111–136.

La Porta, R., Lopez-de-Silanes, F., Shleifer, A., and Vishny, R. (1997). 'Legal determinants of external finance.' *Journal of Finance*, 52: 1131–50.

—— —— —— —— (1998). 'Law and finance'. *Journal of Political Economy* 106: 1113–55.

—— —— —— —— (1999). 'Corporate ownership around the world'. *Journal of Finance* 54: 471–517.

—— —— —— —— (2000). 'Investor protection and corporate governance'. *Journal of Financial Economics* 58: 3–27.

Lasfer, M. (1996). 'Taxes and dividends: The UK evidence'. *Journal of Banking and Finance* 20: 455–72.

Lease, R., John, K., Kalay, A., Loewenstein, U., and Sarig, O. (2000). *Dividend Policy. Its Impact on Firm Value*. Financial Management Association Survey and Synthesis Series, Boston: Harvard Business School Press.

Lehmann, E. (2003). 'Corporate governance in Germany: Problems and prospects', Working Paper, University of Konstanz.

Leithner, S. and Zimmermann, H. (1993). 'Market value and aggregate dividends: A reappraisal of recent tests, and evidence from European markets'. *Swiss Journal of Economics and Statistics* 192: 99–121.

Leland, H. and Pyle, D. (1977). 'Informational asymmetries, financial structure and financial inter-medition'. *Journal of Finance* 32: 371–87.

Levine, R. (1999). 'Law, finance, and economic growth'. *Journal of Financial Intermediation* 8: 36–67.

Lewellen, W., Stanley, K., Lease, R., and Schlarbaum, G. (1978). 'Some direct evidence of the dividend clientele phenomenon'. *Journal of Finance* 33: 1385–99.

Lintner, J. (1956). 'Distribution of incomes of corporations among dividends, retained earnings and taxes'. *American Economic Review* 46: 97–113.

Lipton, M. and Lorsch, J. (1992). 'A modest proposal for improved corporate governance'. *Business Lawyer* 48: 59–77.

Litzenberger, R. and Ramaswamy, K. (1979). 'The effect of taxes and dividends on capital asset prices: Theory and empirical evidence'. *Journal of Financial Economics* 7: 163–95.

—— —— (1982). 'The effect of dividends on common stock prices: Tax effects or information effects'. *Journal of Finance* 37: 429–43.

Lombardo, D. and Pagano, M. (2002). 'Law and equity markets: A simple model'. In J. McCahery, P. Moerland, T. Raaijmakers, and L. Renneboog (eds.), *Corporate Governance Regimes: Convergence and Diversity*. Oxford: Oxford University Press.

London Stock Exchange (1994). *Stock Exchange Quarterly*, London: London Stock Exchange, Spring.

Low, S.-W., Glorfeld, L., Hearth, D., and Rimbey, J. (2001). 'The link between bank monitoring and corporate dividend policy: The case of dividend omissions'. *Journal of Banking and Finance* 25: 2069–87.

MacAvoy, P., Cantor, S., Dana, J., and Peck, S. (1983). 'ALI proposals for increased control of the corporation by the board of directors: An economic analysis'. In *Statement of the Business Roundtable on the American Law Institute's Proposed Principles of Corporate Governance and Structure: Restatement and Recommendation*. New York: Business Roundtable.

McCahery, J. and Renneboog, L. (2003). 'The economics of the proposed takeover directive'. Working paper, Centre for European Policy Studies.

—— Moerland, P., Raaijmakers, T., and Renneboog, L. (2002). *Corporate Governance Regimes: Convergence and Diversity*, Oxford: Oxford University Press.

McConaughy, D., Walker, M., Henderson, G., and Mishra, C. (1998). 'Founding family controlled firms: Efficiency and value'. *Review of Financial Economics* 7: 1–19.

McConnell, J. and Servaes, H. (1990). 'Additional evidence on equity ownership and corporate value'. *Journal of Financial Economics* 27: 595–612.

—— —— (1995). 'Equity ownership and the two faces of debt'. *Journal of Financial Economics* 39: 131–57.

McDonald, J., Jacquillat, B., and Nussenbaum, M. (1975). 'Dividend, investment and financing decisions: Empirical evidence on French firms'. *Journal of Financial and Quantitative Analysis* 10: 741–55.

McDonald, R. (2001). 'Cross-border investing with tax arbitrage: The case of German dividend tax credits'. *Review of Financial Studies* 14: 617–57.

McElvey, R. and Zaviona, W. (1975). 'A statistical model for the analysis of ordinary level dependent variables'. *Journal of Mathematical Sociology* 4: 103–20.

McFadden, D. (1974). 'The measurement of urban travel demand'. *Journal of Public Economics* 3: 303–28.

Maddala, G. (1983). 'Limited-dependent and qualitative variables in econometrics'. *Econometric Society Monographs*. Cambridge: Cambridge University Press.

Marsh, P. (1992). 'Dividend announcements and stock price performance'. Mimeo, London Business School.

Marsh, T. and Merton, R. (1987). 'Dividend behaviour for the aggregate stock market'. *Journal of Business* 60: 1–40.

Martin, K. and McConnell, J. (1991). 'Corporate performance, corporate takeovers and management turnover'. *Journal of Finance* 46: 671–87.

Maug, E. (1998). 'Large shareholders as monitors: Is there a trade-off between liquidity and control?' *Journal of Finance* 53: 65–98.

Mayer, C. (1990). 'Financial systems, corporate finance, and economic development'. In R. Glenn Hubbard (ed.), *Asymmetric Information, Corporate Finance and Investment*. Chicago: University of Chicago Press.

—— and Alexander, I. (1990). 'Banks and securities markets: Corporate finance in Germany and the United Kingdom'. *Journal of the Japanese and International Economies* 4: 450–75.

Mehran, H. (1995). 'Executive compensation structure, ownership, and firm performance'. *Journal of Financial Economics* 38: 163–84.

Michel, A (1979). 'Industry influence on dividend policy'. *Financial Management* 8: 22–6.

—— and Shaked, I. (1986). 'Country industry influence on dividend policy: Evidence from Japan and the USA'. *Journal of Business Finance and Accounting* 13: 365–81.

Miller, M. and Modigliani, F. (1961). 'Dividend policy, growth and the valuation of shares'. *Journal of Business* 34: 411–33.

—— and Rock, K. (1985). 'Dividend policy under asymmetric information'. *Journal of Finance* 10: 1031–51.

—— and Scholes, M. (1978): 'Dividends and taxes', *Journal of Economics*, 6: 333–64.

—— —— (1982): 'Dividends and taxes: Some empirical evidence'. *Journal of Political Economy* 90: 1118–41.

Modigliani, F. and Miller, M. (1958). 'The cost of capital, corporate finance, and the theory of investment'. *American Economic Review* 48: 261–97.

—— —— (1959). 'The cost of capital, corporate finance, and the theory of investment: Reply'. *American Economic Review* 49: 655–69.

Moh'd, M., Perry, L., and Rimbey, J. (1995). 'An investigation of the dynamic relationship between agency theory and dividend policy'. *Financial Review* 30: 367–85.

Morck, R. and Nakamura, M. (1999). 'Banks and corporate control in Japan'. *Journal of Finance* 54: 319–40.

—— Shleifer, A., and Vishny, R. (1988). 'Managerial ownership and market valuation: An empirical analysis'. *Journal of Financial Economics* 20: 293–315.

Murphy, K. (1999). 'Executive compensation'. In O. Ashenfelter and D. Card (eds.), *Handbook of Labor Economics*. Amsterdam: North Holland.

Myers, S. (1984). 'The capital structure puzzle'. *Journal of Finance* 39: 575–91.

—— and Majluf, N. (1984). 'Corporate financing and investments decisions when firms have information that investors do not have'. *Journal of Financial Economics* 13: 187–221.

Nenova, T. (2003). 'The value of corporate votes and control benefits: A cross-country analysis'. *Journal of Financial Economics* (forthcoming).

Nickell, S. (1981). 'Biases in dynamic models with fixed effects'. *Econometrica* 49: 1417–26.

—— (1995). *The Performance of Companies—The Relationship Between External Environment, Management Strategies and Corporate Performance*. Oxford: Blackwell.

Nicodano, G. (1998). 'Corporate groups, dual-class shares and the value of voting rights'. *Journal of Banking and Finance* 22: 1117–37.

—— and Sembenelli, A. (2000). 'Private benefits, block transaction premia and ownership structure'. Working paper, University of Torino.

Noe, T. and Rebello, M. (1996). 'Asymmetric information, managerial opportunism, financing, and payout policies'. *Journal of Finance* 51: 637–59.

Noronha, G., Shome, D., and Morgan, G. (1996). 'The monitoring rationale for dividends and the interaction of capital structure and dividend decisions'. *Journal of Banking and Finance* 20: 439–54.

OECD (1989). *Economic Surveys: Germany*. Paris: OECD, 85–9.

Ofer, A. and Siegel, D. (1987). 'Corporate financial policy, information, and market expectations: An empirical investigation of dividends'. *Journal of Finance* 42: 889–911.

Ofer, A. and Thakor, A. (1987). 'A theory of stock price responses to alternative corporate cash disbursement methods: Stock repurchases and dividends'. *Journal of Finance* 42: 365–94.

Pagano, M. and Röell, A. (1998). 'The choice of stock ownership structure: Agency costs, monitoring and the decision to go public'. *Quarterly Journal of Economics* 113: 187–225.

Pettit, R. (1972). 'Dividend announcements, security performance, and capital market efficiency'. *Journal of Finance* 27: 993–1007.

Porter, M. (1992). 'Capital disadvantage: America's failing capital investment system'. *Harvard Business Review* (Sept.–Oct.), 65–82.

Poterba, J. and Summers, L. (1984). 'New evidence that taxes affect the valuation of dividends'. *Journal of Finance* 39: 1397–415.

Prowse, S. (1990). 'Institutional investment patterns and corporate financial behaviour in the United States and Japan'. *Journal of Financial Economics* 27: 43–66.

—— (1992). 'The structure of corporate ownership in Japan'. *Journal of Finance* 47: 1121–40.

Rajan, R. and Diamond, D. (2000). 'Banks, short term debt and financial crises: Theory, policy implications and applications'. Discussion paper, University of Chicago.

—— and Zingales, L. (1995). 'What do we know about capital structure? Some evidence from international data'. *Journal of Finance* 50: 1421–60.

—— —— (2003). 'Banks and markets: The changing character of European finance'. Working paper, University of Chicago.

Renneboog, L. (1998). 'Corporate governance systems: The role of ownership, external finance and regulation (part I)'. *Corporate Governance International* 1: 37–48.

—— (2000). 'Ownership, managerial control and the governance of poorly performing companies listed on the Brussels stock exchange'. *Journal of Banking and Finance* 24: 1959–95.

—— and Trojanowski, G. (2003). 'The managerial labor market and the governance role of shareholder control structures in the UK'. Working paper, European Corporate Governance Institute.

Rose, C. (2002). 'Corporate financial performance and the use of takeover defences'. *European Journal of Law and Economics* 13: 91–112.

Rosenstein, S. and Wyatt, J. (1990). 'Outside directors, board independence, and shareholder wealth'. *Journal of Financial Economics* 26: 175–84.

Ross, S. (1977). 'The determination of financial structure: The incentive-signalling approach'. *Bell Journal of Economics* 8: 23–40.

Rozeff, M. S. (1982). 'Growth, beta and agency costs as determinants of dividend payout ratios'. *Journal of Financial Research* 3: 249–59.

Rydqvist, K. (1987). 'Empirical evidence of the voting premium'. Working Paper 35, Northwestern University.

Ryngaert, M. (1988). 'The effect of poison pill securities on shareholder wealth'. *Journal of Financial Economics* 20: 377–417.

Scharfstein, D. (1988). 'The disciplinary role of takeovers'. *Review of Economic Studies* 55: 185–99.

Schellenger, M. (1989). 'Board of director composition, shareholder wealth, and dividend policy'. *Journal of Management* 3: 457–67.

Schooley, D. and Barney, L. (1994). 'Using dividend policy and managerial ownership to reduce agency costs'. *Journal of Financial Research* 17: 363–73.

Shivdasani, A. (1993). 'Board composition, ownership structure, and hostile takeovers'. *Journal of Accounting and Economics* 16: 167–98.

Shleifer, A. and Vishny, R. (1986). 'Large shareholders and corporate control'. *Journal of Political Economy* 94: 461–88.

—— —— (1997). 'A survey of corporate governance.' *Journal of Finance* 52, 737–84.

Short, H., Zhang, H., and Keasey, K. (2002). 'The link between dividend policy and institutional ownership'. *Journal of Corporate Finance* 8: 105–22.

Stapledon, G. (1996). *Institutional Shareholders and Corporate Governance.* Oxford: Clarendon Press.

—— and Bates, J. (2002). 'Unpacking the "interest-holders" in a share: Making voting easier for institutional shareholders'. In J. McCahery, P. Moerland, T. Raaijmakers and L. Renneboog (eds.), *Corporate Governance Regimes: Convergence and Diversity.* Oxford: Oxford University Press.

Stulz, R. (1988). 'Managerial control of voting rights: Financing policies and the market for corporate control'. *Journal of Financial Economics* 20: 25–54.

Sudarsanam, S. (1996). 'Large shareholders, takeovers and target valuation'. *Journal of Business Finance and Accounting* 23: 295–314.

Trojanowski, G. (2003). 'Equity block transfers in transition economies: Evidence from Poland'. Mimeo, Tilburg University.

Vermaelen, T. (1981). 'Common stock repurchases and market signalling: An empirical study'. *Journal of Financial Economics* 9: 139–83.

Warner, J., Watts, R., and Wruck, K. (1988). 'Stock prices and top-management changes'. *Journal of Financial Economics* 20: 461–92.

Watts, R. (1973). 'The information content of dividends'. *Journal of Finance* 46: 191–211.

Weisbach, M. (1988). 'Outside directors and CEO turnover'. *Journal of Financial Economics* 20: 431–60.

Wenger, E. and Kaserer, C. (1998). 'The German system of corporate governance—A model which should not be imitated'. In S. Black and M. Moersch (eds.), *Competition and Convergence in Financial Markets.* Amsterdam: Elsevier, pp. 41–78.

White, H. (1980). 'A heteroskedasticity-consistent covariance matrix estimator and a direct test for heteroskedasticity'. *Econometrica* 48: 817–38.

Yermack, D. (1996). 'Higher valuation of companies with a small board of directors'. *Journal of Financial Economics* 40: 185–212.

Yurtoglu, B. (2000). 'Ownership, control and performance of Turkish listed firms'. *Empirica* 27: 193–222.

Zeckhauser, R. J., and Pound, J. (1990). 'Are large shareholders effective monitors? An investigation of share ownership and corporate performance'. In R. Glenn Hubbard (ed.), *Asymmetric Information, Corporate Finance and Investment.* Chicago: University of Chicago Press.

Zingales, L. (1994). 'The value of the voting right: A study of the Milan Stock Exchange'. *Review of Financial Studies* 7: 125–48.

—— (1995). 'What determines the value of corporate votes?'. *Quarterly Journal of Economics* 110: 1047–73.

Zwiebel, J. (1995). 'Block investment and partial benefits of corporate control'. *Review of Economic Studies* 62: 161–85.

Index